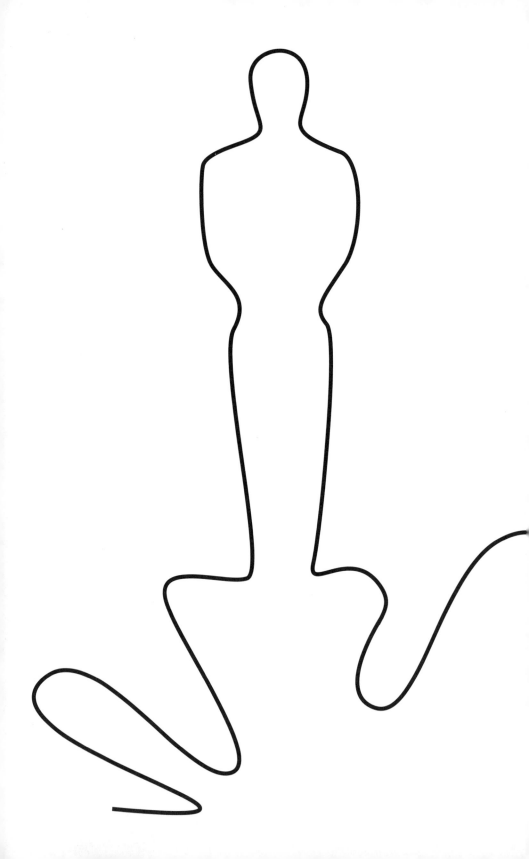

REEL WINNERS
Movie Award Trivia

by Richard Crouse

THE DUNDURN GROUP
TORONTO

Copy-Editor: Jennifer Gallant
Design: Andrew Roberts
Printer: University of Toronto Press

Library and Archives Canada Cataloguing in Publication

Crouse, Richard, 1963-
    Reel winners : movie award trivia / Richard Crouse.

Includes bibliographical references.

ISBN-10: 1-55002-574-0
ISBN-13: 978-1-55002-574-3

    1. Motion pictures--Miscellanea.   I. Title.

PN1993.9.C76 2005   791.43   C2005-903477-7

1   2   3   4   5   09   08   07   06   05

Conseil des Arts
du Canada   Canada Council
for the Arts

Canada

ONTARIO ARTS COUNCIL
CONSEIL DES ARTS DE L'ONTARIO

We acknowledge the support of the Canada Council for the Arts and the Ontario Arts Council for our publishing program. We also acknowledge the financial support of the Government of Canada through the Book Publishing Industry Development Program and The Association for the Export of Canadian Books, and the Government of Ontario through the Ontario Book Publishers Tax Credit program, and the Ontario Media Development Corporation.

Printed and bound in Canada.
Printed on recycled paper.

www.dundurn.com

Dundurn Press
3 Church Street, Suite 500
Toronto, Ontario, Canada
M5E 1M2

Gazelle Book Services Limited
White Cross Mills
Hightown, Lancaster, England
LA1 4X5

Dundurn Press
2250 Military Road
Tonawanda NY
U.S.A. 14150

"You finally made it, Frankie! Oscar night! And here you sit, on top of a glass mountain called 'success.' You're one of the chosen five, and the whole town's holding its breath to see who won it. It's been quite a climb, hasn't it, Frankie? Down at the bottom, scuffling for dimes in those smokers, all the way to the top. Magic Hollywood! Ever think about it? I do, friend Frankie, I do...."

— Hymie Kelly (Tony Bennett) in *The Oscar*, 1966

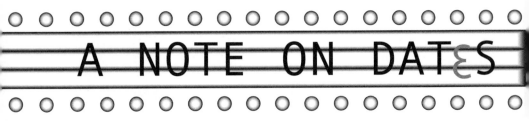

A NOTE ON DATES

Many awards shows take their lead from the Academy of Motion Picture Arts and Sciences, which lists awards shows by the year during which the eligible movies were released. By those standards, the February 2005 ceremony is officially the 2004 Oscars. I find this labelling often leads to confusion, so for clarity's sake I have used the dates of the ceremonies. For example, I refer to the 2004 Academy Awards as the Oscarcast of February 28, 2005.

TABLE OF CONTENTS

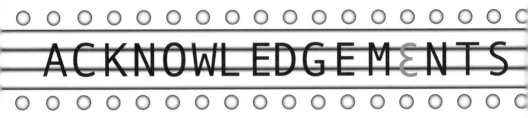

ACKNOWLEDGEMENTS

At the Oscars each year winners are asked to keep their thank-you speeches under forty-five seconds in length. I'll try to do the same — extend a personal thanks to everyone who helped with this book in a list that will take under forty-five seconds to read: Andrea Bodnar; Dara Rowland; Claudio Castro; Geoff Pevere; Katrina Onstad; Ed, Norma, Gary, Christian, and Nicholas; Barry Jowett, Jennifer Gallant, and the crew at Dundurn; my *Groove Shinny* and *Go!* pals Pedro Mendes, Kai Black, David Carroll, and Brent Bambury; Teri Hart; Dean D'aguilar; Erin Gorman; Avi Botbol; the crew at Canada AM, Jeffrey Tam Karning Hum, Seamus and Bev; Ron "Did you see the brick?" Bodnar; Frances and everyone at Southern Accent; Susan Smythe; Laura Quinn; Virginia Kelly; Nancy Yu; Angie Burns; Bonne Smith; Shelly Chagnon; Bryan Peters; Charles Wechsler; and everyone who watches *Reel to Real* each week.

"*Ladies and Gentlemen,
tomorrow's headlines
will be made here tonight.
This is news. This is
movietown's election night.*"

— Oscar broadcast announcer, 1953

GOLD
A-GO-GO

Q What is commonly believed to be the first movie award in history?

A The earliest awards — the ancestor of the People's Choice Awards — were the Photoplay Awards, published yearly in the pages of the magazine of the same name. From 1920 to 1939, the Medal of Honor was voted for by the readers of the popular *Photoplay* magazine. The first winner of the populist award was Cosmopolitan Pictures' *Homoresque*, about a young boy who dreams of becoming a famous violin player.

Other winners of the original Medal of Honor were 1921's silent rural drama *Tol'able David*; Douglas Fairbank's 1922 *Robin Hood*, featuring the largest set built for any silent movie; 1923's *The Covered Wagon*, the first truly epic Western film; 1924's cradle-to-grave bio *The Dramatic Life of Abraham Lincoln*; 1925's *The Big Parade*, the highest grossing silent film of all time, which made $22 million during its worldwide release; Ronald Coleman's 1926 French Foreign Legion epic, *Beau Geste*; 1927's *7th Heaven*, the first film to romantically pair Janet Gaynor and Charles Farrell; John Ford's 1928 family saga *Four Sons*, about three Bavarian brothers who go to war for Germany while the fourth goes to America; 1929's *Disraeli*, the story of the British prime minister and England's purchase of the Suez Canal; *All Quiet on the Western Front*, 1930's powerful anti-war film; 1931's *Cimarron*; *Smilin' Through*, a 1932 romance starring Norma Shearer; 1933's *Little Women*, Katharine Hepburn's coming-of-age drama about four sisters during the American Civil War; 1934's *The Barretts of Wimpole Street*, the true story of poet Elizabeth Barrett's tyrannical father, who tries to prevent her from marrying Robert Browning; *Naughty Marietta*, Jeanette MacDonald's 1935 hit about a French princess who fled to New Orleans to escape an arranged marriage; 1936's *San Francisco*, which also starred Jeanette MacDonald; 1937's *Captains Courageous*, which would later become the first MGM film to be shown on television; 1938's *Sweethearts*, MGM's first full Technicolor feature; and 1939's *Gone With the Wind*, which would later be voted #4 on the American Film Institute's list of the greatest American movies of all time.

Photoplay took the war years off, returning in 1944 (and continuing until 1968) with an expanded list of awards, including Most Popular Male and Female Star, which were based on overall popularity, not a specific performance.

Q Which critics' award did director John Huston call "the greatest honor that anyone in my profession can receive"?

A John Huston was referring to the New York Film Critics Circle Award, and he went on to say that it "means more to me than any other honor."

Huston had good reason to praise the New Yorkers — they had awarded him three Best Director awards over the course of almost forty years. The first NYFCC kudo came in 1948 for his work on *The Treasure of the Sierra Madre*. Eight years later they praised him for his direction of *Moby Dick*, and in 1985 they gave him his third and final prize for *Prizzi's Honor*.

Maverick filmmaker John Ford also had a special fondness for the NYFCC, gravitating toward the east coast critics to show his ambivalence to Hollywood. The New York critics first honoured Ford in 1936 for the grim drama *The Informer*, then again in 1939, 1940, and 1941 for *Stagecoach*, *The Grapes of Wrath*, and *How Green Was My Valley*.

Ford was so dismissive about Hollywood that when he was asked what brought him to Tinseltown from his native Maine he would sarcastically reply, "The train," and to show his disdain for the studios he barred producers from his sets. If any suits ever showed up he would glare at them and ask, "Don't you have an office?"

Q Who has co-hosted the People's Choice Awards since 1975?

Courtesy of AMPAS

Perennial People's Choice Award host Army Archerd with Carlos Santana at the 77th Annual Academy Awards in 2005.

Variety scribe and PCA co-founder Army (short for Armand) Archerd has been a co-host of the People's Choice Awards since 1975. The PCA ceremony is the first awards show of the year, airing in January to honour favourites from the year before.

Archerd has been a columnist with *Daily Variety* since 1953 and hosted the pilot of *Entertainment Tonight* in 1981.

Which awards show did comic Robin Williams once describe as "the Golden Globes on acid"?

Robin Williams was referring to the MTV Movie Awards. The saucy awards ceremony, described by the *Los Angeles Times* as "an engaging mixture of clunky spontaneity and outrageous behaviour," features non-traditional awards categories like Best Kiss — one year comedian D.L. Hughley joked, "The worst kiss is pretty much Whoopi Goldberg and anybody" — and Best Villain.

The show is famous for its unscripted moments, such as when a tongue-tied Keanu Reeves ran out of things to say in his acceptance speech and Ice Cube advised him, "Thank your mama," and when Jim Carrey accepted his award wearing shoulder-length hair, a shaggy beard, and granny glasses. The heavy metal disguise was so convincing that Courtney Love had no idea who he was when he bummed a cigarette from her backstage. There aren't too many other places where Sarah Jessica Parker could introduce a pair of flavour-of-the-week actors with the description, "They're so hot you could fry an egg on their flat little [bottoms]."

Which organization gives out an award called The Actor?

The Screen Actors Guild has handed out naked male actor statuettes known as The Actor since 1994. Each award is cast in solid bronze, stands sixteen inches tall, and weighs twelve pounds. The Actor was originally sculpted by Edward Saenz and was designed by Jim Heimann and Jim Barrett. The statuette is cast at the American Fine Arts Foundry.

The statue is prestigious, but that's not how Tony Shalhoub's daughter saw it. When he was up for a SAG Award for best dramatic actor, his ten-year-old daughter hoped he wouldn't win.

"Right before my category came up, my daughter said, 'I don't want you to win; I don't want you to get that.' I think she's uncomfortable to have this in the house," he joked about the naked male statuette. "Maybe we can make a little doily [and cover him up]. ... I was going to put it up on the mantel, but now I think I'll put it in the shower or something."

Angelina Jolie with her Screen Actors Guild Award for Outstanding Performance by a Female Actor in a Supporting Role for *Girl, Interrupted*.

What was on the menu at the first Academy Awards ceremony?

The first Academy Awards ceremony took place in the Blossom Room at the Roosevelt Hotel — movieland's first luxury hotel — on Hollywood Boulevard, less than a block west of the current site of the Oscars, the Kodak Theatre, on May 16, 1929. The 270 guests shelled out five bucks each for tickets to stargaze and enjoy a meal that consisted of Jumbo Squab Perigeaux, Lobster Eugene, Clear Terrapin, Los Angeles Salad, and Fruit Supreme. Each of the thirty-six banquet tables was decorated with a replica of the Oscar statue made of waxed candy.

The awards were given for films released between August 1, 1927, and August 1, 1928. Awards and winners were announced three months in advance of the ceremony. The banquet was hosted by Douglas Fairbanks, the first president of the Academy, who handed out statues to the winners and honourable mention scrolls to the runners-up.

The only recipient to make a speech was Darryl F. Zanuck, who accepted a special award for producing *The Jazz Singer*, "the pioneer outstanding talking picture, which has revolutionized the industry."

Photo by Richard Crouse

The Roosevelt Hotel on Hollywood Boulevard, home of the first Academy Awards ceremony in 1929.

Up until 2004 how were the winners of the People's Choice Awards selected?

Until 2004 winners were selected through a Gallup poll representing 212 million Americans aged twelve and older. No industry peer group was involved. People were asked for their opinions about their favourite actors, singers, films, and TV programs. Those polled were free to name any star they like; their choices were not limited to a handful of nominees.

Gold A-Go-Go

However, in 2004 the PCAs dropped Gallup and switched to a partnership with *Entertainment Weekly* magazine. Under the new system, nominees are determined by a "front row panel of over 6,000 entertainment enthusiasts" recruited by *EW* editors. The panel votes on the various categories, then people vote via the Internet to select the winners.

When did the Academy ban the use of the term "And the winner is…"?

In 1989 Oscarcast producer Alan Carr replaced the phrase "And the winner is" with "And the Oscar goes to" in an attempt to soften the blow to the losers, or as the Academy quaintly calls them, "the non-winners." The Academy explained that they wanted to recognize the overall high quality of all the nominees and to make the distinction between being awarded an honour and being an actual "winner." After all, they reasoned, every nominee is a winner simply by virtue of being nominated for such an award. The traditional phrase was thought to be politically incorrect.

"They used to say when they opened the envelope, 'And the winner is…,' and you'll notice they've changed it to 'And the Oscar goes to…,'" joked Steve Martin, "because God forbid anyone should think of this as a competition. It might make the trade ads seem crass."

Seating placards at 74th Academy Awards.

15

Despite the Academy's insistence that presenters use the new phrase, there have been several slips over the years. Jim Carrey deliberately used the phrase in 1999 when he presented the award for Best Film Editing, and when Kirk and Michael Douglas presented the award for Best Picture at the 75th Annual Academy Awards the younger actor started with the politically correct intro, "And the Oscar goes to…," but Kirk bellowed, "And the winner is…."

Which is the only televised awards show to honour performers in TV, movies, and music?

The People's Choice Awards pay tribute to performers in the three categories of movies, television, and music. The PCAs first aired on CBS in March 1975 and in subsequent years has often bested the Emmys in terms of ratings clout.

The PCAs mark the beginning of the awards season, airing in January to reward favourites from the year before. To avoid disappointment — and probably to bump up the star quotient of the show — winners are informed in advance. As one cynical writer pointed out in 1998, telling the celebs beforehand that they are guaranteed to win is a strong lure to get them to attend. "Celebrities will turn down accepting an award," he wrote, "just about as frequently as Madonna will turn down a tanned and single Latin poolboy."

Like the Golden Globes, the PCA show is a more casual affair than the Oscars and often makes for entertaining television. When comedian Jim Carrey won the Favorite Comedy Motion Picture award for *Liar Liar*, he leapt up from his table, swung his chair high above his head, and shook it wildly as he danced up to the stage, finally tossing the chair ahead of him before leaping onto the stage and passionately hugging his producer. With the possible exception of Roberto Benigni, few performers would behave like that at the Academy Awards.

What was the prize at the first Canadian Film Awards in 1949?

The Canadian Film Awards (later renamed the Genies) were first awarded on April 27, 1949, at the Little Elgin Theatre in Ottawa, Ontario. Winners received an original painting by a Canadian artist (including several by members of the Group of Seven) valued at roughly fifty dollars each. In that inaugural year twenty-nine films (twenty-eight shorts and one full-length feature) competed for five prizes. Film of the Year went to *The Loon's Necklace*, a twelve-minute short based on an aboriginal legend explaining how the loon got its ring of white feathers.

The Canadian Film Awards organizers dropped the paintings in 1951, citing budget restraints. Instead of works of art, winners were given awards certificates. In 1968, Romanian-born sculptor Sorel Etrog was commissioned to create an award statue for the CFAs. The original statue, an abstract standing figure, was gold-plated and featured a belly button, which over the years inexplicably disappeared. In the artist's honour the award was known as the Etrog until 1980 when it was renamed the Genie.

Who manufactures the crystal People's Choice Award?

The People's Choice Awards stat-uette of two hands applauding is made by glass designers Orrefors of Sweden. At the 25th Annual PCA show, host Ray Romano had *Titanic* director James Cameron weigh the statue. Cameron joked that the crystal award was heavier than two Oscars and a Golden Globe combined.

Courtesy the Hollywood Collection

Tom Cruise with his People's Choice Award for Favorite Dramatic Motion Picture Actor.

What is the Academy of Motion Picture Arts and Sciences?

The Academy of Motion Picture Arts and Sciences (AMPAS) is an American non-profit organization that was started in 1927 to "improve the artistic quality of the film medium, provide a common forum for the various branches and crafts of the industry, foster cooperation in technical research and cultural progress, and pursue a variety of other stated objectives."

The Academy Awards telecast is its most high profile event, but the Academy also preserves films damaged by poor storage and deteriorating film stock, publishes trade magazines, presents annual student film awards and film festivals, administers a scholarship program, and maintains one of the best film libraries in the world.

Courtesy of AMPAS

The Oscar, the symbol of the Academy of Motion Picture Arts and Sciences.

How many branches does the Academy of Motion Picture Arts and Sciences have?

There are fourteen branches to the Academy. In order of number of members, they are Actors, Producers, Executives, Writers, Sound, Public Relations, Art Directors, Directors, Short Films and Feature Animation, Music, Visual Effects, Film Editors, Cinematographers, and Documentary.

Membership of the Academy is by invitation of the board of governors. The criteria for admittance include having film credits of a calibre that reflects the high standards of the Academy, receiving an Academy Award nomination, achieving a unique distinction, earning special merit, or making an outstanding contribution to film. Each branch chooses the nominees for the awards given in its category.

Q: Which award celebrates films that Samuel L. Jackson called "the strange, the weird, the eclectic, the visionary, the new blood"?

A: Hosted annually on the beach in Santa Monica, the Independent Spirit Awards celebrate "filmmakers of independent vision."

Q: Which film festival gives out the Maquina del temps and the Orient Express awards?

A: The Catalonian International Film Festival in Sitges, Spain, which focuses on fantasy films, was established in 1968 and gives out almost twenty awards each year. Maquina del temps (the Time Machine Honorary Award) is awarded to an important figure in the fantasy world in recognition of his or her entire career. Previous winners include the brilliant graphic designer Saul Bass, who served as a visual consultant on Hitchcock's *Psycho* and *North by Northwest*, legendary special effects pioneer Ray Harryhausen, and B movie king Roger Corman.

The Orient Express Award has been presented to the best Asian film of the year since 2001.

Q: Who is eligible to win the Saturn Award?

A: The Saturn Awards are doled out by the Academy of Science Fiction, Fantasy & Horror Films to honour genre films and filmmakers. Established in 1972 (although the first awards weren't given out until the following year), this non-profit organization uses a mix of fans, film professionals, and academics to adjudicate the awards. Founder Dr. Donald A. Reed insisted on this unique blend of judges to determine the award on a fair and level playing field, rather than simply awarding the prize to the most popular films of the year.

Past honourees include Sherry Lansing, Steven Spielberg, Gore Verbinski, Walter Parkes, Nicolas Cage, Brian Grazer, James Cameron, Arnold Schwarzenegger, Whoopi Goldberg, Peter Jackson, Michael Bay, Gale Anne Hurd, Peter Fonda, Stan Lee, and Robert Wise.

What three awards were given during Oscar's first year and were never given again?

Best Artistic Quality of Production (awarded to *Sunrise: A Song of Two Humans*), Best Title Writing (an award for silent films given to Joseph Farnham and George Marion Jr.), and Best Comedy Direction (Lewis Milestone took this one for his work on *Two Arabian Knights*) are the three categories of Academy Awards that were discontinued after Oscar's first year.

What was the first year that celebrities presented the Golden Globes?

The Golden Globes were given out by Hollywood Foreign Press journalists until 1958, when whiskey-soaked Rat Packers Frank Sinatra, Dean Martin, and Sammy Davis Jr. emerged from a cloud of cigarette smoke and hijacked the show. Their wild behaviour went over big and they repeated their performance the following year. Since then, stars have been a staple of the Golden Globes ceremony.

Which New York–based award-granting group began its life as an anti-censorship group?

The National Board of Review of Motion Pictures was founded in 1909 in New York City to protest New York City Mayor George McClennan's revocation of moving-picture exhibition licences on Christmas Eve 1908. The mayor believed that the new medium degraded the morals of community. To assert their constitutional freedom of expression, theatre owners, led by Marcus Loew and film distributors Edison, Biograph, Pathe, and Gaumont, joined John Collier of the People's Institute at Cooper Union and established a National Review Committee that endorsed films of merit and championed the new "art of the people."

In an effort to avoid government censorship of films, the National Board became the unofficial clearing house for new movies. From 1916 into the 1950s, thousands of motion pictures carried the legend "Passed by the National Board of Review" in their main titles.

In 1929, the NBR became the first group to choose the ten best English-language movies of the year and the best foreign films. It remains the first critical body to announce its annual awards.

Who said, "The Golden Globes are fun. The Oscars are business"?

Warren Beatty explained the differences between the two premier movie awards with the quip, "The Golden Globes are fun. The Oscars are business." The Golden Globes ceremony tends to be a looser affair, a glittery gala with dinner and cocktails — Tom Hanks once said, "This evening's about free drinks and shrimp cocktail" — while the Oscars are a bit more staid. An Oscar nomination or win, however, can add millions to a movie's take. Insiders call it Oscar's box-office bounce. Industry analysts estimate that winning an Academy Award for Best Picture will boost a film's box-office revenue by $20 to $40 million. An award for Best Actor or Best Actress is thought to bring in an additional $4 to $5 million.

How much does the Academy offer to pay for returned Oscar statues?

To protect the image of its award, the Academy has a standing rule that if an Oscar winner decides he no longer want his statuette, he must offer to sell it back to the Academy for one dollar.

How much does an Academy Award weigh?

An Academy Award statute weighs 8.5 pounds and measures 13.5 inches in height. It is made of tin and copper but is plated with gold. Approximately one hundred Oscars are made each year in Chicago by the manufacturer R.S. Owens, which also manufactures the Emmy Awards, the Miss America statuettes, the National Football League's

Most Valuable Player trophies, and the Rock 'n' Roll Hall of Fame Awards. If they don't meet strict quality control standards, the statuettes are immediately cut in half and melted down.

Courtesy of AMPAS

The oversized Oscars used as set dressing at the 77th Annual Academy Awards. The actual Oscar trophy is only 13.5 inches tall.

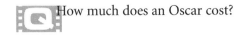 How much does an Oscar cost?

The Oscars cost the Academy of Motion Picture Arts and Sciences about $200 each. The Academy disapproves of artists selling or auctioning off their Oscars and will buy back an Oscar from the recipient for one dollar.

On occasion, however, old Oscars have shown up for sale at auctions, and to date, about half a dozen Oscars have been sold. Marlon Brando's 1954 Best Actor Oscar for *On the Waterfront* sold for $13,500 in 1988, and Vivien Leigh's *Gone with the Wind* Oscar sold for $563,000 in 1993. On December 14, 2002, Steven Spielberg anonymously bought Bette Davis's *Dangerous* Oscar at a Sotheby's auction in New York for $207,500 so he could return it to AMPAS. He had previously rescued two other Oscars from auction: Davis's for *Jezebel* (1938) and Clark Gable's for *Gone with the Wind* (1939).

Q True or false: The Academy Awards are engraved in advance of the ceremony.

A The list of winners is kept top secret until the broadcast, so the awards handed out during the show are blanks. The Academy retrieves the statuettes the day after the show and has them engraved before they are shipped back to the recipients. The personalized engraving is on a small plaque attached to the pedestal on which Oscar stands. The engraving includes the year, the award category, and the name of the recipient. Each statuette is also engraved with a serial number on the back of its base.

Q What group did John Huston call "the conscience of the American film industry"?

A The New York Film Critics Circle's members are NYC-based newspaper and magazine film critics. Founded in 1935, the organization was meant to provide an alternative to the Academy Awards, which were felt to be too influenced by studio politics and local Hollywood taste. The first ceremony was held at the Ritz Carlton in New York and has been a yearly event, except for 1962 when no awards were given because of a newspaper strike.

Q Which co-founder of the Motion Picture and Television Fund has a special humanitarian Oscar named after him?

A The Jean Hersholt Humanitarian Award, named after the character actor — and actor Leslie Nielson's uncle — from *The Four Horsemen of the Apocalypse*, *Greed*, and *Heidi*, is given to a person in the movie business whose humanitarian efforts have brought credit to the industry.

Hersholt, who died in 1956, devoted himself to many humanitarian and charitable causes, including co-founding the Motion Picture and Television Fund, which oversees a retirement community for hundreds of people from the entertainment industry and the construction of the Motion Picture Country Home and Hospital.

REEL WINNERS

Q Which association's yearly ceremony features a taped segment with stars talking about how they earned their membership cards?

A The Screen Actors Guild Awards have several distinctive features that set them apart. For example, SAG is the only organization to offer an ensemble award to recognize collaborative performances in film and television, and during the ceremony the guild pays tribute to actors working in the trenches: commercial actors, background singers, dancers, background performers, animation voiceover performers, and stunt performers. The most popular feature of the annual awards show is the "How I Got My Card" segment, in which actors talk about the first jobs that earned them their SAG memberships.

That segment was inspired by a speech Tom Hanks made in 1994 when he won Best Actor for *Forrest Gump*. He reminisced about *Bosom Buddies*, the television sitcom that earned him his SAG card, and pointed out that the award shows the masks of both comedy and tragedy. "Both will make you lose sleep," he said, "question your motives, wonder why you are there, wonder why you are doing this in the first place. But if you are crazy enough, you can get one of these — a Screen Actors Guild card."

Hanks's speech was so popular that ceremony organizers made the SAG card recollections a regular feature.

Q When did the accounting firm Price, Waterhouse begin tabulating the Oscar ballots?

A Academy president Frank Capra hired the accounting firm Price, Waterhouse to accurately and fairly count the Oscar ballots in 1936. The firm has remained with the Academy to the present day.

Here's how it works. Once the ballots have been filled out and sealed by Academy members, they are carried by armed guard from the AMPAS offices to the offices of Price, Waterhouse (now called PricewaterhouseCoopers). The nominations are tabulated by the firm using what is known as the "preferential" or "weighted average" system, an extremely complicated formula whose only other noteworthy advocate is the Australian parliament. Under the system, nominating votes are weighted differently on virtually every ballot, depending on the votes already counted. The system is so involved that few voters understand it. The final votes to determine Oscar winners are, however, counted in the standard way. "Rolls-Royce still makes cars by hand, and we count our ballots by hand," said Rick Rosas of PricewaterhouseCoopers. During the counting no talking is allowed and no one breaks for lunch; food is delivered to the office.

The results are kept under wraps, known only to the three accountants who make the final tabulations on the day of the telecast and prepare the sealed envelopes that contain the winners' names.

A PricewaterhouseCoopers official then takes the twenty-two sealed envelopes to the awards ceremony and hands them to the presenters just before the winners are announced. A carbon copy set of sealed envelopes is kept by an anonymous backup official in case something happens to the first official. The backup has never been needed. The official and his backup do not travel to the ceremony in the same car in case of an accident.

Courtesy of AMPAS

Representatives from the accounting firm of PricewaterhouseCoopers on the way in to the 77th Annual Academy Awards.

When was the first Golden Globes statue given out?

The Golden Globes statue came about in 1946, when Hollywood Foreign Press president Marina Cisternas came up with an idea for the award's design: a "golden globe" with a filmstrip circling it. One early recipient of the trophy, Olivia de Havilland, said, "This golden replica of the world is romantic. It covers places and cities that I would like to visit but where, so far, only my shadow has been."

Who designed the famous Oscar statue?

The original Oscar statuette — a knight standing on a reel of film with five spokes, representing five branches of the academy: Actors, Directors, Writers, Producers, and Technicians — was designed by Metro-Goldwyn-Mayer art director Cedric Gibbons, who doodled it during an early meeting of the fledgling Academy and who received the award himself eleven times. Unemployed sculptor George Stanley was paid $500 to produce the first batch of Oscars and Frederic Hope the black stand. It stands at 13.5 inches, weighs 8.5 pounds, and is coated with twenty-four karat gold — except during World War II, when the statuettes were made of plaster.

The design has not changed since, save for the number of holes in the film spool on which the Oscar figure stands. In 1929, the spool had only five holes, since the Academy had only five branches at the time; now it has fourteen holes, representing the current fourteen branches.

Who gave the nickname "Oscar" to the Academy Award?

No one knows for sure, although three sources have often been quoted. Actress Bette Davis's assertion that she was responsible for the name after mentioning that the statuette's backside reminded her of her husband Harmon Oscar Nelson was proven false when an Oscar reference was found in print dated three years before her 1937 win.

Another rumour had Hollywood writer Sidney Skolsky, who used the name in a 1934 column in reference to Katharine Hepburn's first Best Actress win, taking credit. Skolsky said he chose the pet name "to negate pretension." "I got tired of using 'statuette' in my story," he said. "I wanted to give the guy a name, not to make it easier to write about, but to give the thing an identity and a personality. I thought Oscar wouldn't be too dignified a name for such a banquet that had so much dignity."

The most likely story involves Academy librarian Margaret Herrick, who claimed that the moniker came from her exclamation that the statuette looked like her uncle Oscar.

In any case, the Academy itself didn't use the nickname officially until 1939.

Q What is the earliest known public reference to the Academy Award as "Oscar"?

A At the March 16, 1934, Academy Awards ceremony Walt Disney won a trophy for Best Short Subject for *The Three Little Pigs*. In his acceptance speech he made the first public reference to the award as "Oscar," a popular nickname among movie insiders, but one that was not yet widely used.

Q Who was awarded the first star on the Hollywood Walk of Fame?

Photo by Richard Crouse

The famous five-pointed Hollywood Walk of Fame star on Hollywood Boulevard.

The Hollywood Walk of Fame is the sidewalk along Hollywood Boulevard in Hollywood, California, which is embedded with over two thousand five-pointed bronze stars featuring the names of celebrities. The Walk of Fame runs north to south on Hollywood Boulevard from Gower to La Brea, and east to west on Vine Street between Yucca and Sunset Boulevard.

Created in 1958, the Walk of Fame has become a tribute to artists working within the entertainment industry, both in front and behind the cameras. Honourees receive a star based on career and lifetime achievements in entertainment as well as their charitable and civic contributions.

Joanne Woodward received the first star on the Walk of Fame at 6801 Hollywood Boulevard on February 9, 1960.

Not all stars are delighted to have their names immortalized on the famous walkway. "Ah, stardom!" said Lee Marvin. "They put your name on a star in the sidewalk on Hollywood Boulevard and you walk down and find a pile of dog manure on it. That tells the whole story, baby."

Still other performers use the opportunity to show their light-hearted side. In October 2002, Jackie Chan attended the unveiling of his star. "To show my appreciation," he said, "I will make better films." In January 2003 Nicole Kidman wisecracked at her star's unveiling, "I've never been so excited to have people walk all over me for the rest of my life."

Photo by Richard Crouse

The Three Faces of Eve actress Joanne Woodward's star at 6801 Hollywood Boulevard. This was the first of more than two thousand stars to be placed on Hollywood Boulevard.

Gold A-Go-Go

Nicole Kidman posing with her Walk of Fame star in January 2003.

Hong Kong superstar Jackie Chan posing with his Walk of Fame star in October 2002.

29

Which film award did George C. Scott consider "the only film award worth having"?

Three months before George C. Scott refused the Best Actor Oscar for *Patton* in February 1971, his wife, Colleen Dewhurst, showed up at the reception to accept a New York Film Critics Circle plaque on his behalf. "George thinks this is the only film award worth having," she said. Scott was unable to attend the ceremony because he was in Spain filming *The Last Run*.

Who is eligible to win the Independent Spirit's John Cassavetes Award?

The John Cassavetes Award, named after the innovative filmmaker of *Husbands*, *Minnie and Moskowitz*, and *A Woman Under the Influence*, is given to the writer, director, and producer of the best feature made for under $500,000. Past winners include identical twins Michael and Mark Polish for *Jackpot* in 2002, director/writer (and playwright Arthur Miller's daughter) Rebecca Miller for *Personal Velocity: Three Portraits* in 2003, and first-time helmer Thomas McCarthy for *The Station Agent* in 2004.

When was the Academy Awards ceremony first broadcast in colour?

The 38th Annual Academy Awards, held on April 18, 1966, was the first to be televised in colour. Emcee Bob Hope joked that one advantage of broadcasting in living colour was that "you can actually see the losers turn green," while veteran costume designer Edith Head worried about the number of female stars who had worn white dresses to show off their tans on colour TV.

"I looked at all those dresses," she said, "and I thought we were doing a reprise of *White Christmas*."

In what year were the Golden Globes founded?

Gold A·Go·Go

A The Golden Globes were founded in October 1943 by eight foreign journalists, under the name the Hollywood Foreign Correspondents Association. The first awards ceremony was held during a luncheon at 20th Century Fox, where the winners in five categories — Best Motion Picture, Best Actor, Best Actress, Best Supporting Actor, and Best Supporting Actress — received scrolls, with *The Song of Bernadette* winning the top prize.

Q Why was the Oscarcast almost cancelled in 1966?

A The 39th Annual Academy Awards were almost scuttled because of a strike by the American Federation of Television and Radio Artists. "It's like directing a Hitchcock movie," said Oscarcast director Dick Dunlap, "except the suspense is killing ME!"

The strike lasted thirteen days and was settled just two hours before the broadcast was to begin. "What drama! What suspense!" joked emcee Bob Hope. "And that's just wondering whether the show would go on!"

Q Who gives out the Golden Frog Award each year?

A The Golden Frog is a cinematographer's award given at Camerimage, a festival held in Toruñ, a medieval town in central Poland. According to legend, the small town of Toruñ was once threatened by a plague of thousands of frogs but was rescued by an artist who led the frogs out of the town. According to the festival website, "Every year [the] finest cinematographers from all over the world compete to prove their art is also the one which saves us."

Q Which Oscar is given to "creative producers whose bodies of work reflect the consistently high quality of motion picture productions"?

A The Irving G. Thalberg Memorial Award is voted on by the Academy's board of governors and is presented to "creative producers whose bodies of work reflect a consistently high quality of motion picture production."

It was named in honour of the man who was one of the thirty-six founders of the Academy of Motion Picture Arts and Sciences; who was the inspiration for the character of Monroe Stahr, the hero of F. Scott Fitzgerald's novel *The Last Tycoon*; and who became vice-president and head of production at Metro-Goldwyn-Mayer while still in his twenties. Under his supervision the studio became Hollywood's most prestigious film studio.

Thalberg died of pneumonia in 1936 at the tender age of thirty-seven. The following year, the Academy instituted the Irving G. Thalberg Memorial Award — a solid bronze bust of Thalberg, resting on a black marble base. It weighs 10.75 pounds and is 9 inches tall.

The Thalberg bust in use today (there were two earlier versions) was sculpted by Gualberto Rocchi in 1957 and was first used in 1961 when Stanley Kramer received the award.

The award is not necessarily given each year. In 1940 studio executive Walter Wanger announced, "There will be no presentation of the Thalberg Award tonight, as the Academy did not think any individual deserved it."

Which Oscar is given to "an individual in the motion picture industry whose technological contributions have brought credit to the industry"?

Gordon E. Sawyer was former head of the sound department at Samuel Goldwyn Studios — he did sound on *West Side Story* and *Gone with the Wind*, among others — and a member of the Scientific and Technical Awards Committee from 1936 to 1977.

After his death at age seventy-five from a heart attack, an honorary Oscar was established in his name — the Gordon E. Sawyer Award — to recognize "an individual in the motion picture industry whose technological contributions have brought credit to the industry." As a rule suggestions for this award are made through the Scientific and Technical Awards Committee.

What is the American Film Institute's highest honour?

In 1973, AFI's board of trustees established the AFI Life Achievement Award, which honours filmmakers and performers "whose talent has in a fundamental way advanced the film art." Twenty years later they extended the criteria to encompass individuals "with active careers and work of significance yet to be accomplished."

Past honourees include Billy Wilder, Elizabeth Taylor, Frank Capra, Barbara Stanwyck, Jack Nicholson, Sidney Poitier, Harrison Ford, Tom Hanks, Robert De Niro, and Meryl Streep.

What did Bob Hope call "the major goof of TV history"?

Hope may have been overstating the case a bit when he called a twenty-minute shortfall in the 31st Annual Academy Awards show (1959) "the major goof of TV history." For the first, and last, time in Oscar history, the show ended early. Really early. *Variety* called the broadcast "a topflight effort this time out — until it ran short. What might have been Hollywood's best Oscar production ended with an embarrassing thud as the two-hour production ran 20 minutes short."

Singer Mitzi Gaynor was doing the show's finale, "There's No Business Like Show Business," accompanied by the evening's winners and presenters, when the show's producer Jerry Wald signalled to emcee Jerry Lewis to keep the number going.

"Another twenty times!" Lewis shouted maniacally, as the all-star ensemble remained onstage, singing and dancing to chorus after chorus.

When the dancing grew tiresome, Lewis tried cracking wise: "We're showing *Three Stooges* shorts to cheer up the losers!" Next he grabbed a baton and started conducting the orchestra, shouting, "We may get a bar mitzvah out of this!"

Lewis valiantly tried to keep things going by mugging for the cameras, but when he produced a trumpet and started playing off-key, NBC put the show out of its misery and pulled the plug. To fill the remaining time they aired an aptly chosen alternative program: a sports documentary on pistol shooting.

How many times did Marilyn Monroe appear on the Oscar stage?

Monroe was never nominated, but she appeared on the Oscar show once as a presenter, on March 29, 1951. At the time, she was a couple of years away from A-list stardom but had appeared in a number of films, including *The Asphalt Jungle* and *All about Eve*.

She almost didn't make it onto the stage, however. She was scheduled to present the award for sound recording, but shortly before she was due onstage, she discovered a rip in her dress and burst into tears.

The rip was repaired, while some of the other presenters tried to calm her. She made it out onstage, but seemed uneasy and barely acknowledged the audience.

Why did Sammy Davis Jr., Sidney Poitier, and Rod Steiger threaten to boycott the 40th Annual Academy Awards?

Four days before the Oscars show was to take place on April 8, 1968, civil rights leader Martin Luther King Jr. was assassinated in Memphis. The funeral was scheduled for April 9, and several presenters, including Sidney Poiter, Sammy Davis Jr., and Rod Steiger, said they would not appear if the show took place before the funeral.

Davis told reporters he found it "morally incongruous" to sing "Talk to the Animals" while King lay in state.

The Academy did the right thing and postponed the show to April 10. "This has been a fateful week in the history of our nation," said Academy president Gregory Peck, "and the two-day delay of this ceremony is the Academy's way of paying our profound respect to the memory of Dr. Martin Luther King Jr."

Appropriately enough the big winner that year was a drama about race relations called *In the Heat of the Night*.

Which Hollywood social club hands out the Sour Apple Award?

A The Hollywood Women's Press Club has been handing out awards at their annual Christmas party since 1941. At the very first ceremony Bob Hope and Bette Davis were given Golden Apples as Most Co-operative Actor and Actress, while Ginger Rogers and Fred Astaire were given the Sour Apple.

The Sour Apple was originally given to the least co-operative actor and actress. In 1967, it was changed to the person who presented a poor image of Hollywood. In 1978, it was switched again to the person who most believed his or her own publicity.

Only one person has shown up in person to collect their Sour Apple dishonour — screenwriter Joe Eszterhas in 1995.

Q Who do the Golden Boot Awards pay tribute to?

A The Golden Boot Awards are a way to recognize the achievements of cowboy film heroes and heroines, as well as writers, directors, stunt people, and character actors who had significant involvement in the film and TV western. Founded in 1983 by Pat Buttram, proceeds from the Golden Boot Awards benefit the health and human services, retirement, and child care programs of the Motion Picture & Television Fund in Woodland Hills, California.

Q When did the Academy begin sealing the winners' names in envelopes to keep them secret?

A From the inception of the Academy Awards, newspapers were given advance notice of the Oscar results so they could publish the winners' names the night of the ceremony. In 1937, Best Actress nominee Gladys George — up for her talkie debut, *Valiant Is the Word for Carrie*, a movie later parodied by the Three Stooges as *Violent Is the Word for Curly* — discovered she had lost to Luise Rainer after she wandered through the press room. Later, in the loo, George spilled the beans to odds-on favourite Carole Lombard that she, too, was going home empty-handed. Three years later, after several attendees got their hands on the 8:45 p.m. edition of the *Los Angeles Times* and learned the results on their way to the Oscar ceremony, the Academy opted for sealed envelopes and secrecy.

The following year, during the February 27, 1941, ceremony, the now-famous words, "The envelope, please," were first uttered on the Academy stage. Host Bob Hope joked about the innovation: "How about these secret ballots? Columnists have exerted every trick to discover the winners beforehand and when the last envelope was sealed, Price, Waterhouse had to open it again to let [gossip columnist] Sidney Skolsky out."

Not everyone thought it was funny, however. Several L.A. newspapers complained that the sealed envelopes prevented them from meeting their deadlines and enabled radio to scoop them by announcing the winners first. *The Mirror* even criticized the Academy for bad manners — they claimed that the awards would be nothing without the press coverage and the Academy's decision to withhold the winners' names from the papers until after press time showed a lack of gratitude. The Academy didn't budge on its new policy, and by the following year the dailies were waiting in suspense just like everyone else.

Who designed the original statue for the British Academy Film Awards in 1948?

The British Academy Film Awards — the BAFTAs — are the U.K.'s chief film awards, founded in April 1947 in a hotel room at the Hyde Park Hotel under the chairmanship of David Lean. Legendary sculptor Henry Moore designed the original BAFTA statuettes, which took the form of a large bronze seated lady and were valued at £550.

In 1958, the British Film Academy merged with the Guild of Television Producers and Directors to form the Society of Film and Television Arts, and in 1976 the Academy was renamed the British Academy of Film and Television Arts. Since 1998, the film awards have been sponsored by the mobile phone company Orange; the ceremony's name officially became the Orange British Academy Film Awards in 2000.

Gold A-Go-Go

Q Which televised awards show gives an award for Favorite Smile and Favorite Animated Movie Star?

A In 2004 the People's Choice Awards freshened up their reward categories, adding fourteen new awards, including Favorite Smile (Julia Roberts), Favorite Hair (Kate Hudson), Favorite Look (Kate Hudson), and Favorite Animated Movie Star (Donkey in *Shrek 2*).

The People's Choice Awards first aired on CBS in March 1975.

Q Which movie awards show features outrageous — and star-studded — parodies of current films?

A The movie parodies on the MTV Movie Awards were the invention of producer Joel Gallen. "Every year I say this is my last year because I think 'How are we going to top last year?'" Gallen says. "But it's still fun because we get to try something new each time."

Memorable parodies include a *Clueless* lampoon performed by the cast of *The Golden Girls*, a *Matrix Reloaded* skit featuring Justin Timberlake and Will Ferrell, and a *Mission: Impossible II* spoof featuring Ben Stiller as Tom Cruise's temperamental stunt double.

The collaboration between Stiller and Cruise almost didn't happen. By the time Cruise committed to doing a sketch with Stiller, Stiller was in Australia on his honeymoon. Trying to find a way to make the skit work, Gallen emailed Stiller.

"I know you're on your honeymoon, but Tom will only do the sketch with you. Is there any chance you would come back early?" Gallen says Stiller replied, "Are you insane? My wife would kill me," but then added, "But, if you're 110 percent sure that Tom will do it..." The satire was such a hit that Cruise later used it on the *Mission: Impossible II* DVD.

Not everyone is as co-operative as Stiller. Gallen tried in vain to team up Warren Beatty and Jack Nicholson for a re-enactment of a scene from *Dude, Where's My Car?* Both declined.

Q Which film festival award fracas led to the creation of the Cannes Film Festival?

A The roots of the Cannes Film Festival go back to 1932, when the first competitive international film festival was held in Venice. In those days, the festival and its awards were highly political. The films were almost secondary to the national prestige of the participating countries, and as the Second World War edged closer, the awards at Venice began to noticeably favour the countries of the fascist alliance, particularly Germany and Italy.

In 1939, France was tipped to win the festival's top prize with the film *Grand Illusion*. The award, or Coppa Mussolini as it was known then, however, ended up being jointly awarded to *Olympia*, a German film produced in association with the Nazi Ministry of Propaganda, and *Luciano Serra, Pilota*, produced by Mussolini's own son. Outraged, the French, British, and American jury members withdrew from the festival in protest.

The snub spurred the French to found a festival of their own. Cannes was not the first choice but was ultimately chosen because of its "sunny and enchanting location." Most people acknowledge, however, that the real reason for its selection was the fact that the City of Cannes agreed to cough up the money to build a dedicated venue for the event.

In June 1939 Louis Lumière, founding father of the cinema, announced that he was prepared to preside over the 1st International Film Festival, scheduled to take place in Cannes from September 1 to 20 with the aim of "encouraging the development of all forms of cinematographic art and foster a spirit of collaboration between film-producing countries."

The festival got off to a rough start. On September 1, guests were treated to an opening night gala screening of *The Hunchback of Notre Dame*, starring Charles Laughton. The next morning Hitler invaded Poland, and the festival was hastily abandoned. The next festival wouldn't take place for seven years.

Q Which is the largest branch of the Academy?

A The Actors branch of the Academy has always been the largest, comprising one-quarter of the total membership. Originally, in 1928, there were just 362 members of the Academy — 91 actors, 78 directors, 70 writers, 69 technicians, and 54 producers — but by 2002 the membership had swelled to 5,739 voting members, with 1,315 (23 percent) being actors.

What was the first movie to campaign with ads in the press for Oscar consideration?

In 1935 MGM was the first studio to campaign with ads in the trade papers for Oscar consideration. The movie was *Ah, Wilderness,* the story of small-town life in turn-of-the-century America based on Eugene O'Neill's only comedy, and it didn't receive a single nomination.

Who was the first Hasty Pudding Man of the Year?

The student-written Hasty Pudding Theatricals have been a staple at Harvard University every year since 1891, the only exceptions being during the world wars. The Man of the Year was introduced in 1967, when comedian Bob Hope was given the now traditional gold pudding pot. Winners attend an afternoon parade and a preview of the season's theatrical performances at the Hasty Pudding Theatre in Cambridge, Massachusetts.

The Man of the Year of 2004, Robert Downey Jr., sang, poked fun at his numerous drug arrests and times in jail, and made out with a drag queen when he picked up his Hasting Pudding Man of the Year Award.

"I haven't been this excited since playing pocket pool and watching *Animal Planet* this morning," he said.

What theatre became the first permanent home of the Academy Awards ceremony in 2002?

The 136,000-square-foot Kodak Theatre, the anchor of Los Angeles' Hollywood and Highland real estate development, is the first permanent

The Kodak Theatre, the permanent home of the Academy Awards at Hollywood and Highland in Los Angeles.

home of the Academy Awards show in seventy-three years — since the first ceremony was held at the Roosevelt Hotel across the street on Hollywood Boulevard.

The opulent Kodak Theatre — the stage alone is one of the largest in the country, measuring 120 feet wide and 75 feet deep — was custom designed to meet the Academy's needs, with camera positions built-in, a direct path from the speaker's podium to the special press room — which can accommodate fifteen hundred journalists for those post-Oscar interviews — separate VIP entrances, and a direct connection to the adjacent luxury hotel.

The red carpet that leads into the Kodak Theatre runs through a shopping mall, past dozens of stores, including Versace, Ralph Lauren Polo, Luxe Lingerie, Neuhaus Chocolatier, Louis Vuitton, Origins, Planet Funk, and the Build-a-Bear Workshop. Stars walking the carpet will not be able to stop and shop. At the request of the Academy, the mall was designed to include removable signs and curtain rods that allow the storefronts to be completely hidden.

The awards ceremony has been bopped around between several different locations over the years. In the early years the Oscar banquets were held in glamorous Hollywood hotels — the Blossom Room of the Hollywood Roosevelt Hotel (first ceremony), the Cocoanut Grove of the Ambassador Hotel (second, twelfth, fifteenth), the Fiesta Room of the Ambassador Hotel (third, fifth, sixth), the Sala D'Oro of the Biltmore Hotel (fourth), the Biltmore Bowl of the Biltmore Hotel (seventh through eleventh, thirteenth and fourteenth) — but once the festivities outgrew hotel ballrooms the event was moved to Grauman's Chinese Theatre for a three-year run in the mid-forties.

A series of homes followed — the Academy Award Theater, at the Academy's former Melrose Avenue headquarters (twenty-first), the RKO Pantages Theatre (twenty-second through thirty-second), the Santa Monica Civic Auditorium (thirty-third through fortieth) — until the Academy decided upon the Dorothy Chandler Pavilion, home to the renowned Joffrey Ballet, in the late sixties. This remained the base for the ceremony for almost twenty years before switching to the larger Shrine Auditorium, which at 6,300 seats has roughly twice the capacity of the Dorothy Chandler Pavilion. During the nineties, and leading up to the opening of Kodak Theatre in 2002, the awards alternated between the Dorothy Chandler Pavilion and the Shrine.

The Oscar ceremony was split between Hollywood and New York in the mid to late fifties. East coast ceremonies took place at the NBC International Theatre, NYC (twenty-fifth), the NBC Center Theatre, NYC (twenty-sixth), and the NBC Century Theatre, NYC (twenty-seventh through twenty-ninth).

What are the requirements for membership to the Actors branch of the Academy?

To become one of the 1,315 (2002 number) members of the Actors branch of the Academy you must have "a minimum of three feature film credits, in all of which the roles played were scripted roles, one of which was released in the last five years, and all of which are of a caliber that reflect the high standards of the Academy." Occasionally exceptions are made — as with the case of Barbra Streisand — when "in the judgment of the Actor's Branch Executive Committee, [they] otherwise achieved unique distinction, earned special merit or made an outstanding contribution as a motion picture actor."

All Academy memberships are for life, although people can be transferred from active members to associate members, who are not allowed to vote in the Oscars.

Q When were the Golden Globes first aired on television?

A The first telecast of the Globes was in 1958, but until 1963 they were aired only locally in Los Angeles. The first national telecasts of the awards occurred during a special segment on *The Andy Williams Show* in 1964 and 1965. *Variety* praised the broadcast for being "smooth and rapid and in color."

Q What was the first award specifically geared to young performers under the age of eighteen?

A The Young Artist Foundation was the first organization to establish an awards show for young artists under the age of eighteen in television, motion pictures, theatre, and music. Founder of the Young Artist Awards Maureen Dragone writes on their website, "During my long standing membership in the Hollywood Foreign Press Association (Golden Globes), I became more aware that the majority of young stars were not receiving the recognition enjoyed by seasoned performers. Two cases in point were Ricky Schroder for *The Champ* and Justin Henry for *Kramer vs. Kramer*, in which they were both placed in the same categories as their adult counterparts. As a champion of youth, I commended the fact that they were at least nominated, but I felt that young artists should have their own special award show."

The first awards — then called Youth In Film/Young Artist Awards — were held in the 1978–79 season. They presented eleven competitive awards — honouring, among others, a then thirteen-year-old Diane Lane for her acting debut opposite Laurence Olivier in the romantic dramedy *A Little Romance* with a Best Juvenile Actress in a Motion

Picture statue — and four special awards for outstanding contributions to youth entertainment. Other boldface names to win include River Phoenix of *The Mosquito Coast,* who took home the Best Young Male Superstar in Motion Pictures in 1988; Christian Bale of *Empire of the Sun,* who won 1989's Best Young Actor in a Motion Picture; and Haley Joel Osment, who won Best Performance by an Actor Under Ten in a Motion Picture in 1995 for his role in *Forrest Gump.*

The Young Artist Foundation is a non-profit organization that also awards scholarships to financially and/or physically challenged young people seeking a future in the entertainment industry.

Who is eligible to win a Taurus Award?

Taurus statuettes are awarded to "the unsung heroes of the movie stunt industry," men and women selected by the members of the World Stunt Academy for doing the most outstanding work in categories that include Best Fight, Best Fire Stunt, Best High Work, and Best Work with a Vehicle.

The ceremony is famous for its spectacular staging of onstage stunt sequences. At the 2004 awards, hosts Dennis Hopper and Carmen Electra opened the show by skydiving onto the stage from an airplane above the Paramount. Later, actor Brendan Fraser leapt off a ten-storey building and through a glass ceiling to present the Taurus award for Best High Work. Action star Michelle Rodriguez crashed onto the stage after a wild car chase through Paramount's back lot to present the award for Best Work with a Vehicle, and finally a stuntman engulfed in flames walked onto the stage to hand the winner's envelope to Adam Brody, who was presenting the award for Best Fire Stunt.

The Taurus World Stunt Awards were envisioned and created by Red Bull Energy Drink CEO Dietrich Mateschitz to honour stunt performers around the world. The show also benefits the Taurus World Stunt Awards Foundation, which was established by an endowment from Mateschitz to provide financial assistance to stunt performers who experience debilitating stunt-related injuries.

REEL WINNERS

Q Which film festival presents the Silver and Golden Bear Awards?

A Internationale Filmfestspiele Berlin (the Berlin International Film Festival, also called Berlinale) adopted the bear as its symbol — the bear is also the official symbol of the City of Berlin — at the inaugural awards in 1951.

The Golden Bears are awarded by the festival's International Jury to the best film in the competition and by the International Short Film Jury to the best film in the short film competition. The International Jury also awards Silver Bears in six categories: the Jury Grand Prix, Best Director, Best Actress, Best Actor, Best Score, and Outstanding Artistic Contribution.

Q Which film festival presents the Leone d'Oro for Best Film?

A The Venice Film Festival is the oldest continuing fête devoted to cinema. With the exception of several short breaks in the thirties, forties, and seventies, the festival, or Esposizione Internazionale d'Arte Cinematografica as it was known in the early days, has rewarded excellence in cinema since 1932. From the first fest to 1942 the Coppa Mussolini was the festival's grand prize and was given for Best Foreign Film and Best Italian Film. In 1949 the Leone d'Oro, or Golden Lion, for Best Film was adopted.

The first Venice Film Festival featured an audience referendum so the public could vote for a variety of categories, including Most Touching Film, Most Amusing Film, and Best Technical Perfection. Some of the performer forms included Mickey Mouse as an option for favourite actor.

There has been a long-standing rivalry between Venice and Cannes over which is the European film festival of record that continues to this day. (See page 38 for details.) Accepting the Leone d'Oro for his film *Vera Drake,* which had been snubbed by Cannes in 2004, Mike Leigh said, "I want to thank most sincerely the Cannes Film Festival for rejecting this film, so that it might be here this evening. Thank you, Venice!" With that remark the crowd erupted into applause and shouts of "Bravo!"

"COULDN'T HAVE DONE IT WITHOUT YOU..."

Best Supporting Actor and Actress Trivia

REEL WINNERS

Q Which 1999 Oscar winner asked Tom Cruise if he knew how much supporting actors get paid during his speech?

A On March 26, 2000, Michael Caine added a second Best Supporting Oscar (the first was for *Hannah and Her Sisters* in 1986) to his collection when he won for his performance as an ether-addicted abortionist in *The Cider House Rules*. He was up against Tom Cruise (*Magnolia*), Michael Duncan Clarke (*The Green Mile*), Jude Law (*The Talented Mr. Ripley*), and Haley Joel Osment (*The Sixth Sense*).

"I was looking watching all the others and thinking back when I saw the performances. I'm thinking of how the Academy changed 'The winner is' to 'The Oscar goes to,' and if ever there was a category where the Oscar goes to someone without there being a winner, it's this one, because I do not feel like being the winner," said Caine in his acceptance speech.

"You have Michael [Duncan Clarke], who I'd never heard of, quite frankly … who is astonishing. You have Jude [Law], who is going to be a big star no matter what happens. You have Tom [Cruise], who, if you had won this, your price would have gone down so fast. Have you any idea what supporting actors get paid? And we only get one motor home — a small one. And Haley Osment, what an astonishing — there he is. Haley, when I saw you, I thought, 'Well, that's me out of it.' So, really, I'm basically up here, guys, to represent you as what I hope you will all be, a survivor."

Later Caine explained the context of his acceptance speech: "I was watching the performances on the big screen right in front of me and when they finished the five of us, I said to my wife, 'I can't win this.' And then when they said my name, I went up there — but we are all very friendly and I had only just met little Haley and I thought, 'This is not fair.' So I wanted to take the edge off it for Haley, because he didn't win and I'm pleased that I said what I did. I was very sincere and I thought all the other performances were extraordinary. They had to pick someone so they picked me."

Later that year Caine was given an even bigger honour — he was formally knighted at Buckingham Palace on November 16, 2000. The actor was knighted under his real name, Maurice Micklewhite, but will be known professionally as Sir Michael Caine.

"Couldn't Have Done It Without You..."

Q: Who thanked the Golden Globes for giving "millions and millions of stringy-haired and toothless people a lot of hope" in 2003?

A: On Monday, January 27, 2003, Chris Cooper won the Best Supporting Actor Globe for his role in *Adaptation*. Cooper, who played an unkempt orchid poacher chronicled in Susan Orlean's book *The Orchid Thief*, offered his thanks, saying, "You've given millions and millions of stringy-haired and toothless people a lot of hope."

Cooper also thanked co-star Nicolas Cage as well as "Nic Cage," a reference to Cage's portrayal of screenwriter Charlie Kaufman and his fictitious twin brother, Donald.

Q: Who claimed to have been nominated for 789 acting awards at the 60th Annual Golden Globe Awards?

A: When Meryl Streep picked up her Best Supporting Actress Globe for her role in *Adaptation* in 2003 she said, after a long standing ovation, "I've just been nominated 789 times, and I was getting so settled over there for a long winter's nap. I didn't have anything prepared, because it's been since the Pleistocene era since I've won anything. Thank you, thank you, thank you, thank you, thank you, thank you!"

Adaptation follows the angst-ridden efforts of screenwriter Charlie Kaufman as he adapts real-life author Susan Orlean's book *The Orchid Thief* for the screen. In the film's climax Kaufman portrays Orlean as a drug-crazed, would-be killer.

"Susan Orlean, I apologize for the second half," said Streep, who played her in the film.

The actress had last won a Golden Globe in 1983 — twenty years earlier — for *Sophie's Choice*.

Q: Who has the longest name of any Oscar nominee?

A: With twenty-five letters, Mary Elizabeth Mastrantonio, who earned a Best Supporting Actress nod for *The Color of Money* on March 30, 1987, has the longest name of the dozens of actors and actresses nominated for Academy Awards since 1927.

Q Who, it was rumoured, won the Academy Award for Best Supporting Actress in 1992 because Oscar presenter Jack Palance read the wrong name by mistake?

A After the 1993 Academy Awards ceremony, a false rumour spread that the award for 1992's Best Supporting Actress had been given to Marisa Tomei by mistake after presenter Jack Palance called out the wrong name.

The rumour was disseminated by film critic Rex Reed, who claimed that Palance was "drunk" or "stoned" when he gave Tomei the award, and who further alleged that a "massive cover-up" was underway to prevent the public from finding out about the mistake. The nasty rumour was fuelled by the belief that Tomei's comic turn as the wisecracking, Brooklynese Mona Lisa in *My Cousin Vinny* was too slender to merit her winning an Academy Award over the other, more experienced nominees — Joan Plowright, Miranda Richardson, Vanessa Redgrave, and Judy Davis.

The Academy has safeguards against this very kind of snafu. During the Oscarcast there are two officials from the accounting firm of PricewaterhouseCoopers (the official tabulators of the Academy Award ballots) posted in the wings. In the event that a wrong name was read, one of the officials would instantly step up to the podium and announce the correct winner.

Years later the stigma of the rumours still lingered. In March 2000, when fifty-five Academy Award statuettes were stolen en route from Chicago to Los Angeles, late-night comedian Craig Kilborn joked, "This is not the first time an Oscar has been stolen. In 1993 Marisa Tomei stole an Oscar for *My Cousin Vinny*."

Q Who, joked Jay Leno, might accept his Best Supporting Actor Oscar with the line, "I see facelifts…"?

"Couldn't Have Done It Without You..."

A "Young Haley Joel Osment was nominated for a Best Supporting Actor Oscar for his role as Cole Sear in *The Sixth Sense*," Jay Leno said on the *Tonight Show* in February 2000. "As he looked around he said, 'I see jealous people.' If he wins the Oscar, he'll look out over the crowd and say, 'I see facelifts!'"

Q Who was nominated for a BAFTA for Best Supporting Actor despite the fact that he died halfway through the filming of the movie and was computer generated for several scenes?

A Oliver Reed, the hard-drinking actor who was as well known for his antics off-screen as he was for his performances onscreen, died in May 1999 after a drinking binge during the shoot for the film *Gladiator*. He passed away from a heart attack after downing three bottles of rum and beating five sailors at arm wrestling.

Reed wasn't quite done shooting his role, but that didn't slow down production. Director Ridley Scott reportedly spent $3 million to digitally recreate Reed's face on a stand-in's body.

On the digital trickery, Mark Morris of the *Observer* wrote, "As Reed wears North African clothing for much of the film, the void is much better disguised than it might have been, but it's still easy to spot. Proof again that the much maligned Ed Wood — who got his wife's chiropractor to complete Bela Lugosi's role *in Plan 9 from Outer Space* — was simply ahead of his time."

The deceased Reed didn't pull in the sympathy vote. He lost the BAFTA to the healthy and very much alive Benicio Del Toro for the film *Traffic*.

Reed's drinking bouts were the stuff of legend. In 1974, Reed invited thirty-six rugby players to a party at his home. Between Saturday night and Sunday lunchtime, they managed to consume sixty gallons of beer, thirty-two bottles of Scotch, seventeen bottles of gin, four crates of wine, and one bottle of Babycham. Reed then led the players on a nude dawn run through the Surrey countryside. On his forty-eight-hour stag night in 1985, Reed claimed to have downed 136 pints of beer. The next year he was forced to dig up nine acres of his back garden after forgetting where he had buried his wife's jewellery when drunk, and during one live television show he drank wine from half-pint glasses, uttered obscenities, and fell over a sofa.

Q Who took out ads in the Hollywood trade papers to convince Academy members to vote for him as Best Supporting Actor that read, "Win, lose or draw, you're all my cousins and I love you all!"

A Cowboy character actor Chill Wills (he was ironically named Chill because the day he was born was the hottest of 1903) became a Hollywood joke when he shamelessly campaigned for an Academy Award for his role in *The Alamo*. In retort to the "cousins" ad, Groucho Marx responded with his own ad, which read, "Dear Chill, I am delighted to be your cousin, but I voted for Sal Mineo."

More ridicule followed his next and more blatant posting. The ad featured a picture of the movie's stars with the text, "We of *The Alamo* cast are praying — harder than the real Texans prayed for their lives at the Alamo — for Chill Wills to win the Oscar." That ad was too much, even for the movie's director, John Wayne. Wayne was no stranger to stumping for *The Alamo*, even going so far as to string up a banner across Sunset Boulevard that read, "This Is The Most Important Motion Picture Ever Made. It's Timeless. It Will Run Forever," but calling on God was too much.

Wayne released a statement that effectively quashed Wills's chances of getting an award. "No one in the Batjac organization [Wayne's producing company] … has been a party to [Mr. Wills's] trade paper advertising. I refrain from using stronger language because I'm sure that his intentions were not as bad as his taste."

Wills was nominated for Best Supporting Actor but lost to Peter Ustinov for his role in *Spartacus*.

Q Who is the only person to win two acting Golden Globes in the same year?

"Couldn't Have Done It Without You..."

A In 1989 Sigourney Weaver was voted Best Actress for *Gorillas in the Mist* and Best Supporting Actress for *Working Girl*. When she collected her second statue of the evening, UPI reported, Weaver told the amused audience that the gorillas in her film really deserved the Golden Globe statuette, but, inasmuch as "they can't eat it or make a nest of it, I think I'll keep it."

Q Who called the 42nd Annual Academy Awards "some sort of masturbatory fantasy"?

A Best Supporting Actor nominee for *Bob & Carol & Ted & Alice* Elliott Gould told reporters he thought the Oscarcast was "some sort of masturbatory fantasy," and added, "I would rather have a good three-man basketball game than sit there in my monkey suit." He nonetheless showed up in a brand spanking new "monkey suit" and presented an award. Gould lost the Oscar to Gig Young, who won for his performance in *They Shoot Horses, Don't They?*

Q Who accepted her 1940 Best Supporting Actress Oscar with the words, "Awards are nice, but I'd rather have a job"?

A Plump character actress Jane Darwell appeared in over two hundred films but was unemployed when she won her Best Supporting Actress Oscar on February 27, 1941. The next day *Variety* followed up on the story, reporting that Darwell "has worked only five weeks since appearing in this picture and has been unemployed for the past seven months." Within weeks of the ceremony, 20th Century Fox had her back on set and she went on to work steadily, appearing in another fifty-nine movies in the next twenty-five years.

Q Who presented Courtney Love with a New York Film Critics Circle Award for Best Supporting Actress with the words of caution, "Cherish this moment later when there are no awards"?

A Love arrived at the 1997 New York Film Critics Circle ceremony at the Rainbow Room with an entourage, including eccentric filmmaker Oliver Stone, in tow. On the way in a mischievous Stone joked with people that Love was a hooker he had picked up outside, but there was nothing playful about the tone of his speech when he gave her the Best Supporting Actress award for her part as Althea Leasure, a bisexual stripper, in *The People vs. Larry Flynt.*

"Cherish this moment later when there are no awards," he said gravely.

There was an audible gasp in the audience at the tone of the remark, which seemed very out of place at a ceremony meant to celebrate film and filmmakers. "Oliver! It's not so tragic," said Love, "I know you don't think I'm an actress."

Q Who was the first Latina actress to win an Academy Award?

A Rita Moreno is listed in the Guinness Book of World Records as the first performer to win an Oscar, a Tony, an Emmy, and a Grammy. She is also the first Latina actress to win an Academy Award. When Rock Hudson called out her name as Best Supporting Actress at the April 9, 1962, Oscarcast she charged the stage, shouting, "I can't believe it! Good Lord! I'll leave you with that."

For her Oscar-winning role as Bernardo's girlfriend Anita in *West Side Story*, critic Leonard Maltin called her a "little charismatic firecracker" who "exploded onto movie screens … delivering a dynamic performance."

Nominated for an incredible eleven Academy Awards in 1961, *West Side Story* took home ten Oscars, including Best Picture, Best Supporting Actor for George Chakaris, Best Supporting Actress for Moreno, and Best Direction for Robert Wise and Jerome Robbins.

Q Who was the first African-American actor to win a Best Supporting Oscar?

A The first African-American actor to be nominated for a Best Supporting Actor Oscar was Rupert Crosse in 1969 for the Steve McQueen action/adventure film *The Reivers*. He lost out to Gig Young in *They Shoot Horses, Don't They?*

The first actor of colour to win a Best Supporting Actor Oscar was Louis Gossett Jr. for his work as the hardassed drill sergeant in *An Officer and a Gentleman*. It had been nineteen years since a black actor had won an Oscar, and in the days before the ceremony a reception was held in Gossett's honour. Sidney Poitier recalled the feeling of being "within touching distance of an Academy Award" and added that Gossett's performance was so strong "it will be inconceivable if he doesn't win."

After his win in a backstage press conference Gossett advised young African-American actors to follow his lead: "Don't just look for black roles," he said. "Just look for good roles."

Q Which second-generation Oscar winner shocked viewers when she gushed, "I am just so in love with my brother" during her acceptance speech?

A When Angelina Jolie was two years old, her father, Jon Voight, scooped the Best Actor Oscar for *Coming Home*. Twenty-two years later Jolie would collect her own Oscar, a Best Supporting Actress trophy for *Girl, Interrupted*. In what gossip columnist Ted Casablanca called a "that's not Hollywood — that's creepy" moment, Angelina thanked her brother, James Haven, saying, "I am just so in love with my brother."

Jolie got spanked in the gossip columns for the offhand remark. Hundreds of column inches were generated, speculating that the actress and her sibling were having an incestuous affair. *Entertainment Weekly* wrote that the disply "just generally gave everyone the heebie jeebies," while *E! Online* said, "What man — or woman, for that matter — wouldn't like to be, even just for a moment, Angelina Jolie's unusually loved brother."

In 2000 Jolie and her brother publicly spoke out to put to bed rumours that the two were having an incestuous love affair, with the actress saying that Jamie "has always supported me and he wanted to make me happy" and that her movie career "wouldn't mean very much if I didn't have him."

Angelina Jolie, who has the letter H tattooed on her wrist in honour of her brother, James Haven.

Brother James added, "I've heard what people are saying, and it's a very weird thing. We love each other. If that's unusual these days, that's sad." He also said that the two haven't slept in the same bed since they were preteens, when "we fell asleep in our mom's bed while watching television."

Who are the only brothers to be nominated for Oscars?

The first (and so far only) brothers to earn acting Oscar nominations are River and his younger sibling Joaquin Phoenix.

River's role as Danny Pope, the son of radicals-on-the-run Judd Hirsch and Christine Lahti, in the 1988 film *Running on Empty* earned him a Best Supporting Actor Oscar nomination. He lost to Kevin Kline's comedic performance in *A Fish Called Wanda*. The actor died on Halloween in 1993 from drug-induced heart failure at age twenty-three.

Thirteen years later Joaquin Phoenix took his mother to the Academy Awards ceremony where he was up for Best Supporting Actor for his role as a selfish, paranoid young emperor in the Roman epic *Gladiator*. But Benicio Del Toro took home the award that night for his work in the film *Traffic*.

"Couldn't Have Done It Without You..."

Who did one-handed push-ups during his Oscar acceptance speech?

In 1991, seventy-two-year-old Jack Palance won a Best Supporting Actor Oscar for his role as the prickly Curly Washburn in the comedy *City Slickers*. The plucky Palance's performance at the award ceremony is probably better remembered than the film he won for. After boasting that he "crapped bigger than [*City Slickers* co-star and Oscar show host] Billy Crystal!" the elderly actor flopped down on the floor and did several one-armed push-ups. Backstage when he was asked about the stunt he shrugged and said, "I didn't know what the hell else to do."

"I was so thrilled that he won," Crystal said later. He sprinkled the rest of the Oscarcast with ad libs scripted on the fly with writer Bruce Vilanch, letting loose a string of one-liners based on the display of virility.

Courtesy of AMPAS

Frequent Oscarcast host Billy Crystal, who once revealed that he always keeps a toothbrush inside his tux during his hosting duties to remind him of his childhood days when he'd go to bed holding his toothbrush on Oscar night. "When I started hosting the show, I'd stow my toothbrush in my pocket because I wanted that big audience to feel like the living room. And it did."

Crystal joked that Palance had bungee-jumped off the Hollywood sign, that he was backstage on the StairMaster, and when a vast horde of children walked out to sing a song, Crystal announced, "He's the father of all these kids."

A year later when Palance provided the voice of Rothbart in the *The Swan Princess* his character was featured doing one-handed push-ups.

Q: Who are the oldest performers to be nominated for Best Supporting Actress Oscars?

A: The earliest born Best Supporting Actress nominee was *Titanic*'s Gloria Stewart — one of the founding members of the Screen Actors Guild — who was eighty-seven when she picked up a nod (but no Oscar) from the Academy for playing the hundred-year-old survivor of the sinking of the Titanic. On Oscar night in 1998 she wore a $20-million, fifteen-karat blue diamond necklace — which came complete with an army of bodyguards to safeguard the gem — supplied by jeweller Harry Winston. "When I graduated from Santa Monica High in 1927, I was voted the girl most likely to succeed," she said at the time of the nomination. "I didn't realize it would take so long."

Jessica Tandy was eighty-two when she was nominated for *Fried Green Tomatoes*, while legendary stage actress and Pulitzer Prize winner Eva Le Galienne was eighty when her quietly touching performance as Ellen Burstyn's grandmother in *Resurrection* earned her an Oscar nomination.

Q: Who are the oldest performers to be nominated for Best Supporting Actor Oscars?

A: Old Vic–trained theatre legend Ralph Richardson was the oldest person to be nominated for a Best Supporting Actor Oscar for his work in his final film, *Greystoke: The Legend of Tarzan*. The 1985 nomination was a posthumous one, however; Richardson had died on October 10, 1983, at the age of eighty.

George Burns was eighty when he won the 1976 Oscar for Best Supporting Actor for *The Sunshine Boys*, and seventy-seven-year-old Don Ameche's exuberant performance as one of the rejuvenated old men in *Cocoon* earned him a Best Supporting Actor Oscar.

Q: Who was the first child to be nominated for an Academy Award?

"Couldn't Have Done It Without You..."

A Bonita Granville was just thirteen years old in 1936 when she was nominated for Best Supporting Actress for her role as Mary, an obnoxious girl who spread lies about her teachers in *These Three*.

Adapted from the Lillian Hellman play *The Children's Hour*, the film explores how a malicious lie disrupts the lives of schoolteachers Karen Wright (Merle Oberon) and Martha Dobie (Miriam Hopkins), both of whom are in love with Dr. Joe Cardin (Joel McCrea). The play's original lesbian theme was considered too hot for the audiences of the day, so Hellman, who also wrote the screenplay, reimagined the story with a heterosexual love triangle.

Granville lost the Oscar to Gale Sondergaard of *Anthony Adverse* but continued acting for another twenty years before retiring from the screen to produce the television series *Lassie*.

Q Which Best Supporting Actor winner said of his role in *Terms of Endearment*, "When I read the part, I knew I'd win the Oscar for it"?

Courtesy of AMPAS

Jack Nicholson, the most Acadamy Award–nominated actor in film history.

A Burt Reynolds was originally offered the part of ex-astronaut Garrett Breedlove in *Terms of Endearment* but turned it down to make *Stoker Ace*. The producers then approached Jack Nicholson, who said, "When I read the part, I knew I'd win the Oscar for it."

"I think you have got to have nutty goals in life," said Nicholson, who prepared for the part of the amorous astronaut by talking with a number of real astronauts while shooting on location in Houston. "I'd like to win more Oscars than Walt Disney, and I'd like to win them in every category."

Terms of Endearment won not only an Oscar for Nicholson — he beat out co-star John Lithgow for Best Supporting Actor — but also a Best Actress statue for Shirley MacLaine and three awards for James Brooks: Best Picture, Best Director, and Best Adapted Screenplay.

Q Which performance by an eleven-year-old actress did Roger Ebert call "one of the most extraordinary examples of a child's acting in movie history"?

A Winnipeg-born, New Zealand–raised Anna Paquin stunned critics with her moving performance as Flora McGrath, the daughter of a deaf-mute, in *The Piano* (1993). Besides the high praise from Ebert, Paquin earned a couple of Best Supporting Actress awards — from the Los Angeles Film Critics Association and the Academy of Motion Picture Arts and Sciences. She was the first New Zealander to receive an Academy Award in that category.

She later told a reporter that she keeps her Oscar in a bedroom closet so her friends won't see it and feel the need to compliment her on it.

Q Who is the youngest person to win an Oscar in a competitive category?

A Tatum O'Neal was just ten years old when she won her Best Supporting Actress Oscar in 1974 for playing the streetwise, cigarette-puffing schemer on the road during the Great Depression in *Paper Moon*, which also starred her father, Ryan O'Neal. In her autobiography, *A Paper Life*, Tatum notes that her father "was truly at the top of his game. He deserved an Oscar nomination at the very least." But the elder O'Neal wasn't recognized by the Academy, and that may have bruised his fragile ego. Peter Bogdanovich summed it up when he said, "Ryan's wonderful in it, and he sat there and watched the kid steal the picture."

"Maybe that's what first tipped the hair-trigger scales of our relationship," Tatum writes in her book. "Jealousy is rife in showbiz families. Legend has it — and people tell me — that when I got the Oscar nomination, Ryan slugged me. I don't remember that, but there are memories that I've blocked."

Who thanked "everyone I ever met in my entire life" as she collected the Best Supporting Actress Oscar on March 29, 1982?

After her Oscar win, *Reds* co-star Maureen Stapleton said, "I expected to win because I'm old and tired and I deserved it." She was a little more humble at the podium, where she breathlessly thanked "everyone I ever met in my entire life."

Who accepted her Best Supporting Actress Oscar on March 30, 1987, with the words, "Gee, this isn't like I imagined it would be in the bathtub"?

"Gee, this isn't like I imagined it would be in the bathtub," said Diane Wiest as she accepted her Best Supporting Actress award for *Hannah and Her Sisters*. She became so caught up in the moment that she forgot to thank her director. She realized the omission when she was almost off the stage and rushed back, shouting, "I left Woody Allen out of my speech!"

Who won an Oscar for playing an Oscar loser in 1978?

In the film *California Suite*, Maggie Smith plays Diana Barrie, an Oscar-nominated actress staying at the Beverly Hills Hotel with her gay companion, Sidney Cochran (Michael Caine). Sidney becomes the victim of Diana's outrage when she loses the Oscar. In real life, however, Maggie Smith, who took home a Best Supporting Actress statue for her role, was more reserved. "I've won two Oscars and I still don't begin to understand film acting," she said. "Oscar doesn't mean a thing in England. They don't know what they are."

 Who won a Best Supporting Actress Oscar despite having the least number of lines in her film — just eighteen — of any acting nominee in history?

Beatrice Straight won an Oscar for her role as William Holden's wife in *Network* in 1976. Straight was a well-respected stage actress who made her Broadway debut in 1935 and won a Tony award in 1953 for playing Elizabeth Proctor in Arthur Miller's *The Crucible*. Her work on *Network* totalled only three days of shooting, and most of what was shot was left on the cutting-room floor. In the end she is onscreen for less than six minutes.

Who was the first Asian actress to win an Oscar?

"I wish someone would help me now," said Miyoshi Umeki as she accepted her Best Supporting Actress Oscar for the film *Sayonara* on March 26, 1958. "I have nothing in my mind. Thank all American people."

The Japanese-born Umeki had been a nightclub entertainer before becoming a regular on the *Arthur Godfrey and His Friends* television variety show. She made the leap from television to the big screen with *Sayonara*, where she played a young girl married to an Air Force sergeant played by Red Buttons. Continuing to act until the early 1970s, she appeared in a number of films and as a semi-regular on the sitcom *The Courtship of Eddie's Father*.

Who left her Best Supporting Actress Oscar in the ladies' room during the 1979 Academy Awards?

"Couldn't Have Done It Without You..."

Meryl Streep left her just-claimed Oscar for *Kramer vs. Kramer* on the back of a toilet during the 1979 festivities. Though she had been nominated the previous year for *The Deer Hunter*, Streep won her first Oscar for her performance as the ex-wife fighting Dustin Hoffman for custody of their son in *Kramer vs. Kramer*.

"It shows how nervous I really am," said an embarrassed Streep after she'd reclaimed her statuette.

The role of the husband-leaving, child-abandoning wife in *Kramer vs. Kramer* had originally been offered to television star Kate Jackson, but she had to bow out because of scheduling problems caused by her role in *Charlie's Angels*. The part then went to Meryl Streep, who didn't see eye to eye with her co-star, Dustin Hoffman.

She told the story of how they met at the audition: "He came up to me and said, 'I'm Dustin — burp'— Hoffman,' and he put his hand on my breast. What an obnoxious pig, I thought."

Their relationship didn't improve during the filming; Hoffman maintained a closer connection with Justin Henry — the actor who played his son — than with Streep. In the edgy scene where Joanna Kramer tells her soon-to-be-ex that she intends to gain custody of their child, an insecure

Dustin Hoffman, who has been honoured with seven Oscar and twelve Golden Globe nominations, says he got into acting "so that I could meet girls."

Hoffman felt that Streep's histrionics and jumpy mannerisms were stealing his thunder. He wrested back control of the scene by throwing a glass of wine, which shattered against the wall. It turned out to be one of the most powerful scenes in the film, and despite their lack of off-screen chemistry both ended up with Oscar gold.

Courtesy the Hollywood Collection

Q What made Linda Hunt's Best Supporting Actress win for *The Year of Living Dangerously* significant in Oscar history?

A Linda Hunt was the first person to win an Academy Award for playing a character of the opposite sex. In *The Year of Living Dangerously* she plays a man, Billy Kwan, photographer sidekick to Guy Hamilton (Mel Gibson), a journalist on his first job as a foreign correspondent.

"They said I would be limited as an actress," said the four-foot-nine-inch Hunt. "No one ever discouraged me from doing it; they only said you must prepare yourself to be limited. And how I feel is that I'm not going to be limited — the sky's the limit."

Hilary Swank received a Best Actress Oscar for playing a woman who was pretending to be a man in *Boys Don't Cry*, and Gwyneth Paltrow really got her gender roles confused in *Shakespeare in Love*, receiving a Best Actress Oscar for playing a woman who was pretending to be a man pretending to be a woman.

Courtesy of AMPAS

Gwyneth Paltrow took the Academy Award–winning role of Viola in *Shakespeare in Love* after actress Kate Winslet turned down the part.

"Couldn't Have Done It Without You..."

Q: Who is the only person to receive two Oscars for the same role?

A: Disabled war veteran–turned-actor Harold Russell won the Best Supporting Actor Oscar for his role as the double amputee Homer Parish in the film *The Best Years of Our Lives*. The same night he received an honorary Oscar for being an inspiration for disabled war veterans throughout the U.S., making him the first (and only) actor to receive two Oscars for the same role.

"I got my award for special contributions," he said, "and I'm hanging around backstage. I found out, months later, that when I was nominated for Supporting Actor, they figured I didn't have a chance — the other guys [Charles Coburn, William Demarest, Claude Rains, Clifton Webb] had too much background. When they got to Supporting Actor, they practically threw me out on the stage."

As Russell was collecting his award, Cary Grant, who was not nominated for an award that year, reportedly moaned, "Where can I get a stick of dynamite."

The Nova Scotia–born Russell had been training paratroopers at Camp MacKall North Carolina in 1944 when he lost both hands in an explosion. His hands were replaced with hooks, and he became so adept with them — he used to joke that he could do anything with them except pick up a dinner check — he was chosen to make an army training film called *Diary of a Sergeant*. William Wyler saw the film and decided to cast him in *The Best Years of Our Lives*.

"There aren't that many parts for a guy with no hands," Wyler told Russell after *The Best Years of Our Lives* wrapped. "You should go back to college and get a degree." Russell took the advice, got a degree from Boston University, and became an ardent advocate for the disabled.

Russell worked with the disabled until his death in 2002. In tribute to his memory the annual award presented by the President's Committee on Employment of People with Disabilities is called the Harold Russell Medal.

Q: Who was awarded a Best Supporting Actress Oscar for a performance that lasted less than eight minutes on screen?

A Judi Dench won a Best Supporting Actress Academy Award in 1998 for her role as Queen Elizabeth in *Shakespeare in Love.*

"I just played her like I imagined she would be," said Dench of the role. "She was a fierce woman. People didn't like messing with her. I was in all those clothes and I couldn't do much but stay very still and pray I didn't have to go to the loo in the middle."

Q Which Best Supporting Actress winner for *The Razor's Edge* was the granddaughter of famous architect Frank Lloyd Wright?

A Anne Baxter was just twenty-three years old when her portrayal of reckless drunk Sophie Nelson Macdonald in *The Razor's Edge* earned her a Best Supporting Actress Oscar on March 13, 1947. She is also the only actress to play two different guest villains on the original *Batman* TV show. (She was seen as Zelda the Great during the first season and Olga, Queen of the Bessarovian Cossacks, during the third season.)

Baxter's mother, Catherine, was the daughter of architect Frank Lloyd Wright. In 1984 the actress narrated a documentary about her famous grandfather titled *The Architecture of Frank Lloyd Wright.*

Q Which Best Supporting Actor from *They Shoot Horses, Don't They?* once summed up his career by saying, "My specialities are corpses, unconscious people and people snoring in spectacular epics"?

A Gig Young had a long and distinguished career before picking up an Oscar on April 7, 1970, for *They Shoot Horses, Don't They?* He began his career in the early 1940s playing supporting roles in dramatic films before switching to second banana parts in light comedies. He longed to headline a movie, and with his Oscar win he hoped to be given the chance. During the next eight years he made only four movies, none of which had his name over the title. In 1978, depressed over the poor state of his career, Young shot and killed his wife of three weeks before turning the gun on himself.

"Couldn't Have Done It Without You..."

Q In Oscar history, what do John Garfield, Sidney Greenstreet, and John Malkovich have in common?

A John Garfield, Sidney Greenstreet, and John Malkovich were all nominated for Best Supporting Actor in their big-screen debuts. Garfield was up for his flashy role as a fatalistic musician in *Four Daughters* (1938). Greenstreet had avoided Hollywood in his forty-year stage career but was lured by John Huston to make his screen debut in *The Maltese Falcon* (1941) as the villain Kasper Gutman, "a man who likes talking to a man who likes to talk." His inaugural screen role knocked out the critics and earned him an Oscar nomination. Although Malkovich made his first appearance on film as an extra in Robert Altman's 1978 feature *A Wedding*, it was his official big-screen introduction in 1984's *Places in the Heart* as the blind Mr. Will that earned him a nomination for Best Supporting Actor.

Other actors that earned a Best Supporting Oscar nomination on their first time out include Robert Morley (*Marie Antoinette*), Richard Widmark (*Kiss of Death*), Don Murray (*Bus Stop*), Terence Stamp (*Billy Budd*), Brad Dourif (*One Flew Over the Cuckoo's Nest*), Howard Rollins Jr. (*Ragtime*), and Ralph Fiennes (*Schindler's List*).

Q In four consecutive years, 1978 to 1982, the women who won the Best Supporting Actress Oscar all had the same initials. Who were they?

A The following actresses won consecutive Best Supporting Actress Oscars and shared the initials M.S.: Maggie Smith for *California Suite* in 1978, Meryl Streep for *Kramer vs. Kramer* in 1979, Mary Steenburgen for *Melvin and Howard* in 1980, and Maureen Stapleton for *Reds* in 1981.

"*Lana Turner is to an evening gown what Frank Lloyd Wright is to a pile of lumber.*"

— Rex Harrison speaking about his fellow
award presenter in 1946

WHO ARE YOU WEARING?

Who Are You Wearing?

Q: Who was named one of America's worst-dressed women on Mr. Blackwell's fashion faux pas list for the outfit she wore to the 2003 Golden Globes?

A: Lara Flynn Boyle was skewered by Mr. Blackwell, who really didn't like the tutu she wore to the 2003 Golden Globes. "Sometimes a single fiasco is all it takes," he wrote. "That tutu terror was one of the all-time worst fashion mistakes! A beautiful face ... but no taste ... what a waste!"

Fashion commentators unanimously voted her the worst-dressed celebrity of the night, but Hollywood legend Jack Nicholson stood by his then-girlfriend, describing the tutu as "startling."

A few days later *Chicago* star Richard Gere astounded audiences by taking a swipe at the tutu terror on *The Tonight Show*, when he danced onto Jay Leno's stage wearing a bright red ballerina's tutu and did a wacky two-minute dance as the audience clapped and cheered.

Q: Who wore a "swan dress" to the 2001 Academy Awards?

A: Icelandic singer Björk laid an egg on the red carpet when she showed up wearing a dress made by Macedonian designer Marjan Pejoski to look like a swan, complete with wings and a beak. The sartorial swan earned the singer — whose song "I've Seen It All" from *Dancer in the Dark* was nominated for Best Song — scads of press. One wag wrote that "she dances in the dark, and dresses there too. Let's dub her *Alice in Blunderland*."

Other style mavens also weighed in. Steven Cojocaru called the dress "probably one of the dumbest things I've ever seen," while Jay Carr of the *Boston Globe* wrote, "Björk's wraparound swan frock ... made her look like a refugee from the more dog-eared precincts of provincial ballet." Bitchy red carpet commentator Joan Rivers said, "Later I saw her in the ladies' room spreading papers on the floor.... This girl should be put into an asylum."

After the ceremony the get-up was fodder for stand-up comedians, who made the dress their joke du jour. Nathan Lane said, "The sad part is, Björk's swan dress was still alive during rehearsal. And, oddly enough, the sound a dying swan makes actually is 'bjork,'" while Jay Leno joked,

"Today we saw the first sign of spring. Björk's dress started building a nest," and "That thing was so bad even heterosexuals are making fun of it."

Not everyone hated the dress. Singer Melissa Etheridge said she loved the dress and loves Björk, and the *New York Observer* style guide gave the dress a "total overall *j'adore!*"

Björk's only comment? "It's just a dress."

Courtesy of AMPAS

Icelandic singer Björk laid an egg on the Academy Awards red carpet when she arrived at the 2001 ceremony in a dress designed to look like a swan.

Q In her acceptance speech, what did director Jessica Yu say cost more than her Oscar-winning film?

A When director Jessica Yu accepted the Oscar for Best Short Subject Documentary for *Breathing Lessons: The Life and Work of Mark O'Brien* on March 23, 1998, she said, "What a thrill. You know you've entered new territory when you realize that your outfit cost more than your film."

"Everything I had on was borrowed," Yu said later. "People sent me cards saying, 'Whatever you paid for this dress it was worth it.' They think I actually bought it!"

Q In 2004 who did fashion maven Steven Cojocaru say looked like she belonged at the Bavarian Academy Awards?

A *Entertainment Tonight* style guru Cojocaru rated Uma Thurman's white tulle Christian Lacroix dress as a total fashion disaster.

Who Are You Wearing?

"What happened? Tonight, I think she made a mistake," he raved. "She didn't have her glasses on. When she got the invitation she went, 'Oh, it's the Bavarian Academy Awards.' Sorry Uma, better luck next time!"

Cojo wasn't the only commentator to diss the dress. One writer said, "Uma Thurman looked like she was auditioning to be a Bavarian waitress. Her fluffy white dress was a total joke — and not the funny ha-ha kind," while another wrote, "Presumably Bill is the stylist who advised her to wear this, hence her animus towards him."

According to friends of the *Kill Bill* star, following the awards the actress was inundated with odd clothes. A friend said, "She's been getting all sorts of offers. One was all leather and another came with a mask. Uma likes to be different, but she's not that different."

Thurman — who once said in an interview that she wanted to borrow Bjork's infamous swan dress — told a reporter that she chose the controversial gown so she could stand out from the crowd. "Everyone looked the same," she said. "Everyone had it down to such a perfect tee in their spaghetti-strapped, sequined or chiffon, body-hugging, gym-hour promoting things. You get bored. I'm glad it was me they panned."

Q Which Oscar winner designed and made the dress she wore to the 1958 Oscar ceremony?

A Joanne Woodward accepted the Oscar for Best Actress for her role in *The Three Faces of Eve* in a dress she sewed herself. "I thought Liz Taylor would walk off with the award for *Raintree County*, so I didn't invest a lot of money in the dress. I was convinced nobody would see it. I spent $100 on the material, designed the dress and worked on it for two weeks. I'm almost as proud of that dress as I am of my Oscar."

Later Joan Crawford seethed that Woodward's outfit "set Hollywood glamour back twenty-five years." Several years later, when Woodward appeared at the Oscars in a dress by designer Travilla, she said, "I hope that it makes Joan Crawford happy."

Q Which Best Costume Design Oscar winner was featured in ads for American Express?

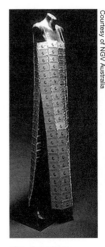

Courtesy of NGV Australia

The American Express dress made of 254 Gold American Express cards was designed by *Priscilla Queen of the Desert* costumer Lizzy Gardiner.

A *The Adventures of Priscilla, Queen of the Desert* costume designer Lizzy Gardiner appeared in American Express ads wearing the gown she made for the 67th Annual Academy Awards. The dress, made of 254 American Express Gold Cards — all with invalid numbers — and metallic links was an attention getter, but didn't come with a couture price tag.

"I'm broke, and I didn't have anything to wear," said Gardiner. "So I went through my list of past good ideas." The gown was originally conceived as a piece for *The Adventures of Priscilla, Queen of the Desert*, but the idea was shelved when American Express wouldn't co-operate. She later convinced AmEx to supply her with three hundred cards — all with her name printed on them and all one number short to make them invalid — when she explained that she'd wear the dress on the Oscar red carpet.

"I was looking for an American symbol," she said. "A Coca-Cola bottle or a Mickey Mouse would have been ridiculous, doing anything with the American flag would have been insulting, and Cadillac hub caps were just too uncomfortable."

After winning the Best Costume Design Oscar, Gardiner was featured wearing the dress in magazine ads that said, "You only need one in your wallet" and beneath in small print, "Congratulations — and thank you."

The AmEx dress was auctioned off in March 1999 for $12,650, with proceeds going to the American Foundation for AIDS Research.

Q Who oversaw the fashions at the Academy Awards for the first sixteen years the show was televised?

A Hollywood fashion guru Edith Head — who won so many Academy Awards that one joker said, "She owns a fifty-acre estate surrounded by a picket fence made of nothing but Oscars" — had to give the thumbs-up to any and all gowns worn by presenters and winners at the Oscars in the early years of the televised awards ceremony. "It wasn't as autocratic as it sounds," she said years later. "Because the television censors were so strict I was appointed guardian of hemlines and bodices. I sat in a little booth right at the entrance to the stage to check each outfit. We had a crew backstage to keep stars from slipping by with irregular attire. I had three seamstresses, a prop man with spray to dim the diamonds, and a large box of cleavage covers. These last were the most important. We couldn't trust the stars who were to go onstage. After I approved their gowns, some would push up their cleavage just before going on."

In 1958, Oscarcast producer Jerry Wald banned cleavage at the Oscars. The previous year, Wald explained, the network had been flooded with complaints about excessively low necklines. Most of the complaints, he said, came from the Midwest.

Q Which February 2005 Best Actor nominee wore a gold gonzo pin in honour of the late anti-establishment icon Hunter S. Thompson?

A Best Actor nominee for *Finding Neverland* Johnny Depp arrived on the red carpet at the Academy Awards in February 2005 wearing a distinctive midnight blue tuxedo with a black velvet shawl collar and a white tuxedo shirt with sapphire studs. In the centre of his black velvet bow tie was a gold gonzo pin he wore to honour his friend, the late Hunter S. Thompson. The gonzo logo — which depicts a six-fingered fist holding a peyote flower with a knife blade for a forearm — was originally used as the symbol of Thompson's unsuccessful Freak Power run for sheriff of Aspen in 1969.

Depp became friends with the legendary gonzo journalist when he moved into Thompson's home in Aspen to prepare for his role in *Fear and Loathing in Las Vegas*, the Terry Gilliam–helmed version of Thompson's most famous work, which detailed a drug-and-alcohol-fuelled journey his alter-ego (Raoul Duke) and his Samoan attorney (Dr. Gonzo) carried out while in Las Vegas to cover a motorcycle race.

"I used to tease him that we were becoming a perversely twisted version of Edgar Bergen and Charlie McCarthy, which really made him uncomfortable," Depp said in *Rolling Stone*. "I had, by this point, purloined an impressive amount of his clothing from the Vegas period and adopted the same mode of dress: the aviator shades, a bush hat, short pants, athletic socks, Converse sneakers, cigarette holder clenched

Courtesy of AAD

Hunter S. Thompson's gonzo logo, originally designed to publicize Thompson's unsuccessful run for sheriff of Aspen in 1969.

tightly between the teeth. We'd saunter out of the house to take a drive in the car like freakish twins.

"So, for good or ill, there we were, a pair of deviant bookends on the prowl. Truly, the man should be sainted for putting up with my continual scratching away at the layers of his life. He stuck it out like a champion and couldn't have been a better friend."

Dr. Hunter S. Thompson took his life with a gunshot to the head at his fortified compound in Woody Creek, Colorado, in February 2005.

Q What medal did Antipodean actor Russell Crowe wear on his Armani tuxedo at the 73rd Annual Academy Awards?

A When Russell Crowe accepted the Oscar for Best Actor for *Gladiator* he wore a Member of the Order of the British Empire medal that had belonged to his grandfather, a cinematographer who was honoured for his work shooting footage in the Second World War.

"My grandfather's name was Stan Wemyss," said Crowe in his speech. "He was a cinematographer in the Second World War. My uncle David, David William Crowe, he died last year at the age of sixty-six. I'd like to thank the Academy for something which is pretty surprising and dedicate it to two men who still continue to inspire me."

Crowe's tribute to his grandfather was touching, but like so many things associated with the rough-and-tumble actor, his wearing the medal caused some controversy.

Clive Cheesman of the British College of Arms and co-author of *Rebels, Pretenders and Impostors* told *People* that Crowe was wrong to wear the medal.

The MBE, originally bestowed to Crowe's grandfather by Queen Elizabeth, should be worn only by its recipient, said Cheesman.

"It's not a criminal offence, but it's not appropriate," he told the magazine.

Style commentators also had a thing or two to say about Crowe's costume. Cynthia Robbins, writing in the *San Francisco Chronicle*, suggested that "Russell Crowe should run his stylist through with that sword from *Gladiator*. He was High Fop with fouffed-up hair, a preacher coat, a string tie and an inexplicable medal hanging on his coat jacket. Get that boy a pair of jeans, a cigarette and a ticket back to his farm in Australia."

Crowe, however, took the criticism in stride. Referring to his unusual tuxedo he told *Entertainment Tonight*, "This is what happens when me and Giorgio Armani have a couple bottles of red wine."

Who said, "As you can see I have received and read the Academy brochure on how to dress as a serious actress" at the 1985 Oscars?

Cher arrived at the 1985 Oscarcast, where she was set to present the Best Supporting Actor award, decked out in a $12,000 Bob Mackie–designed dress that made her look like an angry burlesque-dancing peacock. The startling gown was a midriff-free concoction of beads, hand-woven satin, and jet crystals topped with a headdress made of eight hundred rare hackle feathers. According to the designer, Cher was miffed that her performance in *Mask* had been ignored by the Academy, so she ordered a dress that would make it impossible for them to ignore her.

"They didn't nominate me this year so fuck it," she told him, "Let's have a good time." The getup shocked some, but it had the intended effect: Cher received loads of publicity — both good and bad — even topping Mr. Blackwell's Worst Dressed List for that year.

Which actress wore her black Gap turtleneck to the 68th Annual Academy Awards?

A At the Academy Awards in 1995, Sharon Stone daringly made the Gap glamorous, combining the designs of Armani, Valentino, and the Gap. Nominated for Best Actress for her role in *Casino*, Stone wore a full-length black velvet Armani coat over a full-length black Valentino skirt with a fluted hem and a simple $22 short-sleeved black mock turtleneck from the Gap.

The mass-market getup was a last-minute switch — she had originally intended to wear a white beaded couture Valentino gown or a Fortuny-inspired dress by Vera Wang — that sent the Gap's market share soaring and earned the actress more column inches of publicity than if she had stayed with a couture outfit.

Q Why did Joan Crawford have two versions of the same dress made for one Oscarcast?

A Joan Crawford's distrust of rival Deborah Kerr led her to have costumer Edith Head design two versions of the same $3,000 dress — one in black, the other in white — for the April 5, 1965, Oscarcast. Kerr, who was presenting the award for Best Writing, had informed the Academy that she would be wearing white, but Crawford, who was presenting the award for Best Director, didn't believe her and couldn't stand the idea that they might end up wearing the same colour dress. "I don't trust her," Crawford said. "I think she might change at the last minute." Kerr kept her word and wore white. "Joan switched to the black gown," said Head, "and was the hit of the evening."

"With all the heated rivalry going on, it wouldn't be a bad idea to hold the Oscar ceremonies in a boxing ring."

— *Variety*, 1948

"HELLO, GORGEOUS..."

Best Actress Trivia

Q: What trait has every Best Actress Oscar winner shared since 1996?

A: The last time a Best Actress Oscar went to a performer over forty years old was at the 1995 Academy Awards — held in March 1996 — when Susan Sarandon, who at the time was forty-nine, won for *Dead Man Walking*. Since then all Best Actress Oscar winners have been under forty years old.

Two-time Oscar winner Hilary Swank with *Million Dollar Baby* director Clint Eastwood at the 77ᵗʰ Annual Academy Awards.

Courtesy of AMPAS

Frances McDormand was thirty-nine when she won for *Fargo*, Helen Hunt was thirty-four when *As Good As it Gets* earned her the award, *Shakespeare in Love*'s Gwyneth Paltrow was just twenty-six, Hilary Swank was twenty-five on her first trip to the podium for *Boys Don't Cry*, Julia Roberts was thirty-three when she accepted the trophy for *Erin Brockovich*, Halle Berry was thirty-five when she took it for *Monster's Ball*, Nicole Kidman was thirty-five when she was honoured for *The Hours*, Charlize Theron was twenty-eight when she won for playing Aileen Wuornos in *Monster* on what would have been Aileen's forty-eighth birthday, and Hilary Swank was thirty when she made her second trip to the winner's circle for *Million Dollar Baby*.

Q: Who were the only people to split a Golden Globe win three ways?

"Hello, Gorgeous..."

A The only three-way tie in Golden Globe history happened in 1988, when Jodie Foster (*The Accused*), Shirley MacLaine (*Madame Sousatzka*), and Sigourney Weaver (*Gorillas in the Mist*) shared the award for Best Actress.

Q Which Best Actress winner has the shortest name of any Oscar-nominated performer?

A Cher — winner of Best Actress in 1988 for *Moonstruck* — has the shortest name of any female nominee in Oscar history. In the mideighties, Cherilyn Sarkisian LaPierre Bono Allman had her name legally changed to the easier-to-remember Cher.

The male nominee with the shortest name is the Japanese actor Mako, who was up for Best Supporting Actor in 1966 for *The Sand Pebbles*.

Q Who won an Oscar playing her own distant ancestor, Eleanor of Aquitaine?

A Katharine Hepburn is descended from Eleanor of Aquitaine in numerous lines, from Eleanor's marriage both to Louis VII, King of France, and to Henry II, King of England. Playing Eleanor of Aquitaine in *The Lion in Winter* brought Hepburn a Best Actress statue, her third of four Oscars.

Q Who sent expensive watches to every member of the Hollywood Foreign Press in 1999?

A Sharon Stone's Best Actress in a Comedy or Musical Golden Globe nomination for *The Muse* was marred somewhat when it was revealed that she had given gold watches to each of the eighty-two members of the Hollywood Foreign Press Association. The watches, which cost $350 from jeweller Coach, were returned on December 13, 1999, the same day they were received and a week before she received the nod for her work.

"This watch was way, way, way beyond the edge of the envelope as far as promotional considerations, like T-shirts," said HFPA President Helmut Voss. "We were touched by her generosity, but this is definitely a no-no for a group like ours that wants to protect the integrity of its award."

The HFPA has struggled for credibility since bequeathing a Globe on Pia Zadora for the 1981 stinker *Butterfly*, so Voss says his group is "a little careful with certain gifts or parties because people are very quick to criticize and think it would affect the voting. So rather than take any chances, we'd rather return."

"Now we've got very specific rules," adds former HFPA president and treasurer Philip Berk. "We've eliminated special perks and gifts that we used to get, just to make sure that we're above suspicion. Certainly, we don't attend any parties during the Golden Globe period — they used to invite you to their homes, that sort of thing. We pay for our own trips; the studio pays for our hotels."

Once the story hit the newspapers the finger pointing started. No one was willing to accept responsibility for the inappropriate gifts. Stone's publicist said the wristwatches were actually sent by USA Films, the company that released *The Muse*. But USA Films claimed that Coach provided the watches to the studio gratis to be sent on behalf of the actress. Movado, the company that makes the watches for Coach, said that USA had purchased the watches, while *Variety* reported unnamed sources saying that Stone herself was behind the watch hullabaloo.

"Hardly a day goes by without one of these stupid crises arising," Voss told *Variety*.

Q Which actress has won the most César Awards?

A French star Isabelle Adjani is the only person to have won four Césars, awarded by the French Académie des Arts and the main national film award given in France. She first won in 1982 for her role in Andrzej Zulawski's *Possession* in 1982, followed by *L'Eté Meurtrier* in 1984, *Camille Claudel* in 1989, and *La Reine Margot* in 1995.

Adjani has also twice been nominated for Oscars — first for 1975's *The Story of Adele H.*, and then for *La Reine Margot*, for which she also received the Berlin Festival's Best Actress prize.

Q In her 2004 Golden Globe Best Actress acceptance speech, who was Hilary Swank talking about when she said, "you have such a huge heart and you envelop all the people around you"?

A Swank thanked director Clint Eastwood for her win as Best Actress in a Drama for her turn as a boxer in *Million Dollar Baby*. "I don't want to ruin your 'go ahead, make my day' image, but you have such a huge heart and you envelop all the people around you. … You guided us so brilliantly, while you also, in my humble opinion, gave the performance of your career."

As she finished her speech, Swank joked about a mistake she made in her Oscar acceptance speech five years ago, when she forgot to thank her husband.

"Let's see, is there anyone else?" she said, while looking at actor Chad Lowe. "You're my rock. Your support is … I can't even describe it. You're my everything. Thank you."

Backstage she continued her praise for her director, even joking that she'd love to be one of the guys in his next film. "He's doing a World War II movie and there are no women in it, and I said, 'You know, Clint, I played a boy before,'" she said, referring to her Oscar-winning portrayal of a cross-dressing teenaged girl in *Boys Don't Cry*.

"So, I'm still trying to twist his arm on that one," Swank said. "I don't think it's working so well."

Q Which Best Actress did South African President Thabo Mbeki praise as a figurehead of South African strength?

A Just days after her Best Actress Oscar win for portraying real-life serial killer Aileen Wuornos in *Monster*, Charlize Theron was praised by South African President Thabo Mbeki as a role model. The actress was born and raised on a farm in Benoni, South Africa, and while living there witnessed her mother shoot and kill her abusive alcoholic father, Charles, in 1991.

"It's a triumph of new South African opportunity," said President Mbeki. "In the film we saw her drawing on her innate tough-mindedness and her emotional stamina in overcoming the tragic personal circumstances of her early life to shine. Miss Theron, in her personal life, represents a grand metaphor of South Africa's move from agony to achievement. We rejoice in the recognition by most critical minds in filming that Charlize Theron is pure gold."

Courtesy the Hollywood Collection

Despite the kind words of President Mbeki and the critics, Theron's hometown did not get to see their homegrown Oscar winner in *Monster* because the local film distributor thought the movie was too highbrow.

"The film caters for a particular niche," said a spokesman for South African movie distributor Nu Metro. "The people of Benoni would prefer to see Charlize in movies like *The Italian Job.*"

Best Actress winner Charlize Theron, who thanked "everybody in South Africa, my home country" as she accepted her award for the movie *Monster* at the 76th Academy Awards.

Q Who are the oldest performers to be nominated for Best Actress Oscars?

A When seventy-six-year-old character actress Dame May Robson was nominated for a Best Actress Oscar for her work as Apple Annie in Frank Capra's *Lady for a Day* — one of her rare starring roles — she became the oldest performer to receive a Best Actress Oscar nomination.

Runner-up in the oldster sweepstakes is the daughter of Yiddish stage actress Ester Rachel Halpern and stage producer Avram Izhak Kaminska, Ida Kaminska, who at age sixty-eight was nominated for *Obchod na korze* (*The Shop on Main Street*).

Q Who said, "It doesn't bring out the Einstein moment that you hoped it would" after receiving a Best Actress Oscar?

Courtesy the Hollywood Collection

A Julia Roberts admitted to a brain freeze while she collected her Best Actress Oscar for *Erin Brockovich*. "It doesn't bring out the Einstein moment that you hoped it would," she said, after realizing she forgot to include the real-life legal-eagle Erin Brockovich in her Academy Award acceptance speech.

Backstage Roberts acknowledged the film's title character. "During that out of body experience I just had, I didn't acknowledge her, shamefully, shamefully," said Roberts. "I've said so many things about her and she knows the esteem I hold her which is quite, quite high with great humility I acknowledge her profusely."

Julia Roberts with her Best Actress Oscar for *Erin Brockovich*. In the heat of the moment Roberts thanked everyone involved in the film, except Brockovich.

The real-life Brockovich wasn't there to witness the snub in person; she watched the ceremony on television at home while taking care of a sick child.

Despite omitting Brockovich from her speech, Roberts's acceptance of the award was memorable. In an effort to tighten up the broadcast, producers had asked winners to keep their speeches economical.

Those who droned on, thanking everyone they had ever met during their career, would be interrupted by the orchestra, which had been instructed to start playing after forty-five seconds. The actress's speech clocked in at four minutes.

"They really did try to cut me off, he was twitching a few times," Roberts said about Bill Conti, the symphony conductor who gave her desperate time signals from the orchestra pit. "Everyone tries to shut me up, it didn't work with my parents, it wasn't going to work now."

"I won't have a proper thought for six to ten days," said the excited actress, "which is unfortunate because I start a new movie in three and that's OK because it's with Steven Soderbergh [who won Best Director] and I don't think he'll make sense for at least four or five days either."

Months after the ceremony, when she'd had time to reflect, she said, "I was having an existential moment. I forgot people and I feel bad. But I don't wish I had written anything down. You can't go back in time, you can't fix it, you can't change it. I did write Bill Conti a little note thanking him for his patience. But I don't believe in 'If only I had…'"

Q Which Oscar-winning Best Actress was also nominated for a Grammy Award for singing her film's title song?

A To prepare for her role as country music legend Loretta Lynn in the acclaimed 1980 biopic *Coal Miner's Daughter*, Sissy Spacek joined the singer on tour and spent months observing her behaviour. The research paid dividends — *Coal Miner's Daughter* grossed $79 million at the box office and landed Spacek a Best Actress Oscar. In addition to the acting trophy, Spacek was also nominated for a Grammy in the category Best Country Vocal Performance, Female for her rendition of the film's title song.

Ironically the actress was up against Crystal Gayle, Loretta Lynn's sister, who was nominated in the same category for her song "If You Ever Change Your Mind."

Q Which Oscar-winning Best Actress had a nine-thousand-year-old skeleton named after her in 2004?

"Hello, Gorgeous..."

A In November 2004 Bulgarian archaeologists unearthed a perfectly preserved woman's skeleton — believed to be the oldest ever found in Europe — with a shiny set of teeth that had survived nine thousand years. The scientists nicknamed the find "Julia Roberts" because of her perfect teeth.

The skeleton, unearthed near the village of Ohoden, Vratsa district, in northwest Bulgaria, is believed to be of a young woman from one of earliest agriculture civilizations on the Balkans. "She was a rare beauty and could have competed with today's Hollywood stars with her perfect set of teeth. She is a Stone Age Julia Roberts. She would have had a perfect smile — it really is a puzzle," Georgi Ganetsovski, the expedition leader, said.

Q Which performer, born Virginia McMath, won a Best Actress Oscar for playing the title role in *Kitty Foyle: The Natural History of a Woman*?

A When Ginger Rogers accepted the Best Actress Oscar for *Kitty Foyle: The Natural History of a Woman* she thanked "the one who has stood by me faithfully — my mother."

Rogers was already a well-known hoofer, having made nine pictures with dancing partner Fred Astaire. *Kitty Foyle* only increased her fan base. The year following her Oscar success she was not only RKO's biggest star, but at almost $12,000 a week she was also Hollywood's highest paid star.

Two decades later, in a *Films in Review* article, Miss Rogers joked, "My first picture was *Kitty Foyle*. It was my mother who made all those films with Fred Astaire."

Born Virginia McMath, she was called "Ginger" when her young cousin couldn't say "Virginia," and she combined that nickname with her stepfather's last name to create her stage name.

Q What do Best Actress winners Jane Wyman, Marlee Matlin, and Holly Hunter have in common?

A Jane Wyman, Marlee Matlin, and Holly Hunter all won Best Actress awards for playing wordless roles.

Wyman won for playing sweet deaf-mute *Johnny Belinda* in 1948. "I accept this gratefully for keeping my mouth shut for once," she said in her acceptance speech. "I think I will do it again."

Matlin took home the top honour in 1986 for her film debut in *Children of a Lesser God* as a hearing-impaired student who fends off the romantic advances of one of her teachers. "I feel there are a lot of deaf people jumping up and down," the actress commented after her win.

In *The Piano* Hunter played a mute who leaves her native Scotland for the rugged forests of New Zealand's South Island in an arranged marriage. "I feel really, really happy," said Hunter after her win. "I felt happy before. But now I feel really, really happy. It changes the economics of my career, at least momentarily."

About whom did the *Hollywood Reporter* rave, "This lady is not just a great star. She is not just an ordinary film personality. She is a whole, whirling galaxy. Once there was Mary Pickford, then there was Garbo, now there is Julie"?

Julie Andrews was on a roll in 1964. On the release of her film debut, *Mary Poppins*, she drew rave reviews, with one paper saying she delivered the "kind of performance that creates not fans but evangelists." The good press paid off and she received the Best Actress award at the April 5, 1965, Oscar ceremony.

Dame Julie Andrews, once voted the 59th Greatest Briton ever in a BBC poll.

"Hello, Gorgeous..."

Q Who was the first Colombian to be nominated for an Academy Award?

A Having performed only in Colombian theatre before being cast as a drug mule who swallows plastic-wrapped pellets of heroin in *Maria Full of Grace*, Bogotá, Colombia–born Catalina Sandino Moreno was just twenty-three years old when she became the first Colombian to receive an Academy Award nomination in 2005. Nominated alongside Annette Bening and Hilary Swank, Moreno was in shock when the nods were announced on television.

Catalina Sandino Moreno, the first person from Colombia to be nominated for an Academy Award.

"I was watching my face and my name," she says, "and it was so unreal — a total disbelief that it's happening. It's just unreal. This is unreal! This can't be happening!"

Moreno's natural performance was applauded by critics and festival audiences, including those at the Berlin Film Festival, where she split lead actress honours with last year's Oscar winner, Charlize Theron.

She says the film struck a nerve with viewers because "it's a real story with real human beings with very naturalistic acting. [The actors] are so fresh and so natural and so human and so beautiful. And I think people like that. People don't care about subtitles. People don't care about races. It's the story about Maria and it's a whole point of view that even we Colombians didn't know anything about."

Moreno's performance is in Spanish. There have been twenty nominations and four Oscar wins for performances in foreign-language roles. In addition, Marlee Matlin received the 1986 Oscar for a performance almost entirely in American Sign Language.

Despite all the critical attention, on Oscar night Moreno's chances were KO'd by *Million Dollar Baby*'s Hilary Swank, who took the Best Actress statue.

REEL WINNERS

Q: Why did Best Actress nominee Jeanne Eagels miss the 1928–29 Academy Awards ceremony?

A: Actress Jeanne Eagels earned an Oscar nod for her role as Leslie Crosbie in the 1929 weepie *The Letter*. Unfortunately, she died of a heroin overdose in New York City on October 3, 1929, just days after the nominations were announced. Eagels, born 1894, flipped between Broadway and the movies until the Actors' Equity Association barred her from performing on the Great White Way for a year and a half, citing her constant lateness for performances. The ban didn't prevent her from working in pictures, and in 1929 MGM signed her to a contract. She made two movies for the lion studio — *The Letter* and *Jealousy* — before her death. Nearly all of her films have been lost to time, but her legacy was preserved in the 1957 biopic *Jeanne Eagels*, starring Kim Novak.

Q: Who was the only performer to win an Oscar for acting in an Alfred Hitchcock film?

A: Joan Fontaine — sister of actress Olivia de Havilland — was the only performer to win an Academy Award for appearing in a Hitchcock film. She took Oscar gold for playing the wife of menacing Cary Grant in Hitchcock's *Suspicion*. A loose adaptation of Francis Iles's nerve-jangling *Before the Fact*, about a handsome gambler who might have murder on his mind as he woos an heiress, *Suspicion* was the director's thirty-third film.

Q: Who was the first person to win a Best Actress Oscar?

A: Janet Gaynor won the first Best Actress Oscar for her roles in three silent films — *7th Heaven*, *Sunrise* (both from 1927), and *Street Angel* (1928). "I remember it as being a quiet warm experience," she said many years after the win. "Hollywood was just one big happy family back then, and this was a bouquet — thrown to me, I think, because I was new and because they thought I had a certain freshness. It was nothing then like it is now. My agent didn't call me up the next day with an offer to double my salary; I didn't find a pile of scripts at my door. Photographers weren't camped on my front lawn. I just got up at 5:00 and drove off to the studio as always."

Gaynor was one of the lucky few who made a smooth transition from silent movies to talkies, and she continued to work steadily until her marriage to famed Hollywood designer Gilbert Adrian in 1939. She retired to raise a family and made only one subsequent appearance on film, in 1957's *Bernadine*. Gaynor died in 1984 from injuries sustained in a brutal car accident that also injured actress Mary Martin.

Who accepted her Best Actress Oscar with the words, "This moment is much bigger than me"?

Courtesy the Hollywood Collection

Halle Berry, one of only three actresses to win both an Academy Award for Best Actress — for *Monster's Ball* — and a Razzie Award for Worst Actress — for *Catwoman*. The others are Faye Dunaway and Liza Minelli.

On March 24, 2002, Halle Berry made Oscar history. After seventy-four years the Academy finally saw fit to award an African-American woman a Best Actress statue when they honoured Berry for her demanding role in *Monster's Ball*. "Oh, my God. Oh, my God," Berry sputtered in a weepy acceptance speech. "This moment is so much bigger than me.

"This moment is for … every nameless, faceless woman of colour that now has a chance because this door tonight has been opened. And I thank the Academy for choosing me to be the vessel for which His blessing might flow."

"I wasn't in my right head all night," she told *Entertainment Weekly* some time later. "It was like I was out of my body — but the next morning, when I saw it on tape, I thought, 'Oh my God! I'm out of control.'"

Why did Bob Hope quip, "Julie Andrews is up for *Mary Poppins*, or How I Learned to Stop Worrying and Love Jack Warner" at the 37th Annual Academy Awards?

Many felt that Julie Andrews, star of the Broadway version of *My Fair Lady*, was done a disservice when Jack Warner scooped up the film rights to the musical. He cast Audrey Hepburn, who couldn't sing — her vocals would be dubbed by Marni Nixon, who also provided Deborah Kerr's singing voice in *The King and I* — instead of Andrews in the lead role of Eliza Doolittle. "Someone, somewhere, made the decision to include Andrews out of the film," wrote *Time*. "There is a an evil and rampantly lunatic force at loose in the world and it must be destroyed."

Jack Warner defended his casting decision by saying, "No one in the sticks ever heard of her."

In the end, however, it was Andrews who emerged on top. She had the time to make *Mary Poppins* because Warner hadn't cast her in *My Fair Lady* — both films were shooting at the same time.

She gave Warner a little slap on the wrist in her Golden Globe acceptance speech for *Mary Poppins* when she said, "And finally, my thanks to the man who made all this possible, Jack Warner."

When she won the Best Actress Oscar for Mary Poppins, Bob Hope joked, "Julie Andrews is up for *Mary Poppins*, or How I Learned to Stop Worrying and Love Jack Warner."

Rex Harrison, star of both the movie and Broadway productions of *My Fair Lady*, acknowledged Andrews in his Oscar acceptance speech that year. He dedicated the award to his "two fair ladies" — his stage and screen Eliza Doolittles, Julie Andrews and Audrey Hepburn.

Q Who was the first Oscar winner to use sign language in her Best Actress acceptance speech?

A When Louise Fletcher won her Best Actress Oscar for *One Flew Over the Cuckoo's Nest* at the March 29, 1975, ceremony, she made a gracious and impassioned speech with one little twist. As she spoke the words she also mimed them in sign language.

The sign language version was a tribute to her parents — father Robert and mother Estelle — both deaf from birth. Born in Alabama in 1934, Fletcher was raised as a bilingual child, speaking (taught by her aunt) and using American Sign Language.

Fletcher wasn't the first choice for the role of the villainous Nurse Mildred Ratched. In fact she wasn't the second or even third choice. The part had been refused by Jane Fonda, Anne Bancroft, and Ellen Burstyn.

Winning the Oscar didn't catapult Fletcher onto the A-list. "Most of the time, I have to remind myself I have an Oscar," admits Fletcher. "I never thought that would be the case when I won it."

Not that Fletcher's unappreciative; in fact, she credits her win with giving her a career. "You have to remember that I was probably the least known actress ever to have won the award," she says. "It was a dream come true to win, and everything else has been dessert. Because of the Oscar, I have worked steadily."

Q Who was the first person to win an Oscar for playing a nun?

REEL WINNERS

A After four nominations — *Atlantic City, Thelma and Louise, Lorenzo's Oil,* and *The Client* — Susan Sarandon finally won Best Actress gold on March 25, 1996, for playing Sister Helen Prejean, a death row nun trying to connect with a condemned man in *Dead Man Walking*. Ironically, at the time of the win Sarandon told the press she was a lapsed Catholic.

From Audrey Hepburn as the pious and inspirational Sister Luke in *The Nun's Story* in 1959 to *Sister Act* in 1992, nuns have often been portrayed in film, but *Dead Man Walking* marked the first time the Academy recognized a performer for playing one.

Q Who was the only person to win a Best Actress Oscar for a movie directed by her husband?

A Several lead actresses have been nominated for films directed by their husbands — Julie Andrews directed by Blake Edwards in *Victor/Victoria*, for example — but at the March 24, 1997, ceremony Frances McDormand in *Fargo* became the first actress to win an Oscar for a performance directed by her husband. "I want to thank [screenwriter] Ethan Coen, who made an actor out of me," she said at the podium, "his brother [director/husband] Joel, who made a woman out of me, and my son, Pedro, who made a mother of me."

Since the win, she confided to a reporter, "I've been taking more showers and worrying more about clothes and matching shoes than ever before in my life."

Q Which two sisters were both up for a Best Actress Oscar in 1941?

A "Of course we fight," Olivia de Havilland said of her sister, Joan Fontaine. "What sisters don't battle?" At the February 26, 1942, Oscar ceremony all eyes were on the Tokyo-born sisters (their father was a British patent attorney with a lucrative practice in Japan), who were both nominated in the Best Actress category, de Havilland for *Hold Back the Dawn* and Fontaine for Alfred Hitchcock's *Suspicion*. One reporter noted that "the two girls faced each other, chatting and smiling with forced gaiety and nonchalance."

"Hello, Gorgeous..."

When Fontaine was announced as the winner de Havilland put on a gracious public face — clapping loudly and later shaking her sister's hand for photographers, but sibling rivalry between the two apparently really did exist. "All the animus we'd felt toward each other as children came rushing back in kaleidoscopic imagery," Fontaine said later.

"I married first, won the Oscar before Olivia did, and if I die first," Fontaine added, "she'll undoubtedly be livid because I beat her to it!"

Q Who said, "I admit I do have a gift for gab," after delivering a five-and-a-half-minute acceptance speech at the 1942 Oscars?

A "I am practically unprepared," said Greer Garson as she began her Best Actress acceptance filibuster for *Mrs. Miniver*. She continued for almost six minutes, although it was reported in at least one trade magazine that she rambled for over an hour. It must have just *seemed* like an hour as she thanked everyone even remotely involved in the film and some who weren't.

"I think the reason people remembered it," Garson said later, "is because I somewhat fractured a long-standing rule, which was that a winner should simply say 'thank you' and then dissolve into a flood of tears and sit down."

The filibuster acceptance speech earned the actress the reputation for being a windbag and became a Hollywood joke. For years afterward Greer refused to speak in public.

Q What Oscar snub did Groucho Marx call the "biggest robbery since Brinks"?

A Judy Garland seemed like a lock to win Best Actress at the March 30, 1955, Oscars. Her bravura turn in *A Star Is Born* as a Hollywood star married to an alcoholic has-been was the best of her career. She had given birth to a baby just two days before the ceremony, and NBC was so convinced she would win that they erected a twenty-foot-high platform outside her hospital room where she could lift the blinds and do a quick "thank you" for the home viewers.

On Oscar night, however, she was bested by model-turned-actress Grace Kelly for her performance in *The Country Girl*. A disappointed Garland told reporters, "It's OK. I have my own live Oscar," referring to her new son, Joey.

It was reported that she received one thousand congratulations (on the baby) and consolation (on the Oscars) telegrams from all over the world, including one from Groucho Marx, which read, "Dear Judy, This is the biggest robbery since Brinks."

Which two actresses held up the live broadcast of the Golden Globes, in different years, because they were in the bathroom when their names were announced as winners?

Courtesy of AMPAS

Renee Zellweger in the movie *Chicago*. When she won an Oscar for her role in *Cold Mountain* she said, "I see the Oscar in my bedroom and it's like I bought it at a souvenir shop on Hollywood Boulevard."

Christine Lahti and Renee Zellweger both had inappropriately timed bathroom breaks during the Golden Globes. After *Chicago Hope* star

Christine Lahti was caught with her pants down in 1998, *Nurse Betty's* Renee Zellweger made the same mistake in 2001 when she went to the restroom to powder her nose as her category was announced.

"Where is she? Is Renee under the table?" presenter Hugh Grant improvised, as the camera frantically searched for the actress. "Oh, she's in the bathroom. What do we do?"

As the camera cut to Christine Lahti, Zellweger made her way from the john to the stage. "Omigod, I have lipstick on my teeth!" she said and continued by thanking the Hollywood Foreign Press for "a moment I'll never forget ... a moment I almost didn't have."

Later, when she was asked why she wasn't in the auditorium when her name was called, she said, "I thought I had something in my teeth, so I went to check."

Q Which twenty-something actress won both Best Actress and Best Kiss awards at the 2003 MTV Movie Awards?

A Kirsten Dunst took home Best Actress honours for her role in *Spider-Man* and the coveted Best Kiss award for the upside-down tonsil-hockey match she shared with Tobey Maguire in the same flick. The famous kissing scene appealed to viewers but was no fun to shoot.

"You know, that was actually really uncomfortable because we were in the rain, and it was cold and Tobey couldn't breathe, because I had pulled his mask like to there [indicates upper lip], and he was hanging upside down soaking wet. So [he had this] head rush kind of thing going on. So, yeah, he couldn't breathe through our kisses, so it was like ... kiss kiss kiss, breathing out the side of the mouth kind of thing." The awards for *Spider-Man* were not the first time MTV had honoured Dunst. In 1995, at age eleven, she won her first MTV Award for Best Breakthrough Performance in *Interview with a Vampire*.

Q Who holds the record for the most thank yous in an Oscar acceptance speech?

A At almost six minutes, Greer Garson may have the record for longest acceptance speech, but incredibly she does not hold the record for most people thanked. That honour belongs to Olivia de Havilland for her Best Actress acceptance speech for the 1946 film *To Each His Own*.

"I feel humble, too, as well as proud. I accept this Oscar in the name of my team as well as my own," she said, before thanking twenty-seven people from "her team."

Q Why didn't Sophia Loren pick up her Best Actress Oscar for *Two Women* in person?

A *Variety* reported that sex symbol Sophia Loren chose not to attend the April 9, 1962, ceremony because of a case of nerves.

"I could not bear the ordeal of sitting in plain view of millions of viewers while my fate was being judged," she said. "If I lost, I might faint from disappointment. If I won, I would very likely faint with joy. I decided it would be better to faint at home.

"On Academy Awards night, our house held the atmosphere of the waiting room in a maternity ward," said Loren. "I was smoking cigarette after cigarette and drinking cup after cup of coffee." When she asked her husband, producer Carlo Ponti, what he recommended as a tranquilizer, he suggested chloroform.

After the win she released a statement from her home in Rome. "I started as a sex symbol, but it was as a symbol of mother love that I won an Oscar, and that gives me extra satisfaction."

Loren's Best Actress Oscar for the Second World War drama was the first Academy Award ever given for a performance in a foreign-language film, although she very nearly didn't play the part. Originally the role was offered to Anna Magnani, the doyenne of Italian actresses, with Loren cast as her daughter. Magnani turned the role down because Loren was "much taller than me," adding that she could not perform with a daughter she "had to look up to."

Q Who were the only actresses to tie for an Academy Award?

"Hello, Gorgeous..."

In 1968 Katharine Hepburn and Barbra Streisand tied for Best Actress at the Academy Awards for their roles in *The Lion in Winter* and *Funny Girl* respectively.

The presenter was Ingrid Bergman, who was told by a Price, Waterhouse representative to make sure she "read everything" on the winning ballot.

"I thought he was referring to all the names of the nominees," she said. Seconds later she announced, "It's a tie," which meant that the 3,030 academy voters had been evenly split. Streisand ripped her bell-bottom pants on the stairs on the way to the stage, while director Anthony Harvey accepted for Hepburn.

"Hello, gorgeous," Streisand said to her Oscar before beginning her acceptance speech. "I am very honored to be in such magnificent company as Katharine Hepburn. The first script of *Funny Girl* was written when I was only 11 years old. Thank God it took this long to get it right, you know?"

The tie ruffled some feathers within the Academy. Streisand had been given a special dispensation and was offered an Actors Branch membership before she had even made her first film. Typically only those who had appeared with "a minimum of three feature film credits, in all of which the roles played were scripted roles, one of which was released in the last five years, and all of which are of a caliber that reflect the high standards of the Academy" are invited to join. Streisand was brought in using a little-known Academy bylaw that states, "If in the judgment of the Actors Branch Executive Committee, [the potential member] otherwise achieved unique distinction … [or] earned special merit …" Gregory Peck, then Academy president, defended the decision to allow Streisand early admission by saying, "When an actress has played a great role on stage [*Funny Girl*] and is coming into films for what will obviously be an important career, it is ridiculous to make her wait three years for membership."

When it came to the 1968 tie irate members who felt that Streisand had not paid her dues came up with an interesting take on the whole affair. Presumably, they reasoned, she voted for herself, and since Academy rules require an exact tie, if she hadn't been given early admission, Hepburn would have won by one vote.

It was the first tie since the 1931–32 ceremony, when Wallace Beery (*The Champ*) and Fredric March (*Dr. Jekyll and Mr. Hyde*) tied for Best Actor.

Wallace Beery and child star Jackie Cooper in *The Champ*, which was voted the second best (next to *Grand Hotel*) of 1932 in a Film Daily poll of national critics.

Why didn't Joan Crawford pick up her Best Actress Oscar for *Mildred Pierce* in person?

Crawford was convinced that she was going to lose the Oscar to Ingrid Bergman for *The Bells of St. Mary's* and refused to attend the show.

Crawford stayed home in bed "wrestling with a flock of flu germs," though her hairdresser and makeup artists were beckoned to the house — just in case. When Crawford won, her daughter Christina noted that her mother's health "seemed to improve dramatically."

The groomers went to work, and when the Oscar was delivered after the ceremony, Crawford was ready for her close-up. Her publicist said later, "The photo of her in bed clutching the Oscar pushed all the other winners off of the front page."

"*It's so much fun being nominated —
everyone is a winner. And then —
afterwards — there are four losers.*"

— Liv Ullmann, 1972

IT'S AN HONOUR JUST TO BE NOMINATED – NOT!

Q Who began the 1968 Oscar broadcast with the quip, "Welcome to the Academy Awards, or as it's known at my house, Passover"?

A Host Bob Hope likened the Academy Awards to Passover at his house. He received five Oscars over the course of his career, but none in a competitive category. Upon receiving an honorary award in 1953 he joked, "Imagine, after all these years, me winning an Oscar. It's the first time I ever left a party with a man and was happy about it." Hope hosted the Oscars more than anyone else — eighteen times, starting in 1939.

Q Which movie was named the "Worst Musical of Our First 25 Years" by the Golden Raspberries?

A *From Justin to Kelly*, featuring American Idol "stars" Justin Guarini and Kelly Clarkson, was named worst musical of the last twenty-five years by the Golden Raspberries at their twenty-fifth anniversary ceremony in February 2005. The movie — which the *New York Times* called "the motion picture equivalent of Cheez Whiz," while another writer said, "It's sad that after *Moulin Rouge* and *Chicago* worked so hard to resurrect the musical, *From Justin to Kelly* had to go and kill it all over again" — holds the record for fastest release from theatres to home video/DVD. It went from the big screen to the small screen in just twenty-nine days.

Gigli, the Ben Affleck–Jennifer Lopez bomb that was reviled by critics, was named worst comedy, and the John Travolta–starred *Battlefield Earth* won for worst drama of the last twenty-five years.

California Governor Arnold Schwarzenegger was named the worst Razzie loser of the last twenty-five years for having been nominated eight times and failing to win even once.

THE PERFORMANCES THAT OSCAR FORGOT:
CLASSIC PERFORMANCES THAT WERE NOT NOMINATED FOR OSCARS

1. Bette Davis, *Of Human Bondage*: The hue and cry over Davis's omission from the nomination list led to the first sanctioned write-in.

2. **Myrna Loy, _The Thin Man_:** Despite being named Queen of the Movies and making 128 films, Loy was never nominated for an acting Oscar, although she received an honorary Academy Award in 1991.

3. **Charles Laughton, _The Hunchback of Notre Dame_:** In spite of the huge publicity push behind this movie — at $1.8 million it was the most expensive film RKO had ever made — and Laughton's poignant performance, the Academy stayed true to its neglect of horror and fantasy films and nominated it only for Best Music and Best Sound.

4. **Boris Karloff, _Frankenstein_:** Karloff created one of the most recognizable characters to ever grace the screen — Frankenstein's lumbering monster — but never had to prepare an acceptance speech.

5. **Cary Grant, _The Philadelphia Story_:** Grant was nominated twice, for _Penny Serenade_ and _None But the Lonely Heart_, and while his two co-stars were recognized by Oscar — Jimmy Stewart won for Best Actor, while Katharine Hepburn lost to Ginger Rogers in _Kitty Foyle: The Natural History of a Woman_ — the suave Grant was not.

6. **Humphrey Bogart, _The Maltese Falcon_:** Bogart starred in so many classic films it is surprising that he earned only three Oscar nominations and just one win, for _The African Queen_, at the March 20, 1952, ceremony. His most famous characterization, the P.I. Sam Spade in _The Maltese Falcon_, went unnoticed by the Academy.

7. **Lauren Bacall, _To Have and Have Not_:** Bacall had to wait more than fifty years after her career-making debut — "You just put your lips together and … blow" — in _To Have and Have Not_ to earn any significant awards attention. After a lifetime of solid performances she was finally nominated — although in an upset she lost to _The English Patient_'s Juliette Binoche — for a Best Supporting Actress Oscar for _The Mirror Has Two Faces_ in 1997.

8. **Ingrid Bergman, _Notorious_:** Actors in Alfred Hitchcock films didn't have much luck with the Academy. Only one performance — Joan Fontaine in _Suspicion_ — ever took home the gold. Laurence Olivier, Joan Fontaine, and Judith Anderson were all nominated for _Rebecca_ but lost. Claude Rains earned a Best Supporting Actor nomination for _Notorious_ in 1946, and Ethel Barrymore earned one in 1947 for _The Paradine Case_. The only other Hitchcock-directed acting nomination went to Janet Leigh for _Psycho_ in the Best Supporting Actress category.

9. **Marilyn Monroe, *Some Like It Hot*:** Monroe was never nominated for an Oscar, although she did win a Golden Globe for her role in this movie.

10. **Gene Hackman, *The Conversation*:** Hackman has been rewarded for his performances many times over. He has two Oscars, a few Golden Globes, and a host of other kudos, but one of his greatest performances — as the obsessive Harry Caul in *The Conversation* — was overlooked by the Academy.

BONUS:

Other stars from the Land That Oscar Forgot include Tallulah Bankhead, John Barrymore, Dirk Bogarde, Joseph Cotton, Errol Flynn, Glenn Ford, Rita Hayworth, Peter Lorre, Tyrone Power, Vincent Price, Edward G. Robinson, and Robert Taylor.

Q Which three stars of a multi-nominated film were not invited to the 74th Annual Academy Awards?

A Three British stars of the chart-busting *Lord of the Rings* were refused tickets for the March 24, 2002, Oscars by Academy Award organizers. Billy Boyd, Dominic Monaghan, and Orlando Bloom starred in the first instalment of the fantasy trilogy — which was nominated for thirteen awards — as hobbits Pippin, Merry, and head elf Legolas Greenleaf.

The actors were in Los Angeles and had planned to join their co-stars at the ceremony but were told by Oscar organizers that the 3,500-seat Kodak Theatre in Hollywood was overbooked and there were no seats for the trio. "I'm going out to get drunk anyway," said Bloom, while Monaghan added, "We have plenty of options for a night out. But the Oscars isn't one of them."

The Lord of the Rings: The Fellowship of the Ring earned four — Best Cinematography, Visual Effects, Makeup, and Music (Original Score) — of the thirteen Oscars it was nominated for.

Q Which 2003 film was nominated for thirteen BAFTAs but earned only two awards?

It's an Honour Just to Be Nominated – Not!

The big shock of the February 15, 2004, BAFTA ceremony was American Civil War drama *Cold Mountain*'s performance. After earning thirteen nominations, the Anthony Minghella–directed epic won only Best Actress in a Supporting Role for Renee Zellweger and the Anthony Asquith Award for Achievement in Film Music.

The movie's poor performance at the BAFTAS was echoed two weeks later at the Oscars, when the film went one for seven, with Zellweger once again winning Best Supporting Actress for her Annie Oakley–wannabe performance as scrappy drifter Ruby Thewes.

Later on Oscar night the much-lauded actress celebrated her win at Hollywood restaurant-to-the-stars Morton's but decided to leave her statuette in the safety of her limousine. When some friends requested to see the Oscar in person she ran to get the award but found it missing. She was about to call security when she realized that she had been searching the wrong limo. Apparently she became confused by the sea of black limos parked at the star-filled restaurant.

"With the excitement of winning the Oscar she just wasn't paying attention and briefly panicked," said a reporter who was on the scene.

A relieved Zellweger was later heard telling a friend, "I'm never letting this guy out of my sight."

Cold Mountain seemed have Oscar written all over it — an A-list cast, an epic love story adapted from a literary and bestselling book, a former Best Director winner at the helm — but something put the Academy voters off. After awards season was over an insider who worked on the film leaked to the press that Nicole Kidman's glamorous appearance was the reason Oscar shunned the film.

"During the editing it was obvious that Nicole looked far too glamorous," the source said. "She was playing a down-trodden farm owner struggling to survive during the American Civil War, yet she looked like a cover girl. There was intense debate involving [director] Anthony and executive producer Harvey Weinstein about digitally smudging Nicole's appearance, roughing up her cheeks, that sort of thing. In the end, time and cost ruled it out. Nicole's appearance dents the credibility of the film and may have cost it Best Picture."

Q What Oscar distinction do 1951's *A Place in the Sun* and 1977's *Star Wars* share?

A Both *A Place in the Sun* and *Star Wars* won six Academy Awards but did not win Best Picture.

Q How many Razzie Awards was *Gigli* nominated for in 2004?

A *Gigli* (rhymes with *really*) picked up an impressive nine nominations at the Golden Raspberry Awards. The Martin Brest–directed gangster super-flop was nominated for Worst Picture, Worst Screen Couple for J-Lo and Ben Affleck, Worst Director, Worst Screenplay for Martin Brest, Worst Supporting Actor for both Christopher Walken and Al Pacino, Worst Supporting Actress for Lainie Kazan, and Worst Actress and Worst Actor for Jen and Ben, respectively.

Not surprisingly, *Gigli* was the big "winner" at the February 28, 2004, dishonours, becoming the first film in the history of the Razzie Awards to "sweep" all the top categories: Worst Picture, Worst Director, Worst Actor, Worst Actress, Worst Screen Couple, and Worst Screenplay.

Razzies founder John Wilson attributes Affleck and Lopez's high-profile relationship for their popularity among voters. "Ostensibly, we're talking about their on-screen performances," he said, "but I'm sure all the endless twaddle about their personal lives played into their being nominated. But it is an embarrassingly bad movie, and unfortunately, it's not a fun bad movie."

The parody website *The Onion* ran a fake news story that seemed to sum up most people's feelings about the movie. "Focus groups at advance screenings for *Gigli*, a romantic comedy starring Ben Affleck and Jennifer Lopez set to open nationwide July 30, have demanded a new ending in which both Affleck and Lopez die."

Affleck, who didn't attend the Razzie ceremony, received his Golden Raspberry Award on *Larry King Live*. On live TV the actor was presented with a small box.

"Is this the real thing, or is this some fake?" he asked. "I like it. What do I get this for? It's a little cheap, guys! [Razzies founder John

Wilson said the awards cost $4.79 each and that he "made them the other day on my patio."] That's very kind of them. They were pleased with *Gigli*, I understand. We swept the Razzies for *Gigli* and *Pearl Harbor*." He then told King, "I'm probably gonna leave it here and make you a gift of it, Larry. Because I love you that much, I'm gonna let you have this. Put that on your shelf with your Emmys and the rest of whatever you got there."

But King declined, saying, "It's a piece of crap!"

Affleck ended up breaking the award in half. The pieces were returned to Razzie godfather Wilson, who auctioned off the broken trophy to pay for the twenty-fifth anniversary Razzie ceremony.

BEST LOSERS:
FILMS THAT HAVE WON FIVE OR MORE ACADEMY AWARDS WITHOUT WINNING BEST PICTURE

1. ***Cabaret*** won so many awards on March 27, 1973 — Best Actress (Liza Minelli), Best Supporting Actor (Joel Grey), Best Director (Bob Fosse), as well as Best Art Direction, Cinematography, Film Editing, Sound, and Music — that it looked like the movie had a lock on the Best Picture award. The year's other hot ticket, *The Godfather*, had been expected to sweep all the major categories but had won only Best Actor and Best Adapted Screenplay. The hotly tipped mafia drama was taking a shellacking from the song-and-dance movie. "When they announced Fosse for Director," said *Godfather* producer Albert S. Ruddy, "I was ready to tear up my speech." Then the unthinkable happened: Best Picture presenter Clint Eastwood announced the winner — *The Godfather*. The loss of the Best Picture statuette set a record for *Cabaret* as the film to win the most Oscars — eight — without taking the top prize.

2. ***A Place in the Sun***, based on Theodore Dreiser's novel *An American Tragedy*, was nominated for nine Academy Awards and won six — Best Director for George Stevens, Best Screenplay, Cinematography (Black and White), Dramatic Score, Film Editing, and Costume Design (Black and White). Its other three nominations were for Best Picture, which it lost to Vincente Minnelli's Technicolor musical *An American in Paris*, Best Actor for Montgomery Clift, and Best Actress for Shelley Winters. *New York Times* critic Bosley Crowther was particularly upset

about the drama's loss in the Best Picture department. He was shocked, he wrote, that the Academy had "so many people so insensitive to the excellencies of motion-picture art that they would vote for a frivolous musical picture over a powerful and pregnant tragedy."

3. Decades after its release, **Star Wars** was voted the sixteenth greatest film of all time by *Entertainment Weekly* — the highest ranked of any sci-fi movie on the list — but in 1977 the Academy held true to its disdain for genre pictures and denied it the top prize. Nominated for ten Academy Awards, it won six in mostly technical categories: Best Art Direction, Sound, Music (Original Score), Film Editing, Costume Design, and Visual Effects. Its other four nominations were for Best Picture, Best Supporting Actor for Alec Guinness, Best Director for George Lucas, and Best Screenplay Written Directly for the Screen. The film was also awarded a Special Achievement Award for Sound Effects for Benjamin Burtt Jr. to honour his creation of the alien, creature, and robot voices. *Star Wars* lost Best Picture to Woody Allen's *Annie Hall*.

4. The rise, fall, and rebirth of a boorish Hollywood producer, as told in **The Bad and the Beautiful**, earned six Academy Award nominations and prevailed in five of the categories, excluding Best Actor — Kirk Douglas lost to Gary Cooper for his role in *High Noon*. The winners included Best Supporting Actress for Gloria Grahame, Best Screenplay, Cinematography (Black and White), Art Direction (Black and White), and Costume Design (Black and White). Strangely, this much-praised film failed to grasp a nomination for director Vincente Minnelli or for Best Picture.

5. **Doctor Zhivago** earned some of the worst notices of director David Lean's career. Influential critic Pauline Kael wrote that his "method is basically primitive, admired by the same sort of people who are delighted when a stage set has running water or a painted horse looks real enough to ride," and Judith Crist called it an "ultimately tedious epic type soap opera," while still another grumbled that the "actors have been given almost nothing to do except wear costumes and engage in banal small talk." The reviews were so punishing, in fact, that Lean vowed never to make another film. It must have been a sweet moment when the film grabbed ten Oscar nominations, including Best Picture and Best Actor. When Lean was told he was up for directing, he said, "But how could I have been when the Director's Guild didn't give us a nomination?" On the night of the Oscarcast *Doctor Zhivago* grabbed five statuettes, tying its biggest competitor, *The Sound of Music*, but didn't take Best Director or Best Picture.

6. ***The King and I*** brought in nine nominations and took over half of them — Best Actor for Yul Brynner, Best Sound Recording, Art Direction (Color), Costume Design (Color), and Score (Musical) — but was unsuccessful in the top category. The Hollywood musical spectacular lost Best Picture to *The Bridge on the River Kwai*.

7. With five Oscars out of eleven nominations, ***Mary Poppins*** is Walt Disney's biggest winner ever at the Academy Awards. The magical, musical nanny took Best Actress for Julie Andrews, Best Effects, Best Editing, Best Music (Song), and Best Music (Score), but lost Best Picture to another musical, *My Fair Lady*, which Andrews had starred in on Broadway.

8. Usually when a film earns a Best Director Oscar, as ***Saving Private Ryan*** did in 1998, a Best Picture statuette can't be far behind. *Variety* reported that the Second World War drama had a statistical advantage going in to the awards. "More than any other genre, war films have commanded their disproportionate share of Best Picture Oscars" — nineteen in the first seventy years of the Academy Awards history. *Saving Private Ryan* did well, taking five wins out of eleven nominations, including Best Director for Steven Spielberg, but lost Best Picture to the medieval rom-com *Shakespeare in Love*.

9. Mike Nichols's shocking black comedy ***Who's Afraid of Virginia Woolf?*** was the first film in Oscar history to be nominated in every eligible category. Netting thirteen nominations — Best Picture, Actor, Actress, Supporting Actor, Supporting Actress, Director, Adapted Screenplay, Art Direction (Black and White), Cinematography (Black and White), Sound, Costume Design (Black and White), Music (Original Score), and Film Editing — it was also the first film to have every member of its cast receive an acting nomination, making it the film to beat in the 1966 Oscar derby. On the big night the film won five Academy Awards — Best Actress (Elizabeth Taylor), Best Supporting Actress (Sandy Dennis), and Cinematography, Art Direction, and Costume Design — but it lost Best Picture to *A Man for All Seasons*.

10. ***Wilson*** is the kind of film the Academy likes — a biopic with a good patriotic message. The two-and-a-half-hour, $5.2-million life story of twenty-sixth president Woodrow Wilson was producer Darryl Zanuck's dream project and was even hailed by the American Nobel Committee as "a vital contribution to the cause of world peace." The film gathered ten Oscars nominations in 1944 — tying with a public favourite, *Going*

My Way — and won five for technical achievements, but didn't win any acting wards or the coveted Best Picture. The day after the ceremony Zanuck told friends that the Academy must be "a corps of philistines if they could pass over *Wilson* as Best Picture."

Q Which Oscar host once called the Academy "a small bunch of people with small minds who chose to ignore the obvious"?

A *The Color Purple* star Whoopi Goldberg lashed out at the Academy — and probably wrecked her chances at winning Best Actress — when the film garnered eleven Oscar nominations in a variety of categories except Best Director for Steven Spielberg. The actress stood by her beleaguered director and labelled the Academy "a small bunch of people with small minds who chose to ignore the obvious."

She also admits to being very nervous about her nomination. "I gave myself the hives," she said. "I got them so bad, I had to go to the dermatologist. I was totally freaked out."

Five years later, in 1990, she appeared to have kissed and made up with the Academy when she accepted the Best Supporting Actress award for *Ghost*. In 1994 she hosted the Oscar broadcast, becoming the first female and first solo African-American host of an Academy Awards show.

Q Which group of people was disqualified from winning Academy Awards during the 1950s?

A The 1947 House on Un-American Activities Committee (HUAC) hearings targeted a core group of Hollywood screenwriters and one director, known as the Hollywood Ten: Alvah Bessie, Herbert Biberman, Lester Cole, Edward Dmytryk, Ring Lardner Jr., John Howard Lawson, Albert Maltz, Sam Ornitz, Robert Adrian Scott, and Dalton Trumbo. During the 1950s an Academy rule was instated whereby those blacklisted by Senator Joe McCarthy's HUAC couldn't receive a nomination. This rule was done away with when blacklisted people were nominated and even won under pseudonyms.

It's an Honour Just to Be Nominated – Not!

Q Which Madonna movie swept the 2002 Golden Raspberry Awards, taking home five dishonours?

A Madonna and husband Guy Ritchie "swept away" the competition at the 2002 Razzies, earning five Razzie Awards, among them Worst Picture of 2002, for *Swept Away*, the island-romance bomb that starred Madonna and was adapted from the original screenplay and directed by Ritchie. Madonna tied for Worst Actress with fellow pop queen Britney Spears, who made her acting debut in *Crossroads*, another Worst Picture candidate. Ritchie was chosen Worst Director, while Madonna took a second award for Worst Screen Couple with co-star Adriano Giannini for the film that one critic said "festers in just such a dungpile that you'd swear you were watching monkeys flinging their feces at you."

A remake of an acclaimed Italian film about a rich snob stranded with a hunky sailor, Madonna's *Swept Away* also received the trophy for Worst Remake or Sequel. "Last week the director's cut of Madonna's *Swept Away* was released on DVD," Conan O'Brien joked in 2003. "That's right — the director was unsatisfied with people walking out of the theatre; he wanted people to walk out of their homes!"

That same year Madonna was named Worst Supporting Actress for her brief cameo as a fencing instructor in the James Bond flick *Die Another Day*, for which she also sang the theme song.

"She's not even in the movie for two minutes, but she's so awful in that one scene, that for the whole rest of the movie, you cannot forget that your eyes and ears have been assaulted with the stupidity of her appearance," said Razzies founder John Wilson.

Q Which two British acting legends were nominated for Oscars seven times each but never won?

A Peter O'Toole was first nominated for an Academy Award in 1963 for *Lawrence of Arabia* — about which Noel Coward quipped, "If he [O'Toole] had been any prettier it would have been *Florence of Arabia*" — and then six more times over the next seventeen years for *Becket* (1964), *The Lion in Winter* (1968), *Goodbye, Mr. Chips* (1969), *The*

Ruling Class (1972), *The Stunt Man* (1980), and *My Favorite Year* (1982). "The fact that I have lost five times intrigues me even more," he said after his 1980 loss.

After receiving his first Best Actor nomination for *Lawrence of Arabia* O'Toole made it known he was immediately hiking his fee to $500,000 per movie — unless he won the Oscar, in which case he would ask for $1 million. The escalator clause never kicked in, as O'Toole lost to Gregory Peck for *To Kill a Mockingbird*.

In 2003, the Academy gave O'Toole an honorary award for "remarkable talents [which] have provided cinema history with some of its most memorable characters." O'Toole initially balked, writing the Academy a letter saying he was "still in the game" and would like more time to "win the lovely bugger outright."

Upon hearing of O'Toole's reticence to accept the award, Oscarcast producer (and actress Phoebe Cates's uncle) Gil Cates said, "I wish I were friendly enough with him to call him on the phone and say, 'Awfully silly — you should really take it and your career will be what your career will be.' If he doesn't appear on the show nothing will happen and he will pick up the Academy Award when he wants to. If he does appear on the show we'll prepare a suitable piece to honor him. I have a feeling that it's going to resolve itself probably this week — he'll either say he'll be there or he won't."

In the end the actor caved in and agreed to appear at the ceremony and pick up his Oscar.

"I now have my own Oscar till death do us part," O'Toole said when he accepted his honorary Oscar.

Over the course of twenty-five years Richard Burton earned seven nominations but never won. He was first given a Best Supporting Actor nod in 1953 for *My Cousin Rachel*, followed by six failed bids for Best Actor: *The Robe* (1953), *Becket* (1964), *The Spy Who Came in From the Cold* (1965), *Who's Afraid of Virginia Woolf?* (1966), *Anne of the Thousand Days* (1969), and finally *Equus* (1977). In 1969 John Wayne reportedly came knocking on Burton's door, drunkenly brandishing his Oscar for *True Grit*. "You should have this," he said, "not me."

It's an Honour Just to Be Nominated – Not!

Q: Who is the most filmed author to have not won an Academy Award?

A: It's a bit of a trick question, in that the most filmed author in Hollywood history is William Shakespeare, who died in 1616. A total of 394 feature films and TV movies have been shot based on his plays to date. *Hamlet* is the most popular, with seventy-five versions, followed by *Romeo and Juliet* with fifty-one and *Macbeth* with thirty-three.

In 1998, *Shakespeare in Love* screenwriter Marc Newman joked, "If Shakespeare were alive today, he'd be driving a Porsche, living in Bel-Air, and he'd have a deal with Paramount."

Q: Why was Robert Rich's 1956 Oscar win so controversial?

A: At the 29th Annual Academy Awards, a writer named Robert Rich won Best Writing (Motion Picture Story) for *The Brave One*.

Mr. Rich didn't show up to collect the statuette, so Writers Guild bigwig Jesse Lasky Jr. accepted it, explaining that his "good friend" Mr. Rich was otherwise engaged attending the birth of his first child.

When reporters tried to track down Mr. Rich they found him to be more elusive than your average Oscar winner. In fact, they couldn't find any trace of the writer; even the officials at the Writers Guild eventually admitted they had no record of any such person.

In truth, Robert Rich was a pseudonym for Dalton Trumbo, one member of the infamous "Hollywood Ten" who was blacklisted for his leftist views and spent years writing in anonymity.

The Academy took back the Oscar and held on to it until 1976, when it was belatedly presented to a dying Trumbo.

Q: Why did Best Supporting Actress winner Estelle Parsons say that *Bonnie and Clyde* won only two of its ten Oscar nominations?

A: When the highly praised but brutal *Bonnie and Clyde* won only two awards out of ten nominations on April 10, 1968, Estelle Parsons said the reason was plain: "Nobody likes Warren Beatty."

Bonnie and Clyde was nominated for Best Actor for Warren Beatty, Best Supporting Actor for both Michael J. Pollard and Gene Hackman, Best Actress for Faye Dunaway, Best Supporting Actress for Estelle Parsons, Best Costume Design for Theadora Van Runkle, Best Cinematography for Burnett Guffey, Best Writing (Story and Screenplay Written Directly for the Screen) for David Newman and Robert Benton, Best Director for Arthur Penn, and Best Picture for Beatty as producer.

The movie collected only two awards: Best Supporting Actress and Best Cinematography.

Hollywood may not have appreciated Beatty's film, but the public sure did. It was a box-office sensation, and thousands of berets were sold worldwide after Faye Dunaway wore them in the film.

Q Who was the first woman to co-host an Academy Awards broadcast?

A The first woman to take the Oscar stage as co-host was four-time Oscar nominee Agnes Moorehead, who shared the stage with Dick Powell on March 20, 1948. She was one of Hollywood's premier character actresses, appearing in everything from *Citizen Kane*, in which she played the title character's mother, to *Bewitched*, in which she played Endora, the "mother witch." She earned her first Oscar nomination as a spinster in Orson Welles's *The Magnificent Ambersons* and was nominated three more times for her performances in *Mrs. Parkington*, *Johnny Belinda*, and *Hush … Hush, Sweet Charlotte*.

That year's show was apparently quite dull — although more than 45 million people tuned their radios to the broadcast — so dull, in fact, that *The Hollywood-Citizen News* suggested the Academy spice things up in future by turning the ceremony into a variety show. "Why not have some big production numbers," they wrote, "a few hundred dancing Oscars, say. Or a couple of bird acts maybe."

Q Which 1966 Richard Burton/Elizabeth Taylor film was nominated for seven Golden Globes but walked away empty-handed?

A *Who's Afraid of Virginia Woolf?*, the famous and shocking black comedy, was based on Edward Albee's scandalous play and was nominated for Best Motion Picture: Drama, Best Motion Picture Actor in a Drama for Richard Burton, Best Motion Picture Actress in a Drama for Elizabeth Taylor, Best Motion Picture Director for Mike Nichols, Best Screenplay for Ernest Lehman, Best Supporting Actor for George Segal, and Best Supporting Actress for Sandy Dennis, but was shut out in all categories.

Similarly, *The Godfather, Part III* received seven nominations in 1990 but no Globes.

IT'S AN HONOUR JUST TO BE NOMINATED:
MOVIES WITH SEVEN OR MORE OSCAR NOMINATIONS BUT NO WINS

1. ***The Letter:*** Despite 1940 Oscar show host Bob Hope's remark that "Bette Davis drops in at these affairs every year for a cup of coffee and another Oscar," Davis missed out on Best Actress for *The Letter*. The film — a remake of the Somerset Maugham story that earned a Best Actress nomination for Jeanne Eagels in 1929 — failed to prevail in any of its seven nominated categories.

2. ***The Little Foxes:*** For the second year in a row Bette Davis head-lined a movie that earned a lot of attention from the Academy — nine nominations — but no love. *The Little Foxes* and its study of turn-of-the-century antebellum greed marked the third and last time Davis worked with William Wyler, who had directed her to a Best Actress Oscar for *Jezebel* and a nomination for *The Letter*.

3. ***Random Harvest:*** The tear-jerking story of an amnesiac who becomes romantically reacquainted with his wife did boffo box office, but apparently Academy voters forgot all about it when it came time to choose the 1942 Oscar winners. Greer Garson called it the favourite of all her films, but *Random Harvest* withered on the vine, failing to win any of its seven Oscar nominations. Years later it would weigh in at #36 on AFI's 100 Greatest Love Stories of All Time list.

4. ***The Talk of the Town:*** Director George Stevens described *The Talk of the Town* as "an understood flight with a take-off time and an

arrival time and not too much headwind." That strange analogy sums up the 1942 comedy in which Cary Grant plays a political activist who is wrongly indicted for arson and murder when a factory worker dies in a mill fire — it's easy-breezy and not too taxing on the noggin. It does, though, feature fine performances from the cast, and the director's characteristically adroit touch with comic shenanigans is apparent throughout the film. Perhaps the tone of the film was too undemanding for the Academy to take seriously. Although they gave the film seven nominations, when it came time to dole out trophies none went to Stevens and company.

5. **Madame Curie**: *The Los Angeles Examiner* thought that the story of Madame Curie's discovery of radium raised "motion pictures to the realm of Shakespearean drama." Academy voters, however, seemed to side with most of the other critics, one of whom called it "a two-hour picture reaching a high point when two people stand looking into a saucer," and didn't give the film any of the seven Oscars it was up for.

6. **Double Indemnity**: The quintessential film noir, *Double Indemnity*'s story of murderous adulterers who plot to kill a woman's husband for the insurance money earned seven Oscar nominations in 1944, including Best Director for Billy Wilder, Best Screenplay for Wilder and Raymond Chandler, Best Actress for Barbara Stanwyck, and Best Picture. The subject matter might have been a bit too dark for Academy members, who voted against the film seven times, overwhelmingly favouring the inspirational *Going My Way* over Wilder's dark drama.

7. **Come to the Stable**: This holiday favourite is the story of two French nuns who relocate to the town of Bethlehem, Connecticut, and use a combination of hard work, prayer, and skilled gambling to establish a new children's hospital. The Academy didn't have as much faith in the film, giving *Come to the Stable* seven 1949 Oscar nominations, including three for acting — Best Actress nods for Loretta Young and Celeste Holm and Best Supporting Actress for Elsa Lanchester — but no trophies.

8. **Quo Vadis**: Adapted from the novel by Polish author Henryk Sienkiewicz, 1951's *Quo Vadis* is the epic story of the conflict between pagan Rome and the newly emerging Christian faith in the last years of Nero's reign. MGM was very keen to have the expensive movie snap up some Oscars and pulled out all the stops to influence Academy voters. In ads they called the film "The Greatest Motion Picture of all Time" and

compared it to one of their other touchstone hits, *Gone with the Wind*. The stumping seemed to work when the film harvested eight nominations, including two Best Supporting Actor nods and Best Picture, but it was just a tease. *Quo Vadis* came up empty on Oscar night.

9. ***The Caine Mutiny*:** Based upon Herman Wouk's bestselling and 1951 Pulitzer Prize–winning novel of the same name about a rebellion aboard a naval vessel and the subsequent court-martial trial, *The Caine Mutiny* contains Humphrey Bogart's last great performance. As the jittery Lt. Cmdr. Philip Francis "missing strawberries" Queeg, Bogie wraps his usual tough-guy-in-a-trench-coat persona in a blanket of paranoia as he crumbles under heavy cross-examination in a climactic court scene. So it was no surprise then when Bogart was nominated for Best Actor, his third top acting nomination. Too bad he was up against *On the Waterfront*'s Marlon Brando in a career-defining performance and his fourth consecutive Best Actor nomination. *The Caine Mutiny*, which earned so-so reviews — *The New Yorker* said, "as pictures about the United States Navy go, *The Caine Mutiny* isn't bad" — was popular at the box office and became the second highest grossing movie of 1954. That didn't impress the Academy, who snubbed it in all seven categories it was nominated in.

10. ***Peyton Place*:** In Hollywood lore the failure of *Peyton Place* to win any of its nine nominations at the 1957 Oscars has been overshadowed by the events that followed the ceremony. Lana Turner, up for Best Actress for the romantic picture, chose to attend the ceremony with an entourage that included her mother, her daughter Cheryl Crane, and her public relations person. Noticeably absent was her boyfriend, underworld figure Johnny Stompanato, whom Turner left at home because of his rough image. The night quickly turned into a disaster on all fronts. Not only did her movie get stiffed on all its nominations, but her limousine driver fell asleep, stranding her on the sidewalk outside the theatre after the awards. Worse yet, when she got home the thug Stompanato beat her senseless for not taking him to the ceremony. This thrashing — a "degradation … at the hands of a madman," Turner later described it — put into motion a series of events that would lead to the teenaged Crane stabbing and killing the mobster ten days later.

11. ***Anatomy of a Murder*:** Otto Preminger's sexually charged courtroom drama — *Time* said it was "less concerned with murder than anatomy" — reaped seven major nominations: Best Picture, Best Actor for James Stewart, Best Supporting Actor nods for Arthur O'Connell and

George C. Scott, Best Adapted Screenplay, Cinematography (Black and White), and Film Editing. It had the misfortune, however, to be up against *Ben-Hur*. The three-hour-thirty-two-minute biblical epic was heavily tipped to sweep the awards, and for once the pundits were right. *Ben-Hur* took all but one of its nominations, robbing Preminger and company of their glory and becoming the first of only three films in history to win eleven Academy Awards, the others being *Titanic* and *The Lord of the Rings: The Return of the King*.

12. *The Nun's Story*: Jack Benny was so moved by *The Nun's Story* that he called it "one of the most beautiful pictures I have ever seen." General audiences seemed to agree with Benny's take on the film — it had a good long run at Radio City Music Hall and was one of the biggest grossing films of the year — but Academy voters chose to give *Ben-Hur* six of the eight awards *The Nun's Story* was up for, with the others, Best Actress and Screenplay, going to *Room at the Top*.

13. *Pepe*: Despite having Charlie Chaplin's endorsement as "the world's greatest comedian," Mexican funnyman Cantinflas — he took his stage name from the Mexican verb *cantinflear*, which means to talk gibberish — had little success in Hollywood. His superstar status in the Spanish-speaking world didn't cross over to America, and one critic even wrote that "Cantinflas, in his classic role as the underdog, is funny mostly to other underdogs. And these form the vast majority in Mexico." The 1959 box-office bomb *Pepe*, about a Mexican horse groomer's adventures in Los Angeles, was the comic's last attempt to make a mark in Hollywood. Perhaps because the movie had cameos by half of the members of the Screen Actors Guild, the Academy felt they couldn't completely ignore the movie, but when it came time to actually hand out awards none of *Pepe*'s seven nominations came to fruition.

14. *Mutiny on the Bounty*: Based on Chris Nordhoff/James Norton Hall's factual narrative of the infamous mutiny in 1789, the 1962 remake of *Mutiny on the Bounty* became known in Hollywood as a bottomless money pit. Marlon Brando, in a foppish portrayal of Fletcher Christian that one critic called "just this side of a female impersonation," heads up the cast, and apparently his notorious on-set behaviour disrupted the production and contributed to the bloated budget, which rose from $10 million to a final total north of $20 million. So beleaguered was the production that the *New Yorker* said the film was "famous for its trouble before it was famous for anything else."

The Academy seemed to try to reward the frazzled behind-the-scenes workers on the film for putting up with Brando's claptrap, nominating six of them in technical categories in addition to offering the film a very generous Best Picture nod. The troubled film was trumped by *Lawrence of Arabia* in most categories.

15. ***Hush … Hush, Sweet Charlotte*:** Genre pictures, like action-adventures, suspense-thrillers, Westerns, and comedies, rarely have a chance to grab the big Oscar gold. *Hush … Hush, Sweet Charlotte* is a thriller that echoes the previous collaboration of director Robert Aldrich and star Bette Davis, *What Ever Happened to Baby Jane?* In both films, a victim suffers most of her life for a crime she didn't commit and an old, decrepit house serves as a symbol of mental decay. The Academy is reluctant to reward this kind of film, and although they gave *Hush … Hush, Sweet Charlotte* seven nominations, there was only one acting nod in there — Best Supporting Actress for Agnes Moorehead — while most of the others were in the non-marquee categories, and everyone left empty-handed.

16. ***Hawaii*:** George Roy Hill's adaptation of James Michener's sprawling saga stars Max von Sydow and Julie Andrews as missionary couple Abner and Jerusha Hale who set sail from Massachusetts to bring the Lord's word to Hawaii. This three-hour epic earned seven Oscar nods: Best Music (Original Score), Music (Song), Cinematography, Costume Design, Special Visual Effects, Sound, and Supporting Actress for the non-professional actor Jocelyn LaGarde, a three-hundred-pound Tahitian who portrayed Queen Malama. The 1966 Oscar season was LaGarde's moment in the spotlight; she never made another film. It would be a nicer story if she had won, but unfortunately Academy members voted both her and *Hawaii* off the island on Oscar night.

17. ***The Sand Pebbles*:** Director Robert Wise was so proud of his three-hour epic about a U.S. patrol in 1926 China that he held annual parties with surviving cast members to celebrate the making of the film. The public liked it too. Twelve months after its 1966 release, the look at China on the eve of the Communist uprisings was still raking in $1 million a week at the box office. The Academy couldn't argue with the film's success and gave it eight nominations, including Steve McQueen's first and only nomination for Best Actor. But when Oscar gave *The Sand Pebbles* the cold shoulder on awards night and presented British actor Paul Scofield with the Best Actor trophy, McQueen somewhat cryptically

attributed his defeat to "the honchos digging some Alistair Cooke type, not a grease monkey who grooves on his wheels."

18. ***Star!*:** *Star!* was one of the biggest bombs of 1968. Despite the highly touted reunion of Robert Wise and Julie Andrews (director and star of *The Sound of Music*), the extravagant film based on the life of theatre legend Gertrude Lawrence was met with apathy at the box office — twice. MGM tried to salvage the film a year later by re-releasing it in a re-cut version titled *Those Were Happy Times*, but the attempt was not successful. The film didn't have much luck with the Academy, either. The big-budget production set a record for the largest number of costume changes for an actress in one film, so Oscar observers predicted it would at least take Best Costume. *Star!* did earn a Best Costume nomination, and six others, too, but missed the boat completely on the big night.

19. **The Turning Point:** Going into the Oscar ceremony on April 3, 1978, director Herbert Ross must have been on cloud nine. Not only did he direct *The Turning Point*, which was nominated for eleven Academy Awards, but he also helmed *The Goodbye Girl*, which received five nominations. Out of the twenty acting nominees that year, an astonishing seven were from his two films. It had to be a bitter pill for him to swallow, then, three hours later when the final tally was in — *The Goodbye Girl* took only one award, Best Actor for Richard Dreyfuss, while all of *The Turning Point*'s Oscar nominations had flown out the window.

20. **The Elephant Man:** "Hollywood will probably consider *The Elephant Man* a 'different' movie," said director David Lynch, "but, for me, it is very mainstream." The story of the monstrously disfigured John Merrick, dubbed the Elephant Man during his years in a circus freak show in Victorian England, was much more digestible than Lynch's previous film, the nightmarish *Eraserhead,* but still couldn't be considered conventional. The Academy, however, warmed to the film and nominated it for eight Oscars, including Best Picture and Best Actor for John Hurt in the title role. Shrouded in makeup Hurt is remarkable, conveying a deep pool of humanity from underneath the head-to-toe prosthetics — which were taken from casts of the real Merrick — and likely would have taken the Best Actor Oscar if he had not been up against Robert De Niro's much-lauded performance in *Raging Bull. The Elephant Man* didn't earn any Oscars, but had the film been released the following year it might have taken at least one award. The Best Make-Up category was introduced the next year and surely would have gone to Christopher Tucker for his design of Merrick's body makeup.

21. *Ragtime*: James Cagney and Pat O'Brien weren't exactly as glamorous as Fred and Ginger, but they were a popular Hollywood duo, making seven films together starting in the Golden Era of Hollywood. The first was *Here Comes the Navy* in 1934; the last was almost five decades later in 1981 for *Ragtime*, the hotly anticipated screen adaptation of E.L. Doctorow's bestselling novel of the same name. Helmed by Best Director winner (for *One Flew Over the Cuckoo's Nest*) Milos Forman and with a cast of Golden Globe and Academy Award recipients, the movie seemed to be the kind of picture that Oscar loves — epic literary adaptation, old-time stars with a social message. The Academy gave *Ragtime* eight nods, including Best Supporting Actor, Actress, and Music, but despite the film's pedigree and the Academy's predilection for sentiment — it was Cagney's first film in twenty years and was O'Brien's last big-screen appearance — *Ragtime* fell into the "it's an honour just to be nominated" category.

22. *The Color Purple*: Based on the Alice Walker novel about the struggle of an abused, uneducated black woman to gain control of her life in turn-of-the-century rural America, *The Color Purple* was one of the most talked about films of 1985, and when it came time to dole out awards, the movie scored nominations in eleven different categories, with one notable exception. Director Steven Spielberg's name was missing from the list of nominees for Best Director. "The Spielberg furor came to be seen as the Oscars' biggest scandal since Bette Davis was over-looked for *Of Human Bondage* in 1934," wrote Anthony Holden in the book *Behind the Oscar*. That slight was bad enough, but worse was yet to come. On awards night *The Color Purple* lost in every single category it was nominated in. Of the "other films to have achieved eleven nominations," says Holden, "only a film as weak as *The Turning Point* had previously been so utterly humiliated."

23. *Broadcast News*: After a wildly successful career in television — he created or co-created the sitcoms *Room 222*, *The Mary Tyler Moore Show*, and *Taxi* — James L. Brooks made his feature-film debut writing, producing, and directing *Terms of Endearment*, which won Academy Awards for Best Picture, Best Director, and Best Screenplay. So it looked like he was continuing his winning ways with the Academy when they nominated his second film, *Broadcast News*, a satire of television news rooms, for seven Oscars, including Best Actor, Best Actress, Best Supporting Actor, and Best Picture. Perhaps the voters felt Brooks had been too heavily rewarded his first time out, or maybe it was just the Academy's prejudice against comedies rearing its ugly head, but on Oscar night *Broadcast News* signed off with no awards.

24. ***The Godfather, Part III***: The first two-thirds of Francis Ford Coppola's *Godfather* trilogy is one of the rare exceptions to the rule of diminishing returns that says that you can only make so many sequels before they start to smell like day-old fish. The second one is arguably better than the first and actually won more Oscars than the original. Between them they earned twenty-two nominations with nine wins, including two Best Pictures, one Best Actor, one Best Director, and two writing awards. Then came the conclusion to the series, *The Godfather, Part III*. The Corleone family saga's coda has been called "the most reviled sequel in American cinema" and stands as proof that the law of diminishing returns is fact and not supposition. The Academy bestowed seven nominations on the movie, but in the end *The Godfather, Part III* got whacked by the Oscar voters who took no notice of the film.

25. ***The Prince of Tides***: Barbra Streisand has a long history with the Academy. In the early days of her association with them she was golden — they gave her early admission as a member and later she became the first person to win both a Best Actress and Best Original Song Oscar — but when she stepped behind the camera to direct, relations became a bit frosty. They chose to bypass her 1983 directorial debut, *Yentl*, which Steven Spielberg called the "best directorial debut since *Citizen Kane*." Ditto for her next two films, although 1991's *The Prince of Tides* managed seven nominations. The bittersweet story of a troubled man who falls in love with his suicidal sister's psychiatrist as he discusses their family history earned Best Actor, Actress, Screenplay, Art Direction, Cinematography, and Picture nominations, but despite good reviews and decent box-office returns the Academy's enthusiasm for the film ebbed when it came time to award the gold.

26. ***In the Name of the Father***: Based on Gerry Conlon's auto-biography, *Proved Innocent*, this film tells the tumultuous and wrenching tale of a man wrongfully imprisoned in 1974 for the bombing of a London pub. It marked the reunion of Irish director Jim Sheridan and British-born actor Daniel Day-Lewis, who worked together on *My Left Foot*, which earned Day-Lewis a Best Actor Oscar in 1989 for his portrayal of quadriplegic writer Christy Brown. *In the Name of the Father* was extremely popular in Ireland and earned good notices in America, which led to the Academy bestowing seven nominations — including Best Actor, Supporting Actor, Best Director, and Best Picture — but no awards on the film.

27. *The Remains of the Day*: Producer Ismail Merchant, who passed away in May 2005, director James Ivory, and writer Ruth Prawer Jbabvala joined forces in 1963 and eventually became the *Masterpiece Theatre* of the big screen. Modestly budgeted but lusciously realized literary adaptations have been their specialty, and Oscar has taken notice. Jhabvala has won multipletimes for Best Screenplay, Ivory has earned three Best Director nods, and Merchant has been nominated four times. Their period of greatest success with the Academy began with their 1992 adaptation of E.M. Forster's *Howard's End*, which was nominated for nine Oscars and earned three, including Best Actress for Emma Thompson. They followed up that success with *The Remains of the Day*, re-teaming *Howard's End* stars Anthony Hopkins and Emma Thompson. The adaptation of the marvellous 1988 novel by Kazuo Ishiguro, about an aging English butler looking back at his past as he drives across the country on a rare holiday, earned both actors Academy Award nominations; the film also garnered six other nods, including Best Director, Picture, and Writing. Perhaps the quiet story of unrequited love and loyalty was too subtle for the Academy, who didn't feel duty-bound to award the film any gold.

28. *The Shawshank Redemption*: Not since the 1942 *Citizen Kane* debacle has the Academy blown it so badly. The 1994 Oscars heaped honours on the mawkish *Forrest Gump* in lieu of two much more deserving films — *The Shawshank Redemption*, which earned seven nominations but no wins, and *Pulp Fiction*, which took only one lone prize for Best Screenplay. Director Frank Darabont's *The Shawshank Redemption* — based on the Stephen King novella *Rita Hayworth and Shawshank Redemption* — follows what happens to Andy Dufresne (Tim Robbins) after he's sent to prison for killing his wife and her lover. The film wasn't as big a hit as *Pulp Fiction* and did only modest business in theatres, which probably explains the Academy's indifference to the movie. In spite of poor box-office returns the film found an audience on home video and went on to become one of the highest grossing movie rentals of all time and continues to sell to this day. When asked if the longevity of *The Shawshank Redemption* takes away some of the sting of the Oscar snub, director Darabont says, "That longevity makes up for everything. Everything. Underline everything. It's a very interesting experience to put almost two years of your life into a movie, into something that you really believe in, really care about. And it's really not an easy process to make something and then release it to theatres and have nobody want to show up. That's a really interesting experience and a very disappointing one as you can imagine. To have it then go on to become what it's become for people is beyond validating, beyond redeeming for me."

29. **The Thin Red Line**: The production of director Terrence Malick's adaptation of James Jones's autobiographical 1962 novel, which focuses on the conflict at Guadalcanal during the Second World War, was fraught with tension between the reclusive filmmaker and two of the film's producers. Prior to the film's release, producers Robert Michael Geisler and John Roberdeau allegedly broke a confidentiality clause they had signed with the director and gave an interview to *Vanity Fair* about their long struggle to get the film made. The article reportedly made the enigmatic director apoplectic. To make peace the producing duo signed a second agreement stating they would not attend the Academy Awards that year, and if they did, as a penalty their names would be stripped from the film and video credits. When the movie was nominated for seven Oscars, Geisler and Roberdeau decided to attend the ceremony. Malick countered, saying if they were going to attend, he would stay home. In the end none of them attended the Oscars, which is just as well, as the film lost in every category.

30. **The Insider**: Director Michael Mann's thriller *The Insider* is based on the true story of former scientist Jeffrey Wigand (Russell Crowe), who exposed malpractices in the tobacco industry. Wigand had a considerable amount of input into the making of his life story — for example, he requested that no one be seen smoking onscreen and that the names of his daughters be changed, both of which the filmmakers agreed to — but the true-to-life insider almost found himself to be an outsider when it came to the Oscar ceremony. Despite all the accolades, and the seven Oscar nods — including Best Picture, Best Director, and Best Adapted Screenplay — the whistleblower was not offered a seat on awards night. Wigand called the Academy of Motion Picture Arts and Sciences about attending and was informed the Oscars "are not the Super Bowl" and that there were no passes to be had. *The San Francisco Chronicle* added to the story, reporting that Wigand wasn't invited because Russell Crowe, the actor who played him in the movie, didn't like him. By the time of the Oscarcast, however, Disney had come up with the tickets for Wigand and announced a plan to bring him onstage if the movie won. On the night of the ceremony Wigand remained seated for the entire evening, as *The Insider* failed to take any awards.

31. ***Gangs of New York*:** A disastrous ad campaign may have cost Martin Scorsese and his historical epic, *The Gangs of New York*, a win at the Oscars. Miramax, the studio behind the opus, turned a complimentary article by director Robert Wise (actually ghost-written by publicist Murray Weissman), originally published March 6, 2003, in the *Los Angeles Daily News*, into an ad that ran in the *Los Angeles Times*, *New York Times*, and several Hollywood trade papers. It began with, "Two-time Academy Award Winner Robert Wise declares Scorsese deserves the Oscar for *Gangs of New York*." (Wise actually has four Oscars — two for directing *West Side Story* and *The Sound of Music* respectively; and two for producing Best Picture winners.) Now that might not seem like such a big deal, but the Academy's rules dictate that members are not to divulge their Oscar picks. According to an article in the *Los Angeles Times*, Academy officials were angered by the ad, and some voters asked for their ballots back so they could cross out Scorsese's name. Academy president Frank Pierson said the ad ran six times, enough to cause "real dismay, anger and outrage" among his membership. "[The ad is] an out-right violation of Academy rules," he said. Miramax pulled the ad and said in a statement that they were "completely unaware" the plug would be "offensive" to voters or that it was a violation of rules, but the damage was already done. Out of ten nominations, *The Gangs of New York* didn't prevail in a single category.

32. ***Seabiscuit*:** *Seabiscuit* is the archetype of the kind of film the Academy likes to celebrate. The above-the-title cast are respected and award-winning actors; it is a quintessentially American underdog story, and, perhaps most importantly, it is a biopic. Academy voters seem to be particularly fond of true-life stories, awarding twenty-four — or 32 percent — of the seventy-four Best Pictures in the twentieth century to movies inspired by real events. The true story of an undersized Depression-era racehorse whose victories raised the spirit of the nation was nominated for seven awards, but *Seabiscuit* the film turned out to be as much of a long shot as the horse it was based on and didn't make it into the winner's circle.

Which famous "Frank" embarrassed himself at the Academy Awards ceremony of March 16, 1934?

Lady for a Day, director Frank Capra's comedy about a gambler who tries to transform Apple Annie, a Times Square apple seller, into a lady for a day, was nominated for four awards, including Best Director and Best Picture.

By his own admission Capra became obsessed with winning. "I kept telling myself that I could win four awards," he said. "No other picture had ever won four awards. I would set a record. Hot damn! I wrote and threw away dozens of acceptance speeches. I ordered my first tuxedo and rented a plush home in Beverly Hills — all to be 'seen' by the few hundred Oscar voters."

On awards night host Will Rogers prepared to give away the Best Director award. He tore open the envelope and said, "Well, well, well, what do you know. I've watched this young man for a long time. Saw him come up from the bottom, and I mean the bottom. It couldn't have happened to a nicer guy. Come up and get it, Frank!"

Capra's table exploded with applause, and as if he had just been awarded the 1934 Eager Beaver Award he began sprinting toward the stage. Unfortunately the winner's spotlight was focused elsewhere, on the real winner, Frank Lloyd, who was also making his way to the front of the auditorium.

"Hey, I'm over here," Capra yelled at the lighting operator before he realized the awful truth. He hadn't won. He stood paralyzed in the middle of the room until someone shouted, "Down in front." His face burning with shame Capra slunk back to his seat in what he described as "the longest, saddest, most shattering walk of my life."

Who threw "Come Over and Watch Me Lose Again" parties on Oscar night?

During the period 1951 to 1963 character actress Thelma Ritter was nominated for six Best Supporting Actress Academy Awards but failed to prevail, hence the self-deprecating party. She is one of the most nominated performers to never win an Oscar. She was nominated for *All about Eve* in 1951, *The Mating Season* in 1952, *With a Song in My Heart* in 1953, *Pickup on South Street* in 1954, *Pillow Talk* in 1960, and *Birdman of Alcatraz* in 1963.

It's an Honour Just to Be Nominated – Not!

Q Which 1981 movie was named Worst Picture of the Decade (1980s) by the Golden Raspberry Awards?

A Presented during the 10th Annual Razzie Awards at the Hollywood Roosevelt Hotel's Blossom Ballroom on March 25, 1990, the Golden Raspberry for Worst Picture of the Decade went to the Joan Crawford biopic *Mommie Dearest*. Based on the book by her adopted daughter Christina, the film is the now-legendary tale of Hollywood superstar Joan Crawford (Faye Dunaway) and the lengths she went to preserve her public image.

Mommie Dearest was the first film ever to "sweep" the Golden Raspberry Awards, winning five dis-honours from a then-record nine nominations. This is also the first movie in which one Oscar-winning actress — Faye Dunaway — has played another — Joan Crawford.

Mommie Dearest was reviled by critics, earning some of the nastiest reviews ever. One writer dubbed it "the most loathsome and sloppy screen treatments to ever have been derived from a literary memoir," while another, more charitable, reviewer thought it was "nightmarishly inept, inutterably depressing, but so campy it's compulsively watchable."

Other films nominated for Worst Picture of the Decade included *Bolero* (1984, Cannon Films), Bo Derek, producer; *Howard the Duck* (1986, Universal), Gloria Katz, producer; *The Lonely Lady* (1983, Universal), Robert R. Weston, producer; and *Star Trek V* (1989, Paramount), Harve Bennett, producer.

Q Who was Clint Eastwood referring to when he said: "He's too successful. He's too young; his genius is too great. They'll never give him the gold"?

A Despite industry rumours to the contrary, Clint Eastwood was right when he predicted in 1985 that the Academy wouldn't give Steven Spielberg an Oscar for *The Color Purple*. In fact, the movie was nominated in eleven major categories, all except Best Director. To put the snub into perspective you have to look back to the thirty-two other films that had won eleven or more Oscar nominations in the past. In every case the directors — all thirty-one of them — had been nominated.

In a double-edged campaign Warner Brothers ran an ad in the trade press expressing its "sincere appreciation" in receiving eleven nominations but added, "At the same time, the company is shocked and dismayed that the movie's primary creative force — Steven Spielberg — was not recognized."

When the film failed to garner even one Oscar, the *New York Post* called it "Omission Impossible."

Peter Bogdonovich commented, "Anyone who says that envy didn't affect Spielberg's chances would be crazy."

The day after the shut-out, Spielberg commented, "When I'm 60, Hollywood will forgive me. I don't know for what, but they'll forgive me."

Q With five awards, Rosalind Russell is the most winning actress at the Golden Globes. How many Oscars did she take home?

A Rosalind Russell never won an Oscar or New York Film Critics Circle kudo, but she's the biggest champ among actresses at the Golden Globes (five wins, including Best Actress for *Auntie Mame*), where she won every time she was nominated.

After her third Oscar loss for *Mourning Becomes Electra*, one writer suggested the title should be changed to *Mourning Becomes Rosalind Russell*.

When she was questioned about her winning acting technique, she said, "Acting is standing up naked and turning around very slowly."

Q My mother and father have each won Academy Awards. My aunt and husband have been nominated, and so has my grandfather. But I've never been nominated and neither has my sister. Who am I?

A Natasha Richardson, whose parents are Vanessa Redgrave and Tony Richardson. Her aunt is Lynn Redgrave, her husband is Liam Neeson, and her grandfather is Sir Michael Redgrave. Her sister is Joely Richardson.

It's an Honour Just to Be Nominated – Not!

Which singer-turned-actress did the Golden Raspberry Awards give the "Worst Actress of the 20th Century" honour to?

Madonna beat out Brooke Shields and Bo Derek to take home the Worst Actress of the 20th Century Golden Raspberry in a ceremony held in Los Angeles. Madonna's thespian skills were summed up by *Globe and Mail* writer Rick Groen: "What Madonna does here can't properly be called acting — more accurately, it's moving and it's talking and it's occasionally gesturing, sometimes all at once."

Sylvester Stallone was named Worst Actor of the 20th Century over contenders Kevin Costner, Prince, William Shatner, and Pauly Shore of *Bio-Dome* and *Encino Man* notoriety. Writing in the *Washington Post*, critic Desson Thomson seemed to agree with the Razzies when he wrote, "Stallone is so artificial, tanned and leathery you could replace his mouth with a zipper and sell him as a pocketbook."

BEST OSCAR

1 "The Oscars are absolutely the best institution in Hollywood."
— Norma Shearer, 1934

2 "The Oscar is a cruel joke hatched up by a cruel town and handed out in a cruel ceremony." — Marion Davies, 1943

3 "Oscar night is just another excuse to get drunk."
— Gary Busey, 1978

4 "It's so much fun being nominated — everyone is a winner. And then — afterwards — there are four losers."
— Liv Ullmann, 1972

5 "It was like having two hours of foreplay and no orgasm."
— *Fatal Attraction* director Adrian Lyne on the 1987 Oscar ceremony, where he lost to Bernardo Bertolucci

6 "Of course, it is always great to win an Academy Award. Everyone in the business wants one. If they say they don't, they're probably lying." — Ingrid Bergman, 1979

7 "When they sign you up for one of those so-called special awards, you know it's time to cash it in."
— Joan Crawford, 1957

8 "The Academy awards are obscene, dirty ... no better than a beauty contest." — Dustin Hoffman, 1975

QUOTES

9 "As long as they keep handing them out, I'll keep showing up to get them." — Shirley MacLaine, 1984

10 "After I won the Oscar my salary doubled, my friends tripled, my kids became more popular at school, the butcher made a pass at me, and my maid asked for a raise."
— Shirley Jones, 1977

11 "Nothing would disgust me more morally than receiving an Oscar. I wouldn't have it in my home." — Luis Buñuel, 1970

12 "The solemnity of the annual Nobel ceremonies in Stockholm with the cheerful bad taste of the grand opening of a shopping center in Los Angeles." — film critic Vincent Canby, 1983

13 "Watching it on television … I felt disgusted — as though I were attending a public hanging.… No one should have a chance to see so much desire, so much need for a prize, and so much pain when it was not given."
— Glenda Jackson, 1979

14 "It should be fun to go to — not agony. There's something barbaric about it." — Paul Newman, 1969

15 "Two hours of sparkling entertainment spread over four hours." — Johnny Carson, 1979

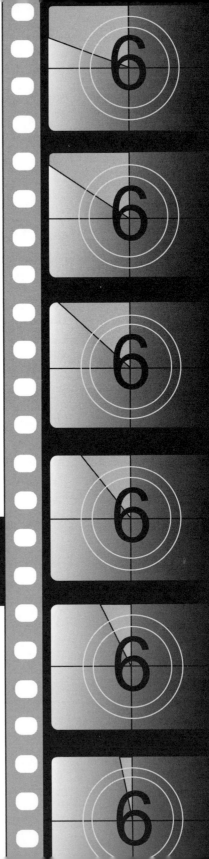

"Of all the noises, I think music is the least annoying."

— Presenter Jerome Kern, 1938

BEST SONG

Q Which R&B singer did Oscarcast producer Lili Zanuck fire during rehearsals for the big show in 2000?

A Multi-Grammy-Award-winning singer Whitney Houston's bizarre behaviour exasperated Burt Bacharach, the musical director of the 2000 Oscars. In one rehearsal, when Bacharach launched into "Over the Rainbow" on the piano, Houston began singing "The Way We Were." In his book *The Big Show: High Times and Dirty Dealings Backstage at the Academy Awards*, Steve Pond reports, "Houston's voice was shaky, she seemed distracted and jittery, and her attitude was casual, almost defiant."

Pond continues, "Finally, Bacharach [at the end of his rope] slumped over the piano, [putting] his head down on the keys." Producer Lili Zanuck called off Houston's appearance at the ceremony, explaining, "We didn't want to work for six months for this to be a show about how fucked-up Whitney Houston was."

"Certainly she was loaded," Oscar co-musical director Don Was told Pond, "but I wouldn't want to do urinalysis on a number of people involved in the show."

To counter the nasty rumours flying around Hollywood, Houston's publicist issued a statement claiming that the singer arrived in L.A. with a sore throat and that "after participating in rehearsals ... both Thursday and Friday nights, she was unsure that she would be better by Sunday. She therefore regretfully withdrew from the performance."

Q Who sang the opening number, "Fugue for Tinhorns" from the musical *Guys & Dolls*, at the 59th Annual Academy Awards?

A Neophyte Oscar producer Samuel Goldwyn Jr. wanted to open the show with an upbeat version of "Fugue for Tinhorns" from the musical *Guys & Dolls*. Frank Sinatra and Dean Martin declined his invitation to sing the song, as did Steve Martin and Rodney Dangerfield. Apparently everyone on the Hollywood A-list also turned him down, leaving Goldwyn to choose three actors not known for their singing voices — Telly Savalas, Pat Morita, and Dom DeLuise.

Q Who sang a duet of "Proud Mary" with Snow White in the disastrous opening musical number of the 61st Annual Academy Awards?

A Oscarcast producer Allan Carr wanted an opening number that television viewers would never forget. Instead he got a spectacle that he would probably like to forget.

The flamboyant showman conceived the number as a tribute to the 1940s Hollywood hotspot the Cocoanut Grove, complete with dancing waitresses in Carmen Miranda–style headdresses and ushers high-kicking like the Rockettes.

The twelve-minute tableaux featured Snow White and a tone-deaf Rob Lowe performing a ridiculous "Proud Mary" duet — "Used to work a lot for Disney/Starring in cartoons every night and day/But you said goodbye to Doc and Sleepy/Left the dwarf behind, came to town to stay" — that impelled Disney to sue because the producer had neglected to get permission to use a likeness of Ms. White; Merv Griffin singing "I've Got a Lovely Bunch of Coconuts" as Roy Rogers; *Variety* columnist Army Archerd interviewing Snow White; audience members Tom Hanks, Sigourney Weaver, and Michelle Pfeiffer enthusiastically shaking Ms. White's hand; and cameos from Vincent Price, Dorothy Lamour, and Lily Tomlin.

The crazy number soon became known as the strangest Oscar opening ever. One comic joked, "I was sitting right next to Meryl Streep. When she saw Snow White, she said, 'Give her an apple.'"

Later, Carr said that former president Ronald Reagan had called the broadcast "the best television show I've ever seen," but the Academy didn't agree. After Gregory Peck threatened to return his two Oscars if subsequent Oscar shows were going to look like Carr's and several other high-profile complaints were lodged, a special committee was assembled to determine just what went wrong and how to keep it from happening again.

The next year host Billy Crystal kicked off the show with a sly reference to the Snow White fiasco. "Is that for me," he asked as the audience cheered, "or are you just glad I'm not Snow White?"

Q Which Oscar-nominated song calls Canadian songbird Anne Murray "a bitch"?

A "Blame Canada," the irreverent anthem from the rude and crude animated musical *South Park: Bigger, Longer and Uncut* was an unlikely choice for Best Song — the lyrics called Canadian singer Anne Murray "a bitch" and were littered with prime-time unfriendly words like *fart* and *fuck*. The Academy warmed to the song once comic Robin Williams agreed to sing it on the Oscarcast.

"Once Robin was in, it changed everything," said the song's co-writer Marc Shaiman. "That's when you learn about the Academy Awards: all they're trying to do is get ratings. They're like selling fucking dish soap, and once Robin Williams was on, it was like 'Great, we're gonna sell more dish soap.'"

The Academy went ahead with the performance once censors gave the producers permission to save the word *fart*, Anne Murray sent word that she was okay with being labelled a bitch in front of hundreds of millions of people, and Williams promised not to say or mouth the word *fuck*.

Despite a rousing production number headed by Williams, "Blame Canada" lost out to Phil Collins's *Tarzan* ditty, "You'll Be in My Heart." *South Park* creators Trey Parker and Matt Stone — who were dressed in drag for the evening's festivities — made a hasty exit after their song failed to win. As one writer joked, "Who would want to stick around once you've lost to Phil Collins?"

As the dress-donning duo left the ceremony Stone told a reporter that his pink spaghetti-strap frock was "cold and uncomfortable." Earlier in the evening the pair's sartorial choices — based on dresses worn by Jennifer Lopez and Gwyneth Paltrow in previous years — earned stares and sneers from the red carpet crowd. Paltrow was not amused and shot the guys a dirty look, but Michael Caine made a point of telling them that they looked "awesome."

Q Why did Mexican actor Gael Garcia Bernal boycott the 2005 Oscar ceremony?

Gael Garcia Bernal was scheduled to introduce the performance of "Al Otro Lado del Rio," the theme from *The Motorcycle Diaries*, but backed out when it was announced that the song's composer, Jorge Drexler, would not be allowed to sing the song during the broadcast. "At the time his song is being honored, all a sudden, that's the moment he does not exist?" he said. "It was impossible for me to be there as part of the film. I didn't want to pretend the song was not part of it; that would have been like an act of murder in the family. And secondly, the film and the song are about respecting people's identity."

Courtesy of AMPAS

Jorge Drexler at the 77th Annual Academy Awards. His song "Al otro lado del Rio" from *The Motorcycle Diaries* is the first Spanish Best Song winner.

The controversial Antonio Banderas and Carlos Santana performance of the nominated song "Al otro lado del Rio" from *The Motorcycle Diaries* at the 77ᵗʰ Annual Academy Awards.

In a controversial move, Oscarcast producer Gil Cates decided against using Uruguayan singer/songwriter Drexler because he was not well known enough. Instead Cates hired audience-friendly Spanish actor Antonio Banderas and Mexican-born rock guitarist Carlos Santana to interpret the tune.

The Motorcycle Diaries' Brazilian director, Walter Salles, immediately voiced his displeasure, issuing a statement calling Drexler's exclusion "unethical," "disrespectful to the author," and "ignorant of the cultural diversity that exists in Latin America." He went on to describe the choice of Banderas as "not only ethically, but aesthetically unacceptable."

Clarín, an Argentine daily, reported that some of the singers suggested by producers filled the composer with "literal dread because they have no connection to what I do. I proposed Caetano Veloso; they offered me Enrique Iglesias."

The *Los Angeles Times* mocked the awkward Oscar performance, writing, "Santana and Banderas, Mexican and Spanish by birth, struggled to perform a song whose roots lie in the slow, pulsating rhythms of folk music from southern South America. Imagine a Scotsman trying to wrap his brogue around hip-hop from Brooklyn or South Los Angeles."

Ironically, Drexler and his composition won an Oscar that night, beating out Andrew Lloyd Webber and Counting Crows to become the first Spanish song to receive an Oscar for Best Original Song. When Drexler took the stage to accept his award — he had been seen cringing earlier during the performance of his song — his speech was simply a brief a cappella version of the first few bars of his own song, delivered in a clear, beautiful tenor that allowed the song to be heard the way it was written and allowing its tantalizing melody to shine.

Q Which tune from the *Saturday Night Fever* soundtrack was nominated for Best Song?

A Trick question. Nothing from the *Saturday Night Fever* soundtrack — one of the bestselling albums in history — was nominated at the 50th Annual Academy Awards. Instead the nominees consisted of the James Bond theme, "Nobody Does It Better"; Debbie Boone's schmaltzy "You Light Up My Life"; and three songs from kids' movies — "Candle on the Water," "The Slipper and the Rose Waltz," and "Someone's Waiting for You."

The following year, the Academy acknowledged some of the glaring oversights from previous years in the Best Song category by including a medley — titled "Oscar's Only Human" — of notable songs that had failed to earn a nomination.

BEST SONGS:
TUNES ABOUT AWARD-WINNING ACTORS

1. Elizabeth Taylor is name-checked in the song "Lady Nina" by rock band Marillion.

2. British ska band Madness scored a top-ten song in Britain in the mid-eighties called "Michael Caine." The band had his "My name is Michael Caine" quote sampled into the song.

3. Hip hop supergroup Gorillaz called their biggest hit "Clint Eastwood" after the Oscar-winning tough guy.

4. Marlon Brando has had many songs written about him, including "Stuck in a Condo with Marlon Brando" by The Dickies, and is mentioned in Neil Young's song "Pocahontas," in David Bowie's song "China Girl," and in Bruce Springsteen's song "It's Hard to Be a Saint in the City."

5. Jive-talking, piano-pounding hepcat Harry the Hipster wrote "Get Hip to Shirley MacLaine" for the Oscar-winning actress, but he's not the only one to pay tribute to her. Post-punkers Helmet sang about MacLaine's "bestselling advice" on the album "Born Annoying."

6. Canadian singer/songwriter Chantal Kreviazuk wrote her song "Julia" about Julia Roberts after seeing the Oscar winner at a Los Angeles restaurant.

7. Gary Cooper is mentioned in the Irving Berlin song "Puttin' on the Ritz."

8. Kim Carnes had a number one hit with "Bette Davis Eyes" in 1981.

9. John Wayne is referenced in the Paula Cole song "Where Have All the Cowboys Gone?" and is the subject of the tune "John Wayne Is Big Leggy" from quirky eighties pop group Haysi Fantayzee.

10. Heavy metal band Blue Oyster Cult featured "Joan Crawford," a tune about the actress rising from the grave, on their *Fire of Unknown Origin* album.

11. British punk band Toy Dolls sang about the Oscar winner from *The King & I* in "Yul Brynner Was a Skinhead": "he's just a baldy geezer from *The King & I*."

Courtesy of AMPAS

Yul Brynner in his most famous role as King Mongkut of Siam in 1956's *The King and I*.

12. "Nicole Kidman Shades," a tune by New York no-wave band Dynamite Club is described by one Internet writer as "heard best with an extremely dry martini with two pickles, a Cuban cigar, and a smut queen giving you an astonishing toe sucking."

13. "Gene Hackman," a tune by Australia's Hoodoo Gurus, is not just a tribute to the multiple Oscar winner, but also to the Ramones.

14. British troubadour Billy Bragg and American roots-rockers Wilco took some of Woody Guthrie's unpublished lyrics and set them to music on the album *Mermaid Avenue*. Among the songs is a sweet tune called "Ingrid Bergman."

15. British eighties pop group Bananarama — Siobhan Fahey, Sarah Dallen, and Karen Woodward — had a big hit with a song dedicated to De Niro, called "Robert De Niro's Waiting."

BONUS:

Oscar winner Russell Crowe doesn't have any songs written about him as far as we know, but he has written and recorded a couple of tunes about actors he admires. Crowe wrote a song about his friend Jodie Foster called "Other Ways of Speaking," which he performs with his band, 30 Odd Foot of Grunts. At the age of sixteen, under the name Russ Le Roq, Crowe recorded a single called "I Just Want to Be Like Marlon Brando." "I released a few records that went rocketing straight to the bottom of the charts," said Crowe about his Le Roq alter ego.

Courtesy The Hollywood Collection

Crowe's rock group, 30 Odd Foot of Grunts, played their first concert in America following the success of *Gladiator* in Austin, Texas, in August 2000. The tickets for the concert sold for as much as $500 on eBay.

Who accepted his Oscar with the words, "I was going to thank all the little people, but then I remembered I am the little people"?

Known for timeless classics such as "We've Only Just Begun," "Rainy Days and Mondays," "Just an Old Fashioned Love Song," and "Rainbow Connection," the five-foot-two songwriter Paul Williams shared an

Academy Award with Barbra Streisand for Best Song at the March 29, 1977, ceremony for "Evergreen," the love theme from *A Star is Born*. Streisand gushed, "In my wildest dreams I never thought I'd win an Oscar for writing a song," while the diminutive Williams added, "I was going to thank all the little people, but then I remembered I am the little people."

Robert Altman's *Nashville* was nominated for a then record ten Golden Globes. How many did it win?

On January 24, 1976, *Nashville* — an ensemble piece telling the intersecting stories of various people connected to the music business in Music City, U.S.A. — set a record, earning the most Golden Globe nominations for a film. Up for ten awards — Best Picture (Drama), Best Director for Robert Altman, Best Supporting Actor for Henry Gibson, three Best Supporting Actress nods (Geraldine Chaplin, Barbara Harris, and Lili Tomlin), two Best Female Acting Debut nominations (Ronee Blakley and Lili Tomlin), Best Screenplay for Joan Tewkesbury, and Best Song — it prevailed in only one category. Keith Carradine won Best Song for "I'm Easy."

How did sugary-sweet singer Debbie Boone cause a stir at the April 1978 Oscars?

During the 1978 Oscars Debbie Boone, daughter of born-again crooner Pat Boone, brought down the house by performing a rendition of her hit "You Light Up My Life," surrounded by ten-year-old girls who interpreted the song in sign language. By the end of the song there was not a dry eye in the house, and when host Bob Hope announced that the girls were from the John Tracy Clinic, named for the deaf son of Spencer Tracy, it seemed like the perfect show business moment. Trouble was, the sign language was ham-fisted and made no sense. When thousands of complaints poured in the Academy had to admit that the girls weren't deaf and had actually been enlisted from a nearby public school.

The president of the Alliance for Deaf Artists was outraged. "We're offended because we have many, many deaf children who could have done the same thing if only they'd been given the opportunity," he said. "What happened on the Oscar show was really the last straw in that it represented the industry's traditional misrepresentation of the deaf."

"After all," said an Academy spin doctor, "nobody actually said the children were really deaf. And a doctor from the Tracy Clinic did recruit them."

Q Who sang Barbra Streisand's Oscar-nominated song "I Finally Found Somebody" at the 1997 Academy Awards?

A Oscar producers had planned to have Natalie Cole sing "I Finally Found Somebody" from the Barbra Streisand movie *The Mirror Has Two Faces* after Babs refused to perform the tune, furious that she had not been nominated in the bigger marquee categories of Best Director and Best Picture. The day before the broadcast Cole called in sick, unable to perform. Less than twenty-four hours before show time Celine Dion — who was already set to perform "Because You Loved Me" from the film *Up Close and Personal* — was asked to sub for the ailing Cole.

With little rehearsal Dion sang the song while Streisand watched from the wings. Days after the ceremony a bouquet of flowers accompanied by a note arrived at Dion's home. "You sang my song beautifully," the note read. "Next time let us make one together … you are a wonderful singer." It was signed Barbra Streisand.

Q Which rap superstar was not present at the March 23, 2003, Oscarcast to accept his award for Best Music (Original Song)?

A Rapper-turned-actor Eminem slept through his Oscar win on March 23, 2003. The *8 Mile* star was competing in the Best Original Song category with the tune "Lose Yourself" next to pop legends U2 and Paul Simon and music from the films *Chicago* and *Frida*. His record label, Interscope Records, said the controversial star was taking a break from showbiz and would stay away from the ceremony at Hollywood's Kodak Theatre, but "Lose Yourself" co-writer Luis Resto — who accepted the

Oscar from presenter Barbra Streisand — told a different story. When Resto called the rapper to congratulate him he found him fast asleep at his home in Detroit. "He was asleep," Resto said. "It wasn't out of any disrespect. We just didn't expect to win."

Which pop singer allegedly flew into a rage during rehearsals for the 1991 Oscarcast?

According to writer Steve Pond's book *The Big Show: High Times and Dirty Dealings Backstage at the Academy Awards*, Madonna went ballistic when two stagehands at the 1991 Oscars made mistakes that inconvenienced her.

Pond says a female camera operator was badly hurt after tumbling off the stage and into the orchestra pit while Madonna was preparing to rehearse the Stephen Sondheim–penned *Dick Tracy* tune "Sooner Or Later (I Always Get My Man)." Instead of showing concern, the singer became incensed when she was told that her performance would be delayed by the accident. "But she's just lying there," she supposedly fumed. "Can't we just do this?"

Later, the situation went from bad to worse when a technician fell asleep and wrecked a planned stunt in which the singer's microphone would appear out of thin air. "[Madonna launched] into an astonishingly profane tirade, despite the fact that the area below the stage was also occupied by a group of children," Pond reports. "Furious, she grabbed [the bearer of the bad news] around the neck and lifted him bodily off the ground, not relinquishing her grip until the trapdoor opened and she began to rise."

In 2002 which composer broke the all-time record for most Oscar nominations without any wins?

At the 2002 Academy Awards, Randy Newman took home an Oscar for his song "If I Didn't Have You" from the *Monsters, Inc.* soundtrack. It was Newman's first Oscar after sixteen nominations.

Best Song

"Thank you," Newman said at the podium. "I don't want your pity. I want to thank first of all the music branch for giving me so many chances to be humiliated over the years. I have nothing [to say]. I'm absolutely astounded that I've won for this, though the picture deserves recognition. ... Walking out here and having someone this beautiful [presenter Jennifer Lopez] give me an award, I'll never get to heaven but that's as close as you get I think. Thanks very much. I'm thrilled."

That year acceptance speeches were limited to forty-five seconds in an attempt to shave off some time from the show's usual four-hour running time. When the orchestra began to play during Newman's speech — a signal that his time was up — he looked down into the pit and saw many musicians he had hired over the years to play on his film scores. "Don't play," he said, and they didn't.

Which Charlie Chaplin film won an Oscar in 1973 despite being twenty years old?

Limelight, Chaplin's 1952 film about a fading comedian and a suicidal ballet dancer became eligible for the 1973 Academy Awards because the film was not released in Los Angeles — it had been banned in the United States because of Chaplin's alleged communist sympathies — until 1972. Under Academy rules at the time, this allowed it to be nominated even though it was two decades old.

The Academy Award Chaplin won for composing this film's score (shared with Ray Rasch and Larry Russell) is the only competitive Oscar the comic ever received; his other awards were given to him for special achievement outside of the established categories.

Charlie Chaplin statue on Hollywood Boulevard in Los Angeles.

"There are two types of people [who win awards]. One type asserts that awards mean nothing to them. The second type breaks into tears upon receiving an award, and thanks their mother, father, children, the producer, the director, and — if they can crowd it in — the American Baseball League."

— Dore Schary, 1956

"I'D LIKE TO THANK THE ACADEMY..."

Best Actor Trivia

"I'd like to Thank the Academy..."

Q Who was the first person to win a Best Actor Academy Award?

A With the words, "Hand me now already the statuette award," German silent movie actor Emil Jannings became the Academy's first Best Actor awardee — in those days actors received one Oscar for multiple films, and Jannings won for *The Way of All Flesh* and *The Last Command*. The burly actor accepted the award in advance of the ceremony — making him the first winner to be absent on presentation night.

His thick accent and propensity for malapropisms made the Academy's first Best Actor unemployable in Hollywood talkies, and by 1930 he had returned to Germany. Several notable film roles followed, including that of the self-important college professor smitten with Marlene Dietrich in Josef von Sternberg's *The Blue Angel*.

Unfortunately Jannings fell under the spell of Hitler in 1933, accepting an offer from propaganda minister Goebbels to appear in pro-German, anti-Semitic movies. He appeared in a number of these films throughout the 1930s and early 1940s and was named "Artist of the State" by Goebbels in 1941. After the war Jannings was shunned by the international film community and died of cancer in 1950.

Q Which 2003 Golden Globe winner for Best Actor in a Drama said, "I thought we made a comedy"?

A The frontrunners for the 60th Annual Golden Globe Best Actor in a Drama award were Jack Nicholson for the title performance in *About Schmidt* and Daniel Day-Lewis for his work as Bill the Butcher in *The Gangs of New York*. In the end it was Nicholson who took home the award.

"Well, I don't know whether to be happy or ashamed, because I thought we made a comedy," said Nicholson in his rambling acceptance speech.

"We had a wonderful cast ... we had the 'Bates Motel,' Kathy ... June Squibb, who played my wife ... Dermot Mulroney, whose haircut alone should have let you know it was a comedy, I thought. I know the evening's getting short, but I took a Valium tonight, so ... thank you all very much for this."

Q Which Puerto Rican–born actor won both an Oscar and a Tony for his portrayal of Cyrano de Bergerac?

A In addition to being heartthrob George Clooney's uncle, José Ferrer achieved renown as Cyrano de Bergerac, playing the role many times in different mediums and languages. He was first seen as Rostand's famous long-nosed hero on stage in 1946, then on film in 1950 (winning the Oscar for his performance), and on TV in 1949 and 1955. In 1963 he played Cyrano again in the French movie *Cyrano et D'Artagnan*. He reprised the role for a final time in the 1974 animated ABC Afterschool Special, *Cyrano*.

Ferrer won the Tony for *Cyrano de Bergerac* in 1947 and is one of only a handful of actors to win both awards for the same role in a play and a movie. The other multiple winners are Rex Harrison as Professor Higgins in *My Fair Lady*, Joel Grey as Master of Ceremonies in *Cabaret*, Shirley Booth in *Come Back, Little Sheba*, the chrome-domed Yul Brynner in *The King and I*, Anne Bancroft as Anne Sullivan in *The Miracle Worker*, Paul Scofield as Sir Thomas More in *A Man For All Seasons*, and Jack Albertson in the post-war drama *The Subject Was Roses*.

Q Whom did Marlon Brando send to speak on his behalf at the 45th Annual Academy Awards ceremony?

A On March 27, 1973, Marlon Brando sent "Indian Princess" Sacheen Littlefeather to the Oscar ceremony to refuse the Best Actor statue for his portrayal of Vito Corleone in *The Godfather*. Ms. Littlefeather announced the reason for the refusal and delivered a prepared speech on Native rights.

"Marlon Brando ... has asked me to tell you, in a very long speech which I cannot share with you presently — because of time — but I will be glad to share with the press afterward, that he must ... very regretfully cannot accept this very generous award. And the reason for this being ... are the treatment of American Indians today by the film industry ... excuse me ... and on television in movie re-runs, and also the recent happenings at Wounded Knee. I beg at this time that I have not intruded upon this evening and that we will, in the future ... our hearts and our understanding will meet with love and generosity. Thank you on behalf of Marlon Brando."

It was later uncovered that Ms. Littlefeather wasn't Native-American. Gossip columnist Rona Barrett wrote in her widely read column that Littlefeather was actually a professional actress named Maria Cruz, who had once been picked as Miss American Vampire of 1970, and as such had made promotional appearances for the MGM film *House of Dark Shadows*.

Presenting the next award after the Brando snub, presenter Clint Eastwood joked before he opened the envelope to reveal the Best Picture winner, "I don't know if I should present this award on behalf of all the cowboys shot in John Ford westerns over the years."

The Oscar was never collected by Brando and is still in the Academy's possession.

Who accepted 2003 MTV Movie Awards for Best Actor and Best Breakthrough Actor with the words, "I can't believe I beat Mariah for *Glitter*."

Rapper Eminem won the 2003 MTV Movie Awards for Best Actor and Best Breakthrough Actor for his role as Jimmy "B-Rabbit" Smith Jr. in the film *8 Mile*. In a pre-taped speech he thanked his fans and took a jab at Mariah Carey's film *Glitter*, which had been released to some of the worst reviews of the year. Opinions of the critics ran the gamut from calling *Glitter* "hilariously inept" to "disappointing and dull."

Who is the only first-time nominee to win a Best Actor Oscar when up against four previous Oscar winners?

On March 23, 2003, *The Pianist*'s Adrien Brody found himself up against Oscar veterans Nicolas Cage for his dual role of the bickering Kaufman twins in *Adaptation*, Michael Caine for *The Quiet American*, Daniel Day-Lewis for his performance as Bill the Butcher in *Gangs of New York*, and Jack Nicholson for *About Schmidt*.

Courtesy of AMPAS

Adrien Brody, Oscar's Best Actor for *The Pianist*, said, "It's interesting, winning an Academy Award as a young man — life-changing, but I'm just me within that. It's been very helpful for my career, but I'm trying to stay on the path I was on before."

Brody, who at twenty-nine was the youngest Best Actor Oscar winner to date, accepted the trophy with exuberance. After giving presenter Halle Berry a long, passionate kiss he said, "There comes a time in life when everything seems to make sense — and this is not one of those times."

Q Who claimed to be the illegitimate child of John Ashcroft, who was soon to be appointed Attorney General, at the January 21, 2001, Golden Globes?

A George Clooney picked up the Best Performance by an Actor in a Motion Picture, Comedy or Musical Golden Globe for the Coen brothers' quirky take on Homer's *Odyssey, O Brother, Where Art Thou?*

"I think when you list the names of the people in my category … you gotta figure I'm gonna win this," said Clooney in his amusing acceptance speech. "Carrey, Cusack, De Niro … What have they done?"

Clooney continues with a mock confession about the Coen brothers. "They're not really brothers, that's a lie," he said. "I'm actually the illegitimate child of [attorney general nominee] John Ashcroft."

Later in the show a newly sober Robert Downey Jr. won Best Performance by an Actor in a Supporting Role in a Series, Mini-Series or Motion Picture Made for TV. "It's really nice not to be under a table tonight," Downey joked, "and congrats to George Clooney, even though he didn't have me as a technical adviser for the convict part [in *O Brother, Where Art Thou?*]."

Q Who was the first native Californian to win an Academy Award for Best Actor?

A La Jolla, California–born Gregory Peck was the first native Californian to win an Academy Award for Best Actor when he picked up a statue for his performance in *To Kill a Mockingbird*.

In May 2003 Peck's character from *To Kill a Mockingbird*, Atticus Finch, a lawyer in the Depression-era South who defends a black man against an undeserved rape charge and teaches his kids to fight prejudice, was voted the greatest screen hero of all time by the American Film Institute. The filmic Finch beat out Indiana Jones, who placed second, and James Bond, who placed third, to take the list's top spot.

Peck's powerful performance in *To Kill a Mockingbird* is so memorable it is hard to imagine anyone else in the role, but he wasn't the first choice. The studio originally wanted to cast Rock Hudson.

Q Which Oscar winner from Austria-Hungary was nominated for both his first and last screen performances?

A Born Meshilem Meier Weisenfreund in Lwow, Galicja, Austria-Hungary (now Lviv, Ukraine), actor Paul Muni and his family immigrated to the United States in 1902. At age twelve Muni made an auspicious stage debut at New York's Yiddish Art Theatre, playing an eighty-year-old man. By 1926 he was performing English-language roles on Broadway, and he signed with 20th Century Fox in Hollywood three years later. In 1929 the Academy recognized his work in his first film, *The Valiant*, playing a man condemned to execution who tries to convince two women that he is not their son and brother and that they must get on with their lives.

Unhappy with the film roles he was being offered, he retreated to Broadway for several years, returning to Hollywood in 1932. His performance as a wrongly accused escapee in *I Am a Fugitive from a Chain Gang* earned him a second Best Actor nomination. By the end of the 1930s he was feted by the Academy two more times — a Best Actor nomination for *The Life of Emile Zola* and a win for *The Story of Louis Pasteur*.

He flip-flopped between the stage and screen until 1959, when he made his last movie, *The Last Angry Man*. He retired from acting shortly after receiving his final Academy Award nomination for his final film.

Who is the only Best Actor Oscar winner to keep his mouth shut and say nothing on stage while accepting his award?

At the March 6, 1946, Oscar ceremony Ray Milland accepted his Best Actor statue for his performance as an alcoholic writer in *The Lost Weekend* wordlessly. Instead he casually bowed his head in appreciation and exited the stage. It has been speculated that he was too overwhelmed to speak, that he didn't expect to win the Oscar, but that doesn't seem likely, as he had swept all three major Best Actor awards — the National Board of Review, New York Film Critics Circle, Golden Globes — and the Oscar was the icing on the cake. Perhaps he was just a man of few words.

Seven years later William Holden almost matched Milland's brevity. When he won the Best Actor Oscar for his role in *Stalag 17* he accepted his statue with a simple "Thank you" and walked off.

Whose 1993 Best Actor acceptance speech was the inspiration for the comedy *In & Out*?

In *Philadelphia* Tom Hanks played a young lawyer with AIDS who must confront not only homophobia but also his own mortality. His teary Best Actor acceptance speech for the film was called "one of the most dramatic acceptance speeches of any Oscar year" by the *Hollywood Reporter*.

Andrew Beckett, the heroic character dying of AIDS played by Tom Hanks in an Oscar-winning performance in *Philadelphia*, was ranked the #49 hero on the American Film Institute's 100 Years ... 100 Heroes and Villains list.

In his speech he thanked and outed his former high school drama teacher, Rawley Fransworth, who, he said, "taught me 'to act well the part, there all the glory lies,'" and former classmate John Gilkerson, "two of the finest gay Americans, two wonderful men that I had the good fortune to be associated with." Contrary to published reports, Hanks did not surprise his former teacher by outing him on national television. The actor called the retired sixty-nine-year-old teacher days before the show and asked permission to include him in the speech.

When producer Scott Rudin heard the speech, he had an immediate idea for comedy. What if the teacher either wasn't gay or wasn't known to be gay?

The resulting comedy, *In & Out* by writer Paul Rudnick, stars Kevin Kline as a drama teacher outed by a former student (Matt Dillon) during an Oscar speech. He claims not to be homosexual, but Tom Selleck as an openly gay reporter tries to get to the bottom of the story.

The statuette used in Matt Dillon's Oscar scene is real. Kevin Kline loaned the production the one he won in 1988 for Best Supporting Actor in *A Fish Called Wanda*.

Q Which Best Actor Oscar winner was the first centre square on the game show *Hollywood Squares*?

A Paul Lynde had a recurring role on the hit show *Bewitched* but was best loved by television audiences as the wisecracking centre square throughout most of the original *Hollywood Squares* run. He was not, however, the first person to take that position. Oscar-winner Ernest Borgnine held that coveted spot during the show's premiere week in October 1966. (The centre square in the pilot was Jim Backus, who at the time was appearing as Thurston Howell III in *Gilligan's Island*, but that show never aired in its entirety.)

In 1970, after two years on the show, Lynde became the regular centre square. His droll delivery of punchlines to host Peter Marshall's set-ups made him a star. For instance, when Marshall asked, "Paul, can you get an elephant drunk?" Lynde replied with a wink, "Yes, but he still won't go up to your apartment." Some of his answers were more risqué. When Marshall asked, "Paul, Snow White, was she a blonde or a brunette?" the comic shot back, "Only Walt Disney knows for sure."

Lynde was the only panellist on the show to win two daytime Emmy Awards — in 1975 and 1979.

Q Who is the only actor to win an Oscar for a role he had originally played on television?

A Maximilian Schell's Best Actor Academy Award for *Judgment at Nuremberg* made him the first actor to win an Oscar for a role he originally performed on television. Schell played the role of lead defence attorney Hans Rolfe in a 1959 episode of *Playhouse 90* before reprising the role for the film.

Schell's Oscar also made him the lowest billed lead category winner in history — he is billed fifth, after Spencer Tracy, Burt Lancaster, Richard Widmark, and Marlene Dietrich.

Q Who called winning the Best Actor Oscar the "highlight of my day"?

"I'd like to Thank the Academy..."

In 1999, Kevin Spacey won a Best Actor Oscar for his performance as Lester Burnham, a middle-aged corporate cog on the brink of psychological meltdown, in Sam Mendes's *American Beauty*.

"This," he said in typically understated fashion, "has definitely been the highlight of my day. I hope it's not all downhill from here."

Several years later in an interview with *Total Film* Spacey wasn't so flip when asked whether his Oscars mean a lot to him. "How could they not?" he said. "How can you even frame a question like that? I'm asked that question so often. I'm like, 'What do people want me to say?' 'Oh, it means nothing.' It means a huge amount. It's a remarkable achievement. All you have to do is look at the actors who've won that little golden statue over the years. It's unbelievable to be thought of in the same company as them."

Who was the first performer to win Best Actor Oscar for a foreign-language role?

Roberto Benigni's performance as Guido Orefice in *La Vita è bella* (*Life Is Beautiful*) was almost as memorable as his antics at the 71st Annual Academy Awards.

After accepting the award for Best Foreign-Language Film — just one of seven nods the movie earned — Benigni was once again called to the stage to collect the first Best Actor Oscar ever awarded for a non-English-speaking role.

"Thank you," he said, taking the stage after leaping over several rows of seats. "This is a terrible mistake, because I used up all my English! ... I would like to be Jupiter and kidnap everybody and lie down in the ground making love to everybody — because I don't know how to express — it's a question of love. You are really ... this is a mountain of snow, so delicate, the suavity and the kindness, it is something I cannot forget!"

He continued backstage. "I'm so happy," he said, "that every organ in my body is moving in a very bad way!"

Peter Gabriel and Randy Newman were scheduled to perform after Benigni's speech. While they stood off to the side of the stage watching the Italian actor's crazy display Newman said, "It'll be like following an animal act."

Q Which 1992 Golden Globe Best Actor is a convicted felon and cannot vote in U.S. elections?

A In 1962 Nick Nolte, who thirty years later would win a Golden Globe for Best Actor in a Drama for *Prince of Tides* — was given five years' probation for selling fake draft cards. As a convicted felon, Nolte cannot vote in the U.S.A.

"I was pretty active politically in the sixties, sold some draft cards," says Nolte. "They nailed me for counterfeit government documents. They gave me a 45-year sentence and a $75,000 fine [all] suspended. I was a felon. So I got into acting."

Q Which February 2005 Oscar loser told the press that he had rehearsed losing the Best Actor trophy to Jamie Foxx?

Courtesy of AMPAS

Leonardo DiCaprio lost Best Actor to *Ray*'s Jamie Foxx at the 77th Annual Academy Awards. "I wasn't surprised that Jamie got the award," he said. "But I knew that cameras would be stuffed up my face so I had my response ready. Anyone who says they don't practice is a liar."

"I'd like to Thank the Academy..."

A *The Aviator* star Leonardo DiCaprio told reporters that he spent hours practising his losing smile for the February 2005 Oscars — because he knew Jamie Foxx was going to take the prize.

It was worth the effort, he said, because the cameras stayed focused on him as Foxx collected the trophy for his work in *Ray*. "I wasn't surprised that Jamie got the award," he said. "But I knew that cameras would be stuffed up my face so I had my response ready. Anyone who says they don't practice is a liar."

DiCaprio's girlfriend, Brazilian supermodel Gisele Bundchen, wasn't quite as gracious. "I was really there to support [DiCaprio]. He's not just my boyfriend but he's an amazing actor. He's really talented and I was so proud of him. I figured I should go and support my man so I went there just for that reason. I don't think he was expecting to win. I think I was more upset because I thought he deserved it more than [Foxx]. I was like, 'He did a better job than [Foxx]!'"

Q Who called himself "the Tom Hanks of the Golden Globes" in 1999?

A Jim Carrey proclaimed himself "the Tom Hanks of the Golden Globes" as he accepted the 1999 Best Actor, Comedy or Musical Golden Globe for his performance as eccentric comic Andy Kaufman in *Man on the Moon*. It was his second Best Actor statues in two years, echoing Hanks's back-to-back triumphs at the Oscars in 1994 and 1995.

"What's going on here?" he said. "I'm the establishment I once rejected!"

Q What did the original inscription on Spencer Tracy's Oscar for *Captains Courageous* read?

A At the March 10, 1938, Academy Awards ceremony Spencer Tracy won the Best Actor statue for playing Manuel Fidello in *Captains Courageous*. Tracy wasn't at the ceremony — he heard the news from a bed in the Good Samaritan Hospital and became so annoyed by the dozens of congratulatory phone calls that poured in that he had his phone disconnected — and didn't see the statue, which was mistakenly engraved "Dick Tracy." The error was caught and corrected before Tracy was given the Oscar.

Later Bob Hope joked that the much-nominated Tracy "needs another Oscar like Zsa Zsa Gabor needs Ann Lander's lovelorn advice."

In 1955 *Captains Courageous* became the first MGM film to be shown on television.

Who accepted a 2003 MTV Movie Award for Best Virtual Performance with the heavily bleeped words, "Frankly, nothing can compensate for the lousy low pay and miserable experience we've had making this fucking movie and if you think a shitty little tub of gold popcorn is going to remotely make up for everything WE'VE suffered YOU'RE SADLY FUCKING MISTAKEN! YOU'RE ALL BASTARDS! MTV SUCKS! WE HATE YOU ALL!"?

Schizophrenic villain Gollum from *Lord of the Rings: The Two Towers* won the first ever MTV Movie Award for Best Virtual Performance in 2003. The category was introduced because of the increase of special-effects performers. Other nominees that inaugural year included Scooby-Doo, Yoda from *Star Wars Episode II: Attack of the Clones*, Kangaroo Jack, and Dobby from *Harry Potter and the Chamber of Secrets*.

Actor Andy Serkis — whose voice and movements brought the animated character to life — began a pre-taped thank you, before Gollum appeared and grabbed the "precious" trophy from the actor's hands.

"You're a liar," said Gollum, "and a thief! It's mine. I won. It was me. We only won because of me!"

Which 1959 Best Actor Oscar winner said, "I felt as out of place among the other nominees as Zsa Zsa Gabor at a PTA meeting"?

"Loved him, hated Hur" is the apocryphal quote most often associated with the sword-and-sandal epic *Ben-Hur*, which won eleven Oscars, including Best Actor for its star Charlton Heston. Heston was competing against Laurence Harvey for *Room at the Top*, Jack Lemmon for *Some*

Like it Hot, Paul Muni for *The Last Angry Man*, and James Stewart for *Anatomy of a Murder*.

Heston's woodenly macho performance as the Jewish prince who is betrayed by a former friend and condemned to the Roman galleys earned him praise and his only Oscar, but he almost didn't get the role. The part of Judah Ben-Hur was first offered to Rock Hudson, who passed; Burt Lancaster turned down the role because he "didn't like the violent morals in the story," and Paul Newman said he rejected it because he didn't have the legs to wear a tunic.

Heston played so many larger-than-life characters — including Michelangelo, Ben-Hur, and Moses — that he once joked, "If you need a ceiling painted, a chariot race run, a city besieged, or the Red Sea parted, you think of me."

Which BAFTA Award–winning Best Actor once worked as a piece of living art in a Soho nightclub in New York City?

Years before Robert Downey Jr. won a BAFTA Award for playing the title role in the biopic *Chaplin*, he was a struggling actor in New York City with lots of crappy jobs on his resumé. One of the stranger jobs saw him hire himself out as a living piece of art.

"It was in a club called Area," he said, "and I wore an orange jump-suit and I sent Gumby dolls down a conveyor belt behind a piece of glass for ten bucks an hour. Everyone was going to that club … I got a lot of exposure. I wasn't hip enough to go [there], just hip enough to work there behind glass for four hours."

He also ran a Thrifty's Ice Cream stand, but quit after just a short while because "you just smell like a dead baby cow at the end of the night."

Who refused to clap when Sean Penn won the 2004 Best Actor Oscar for his work in *Mystic River*?

Bill Murray surprised guests at the 2004 Academy Awards when he sat on his hands as rival nominee Sean Penn was named Best Actor. The

Courtesy of AMPAS

Sean Penn took home the Best Actor Oscar at the 76th Annual Academy Awards. "The horror of the Academy Awards is what the press does leading up to it to make it a popular TV show," he said at the time. "Where they'll actually make it like it's an arm-wrestling event between two actors."

Lost In Translation star had a sour look on his face when Nicole Kidman read out Penn's name instead of his as winner and didn't clap.

Later, British newspaper *The Sun* reported that Murray shouted at organizers, "If I knew this was going to happen, I wouldn't have bothered coming." The comedian has often spoken of his dislike of awards shows. "Awards are meaningless to me," he said, "and I have nothing but disdain for anyone who actively campaigns to get one. It's a really unattractive sight to see an actor or actress who really wants an Oscar. And you often see it on the show. You see their faces and the desperation is so ugly."

Who threatened to "steal the sound editing Oscar" for Jamie Foxx if he didn't win Best Actor for *Ray* in 2005?

"I'd like to Thank the Academy..."

Comedian Chris Rock wasn't even an Academy member when he was asked to host the February 27, 2005, Academy Awards. Despite acting turns in *Head of State, Bad Company, New Jack City, I'm Gonna Git You Sucka!*, among others, he had never joined. When asked why, he said, "If you're darker than a paper bag, you can't get in."

How, then, did Rock end up hosting the show? "Billy [Crystal] is doing a show in New York and Steve Martin is doing a movie," producer Gil Cates explained at a press conference before Rock cut him off. "Ellen DeGeneres has crabs," the comic said. "Jay Leno's got a gig. They got to the R's. Burt Reynolds said no."

Despite his joking, Rock says he used to watch the Oscarcast when he was young — sort of. As a kid in Brooklyn, New York, Rock would tune into the Oscar show for the opening monologue, then switch off the television. "Any black people nominated? No, oh, back to bed," he said.

When asked what the worst thing that could happen during the broadcast was, Rock replied, "Being gang-raped by the cast of *Sideways*."

The 2005 Oscarcast broke a record for African-American nominations with five nods, including Best Actor for Don Cheadle and Best Supporting Actress for Sophie Okonedo of *Hotel Rwanda*, Best Supporting Actor for

Jamie Foxx was a clear favourite to take home the Best Actor Oscar at the 77th Annual Academy Awards for his portrayal of singer Ray Charles in the biopic *Ray*.

Morgan Freeman of *Million Dollar Baby*, and dual nominations for Jamie Foxx. Foxx was up for Best Actor for *Ray* and Best Supporting Actor for *Collateral*. Foxx was considered the front-runner for Best Actor, and Rock certainly made no secret of whom he would be pulling for.

"If he [Foxx] doesn't win, I will steal the sound editing Oscar [and give it to him]," Rock said.

Q Which Best Actor Oscar winner name-checked American soldier Tommy Zarobinski in his emotional acceptance speech?

A Newcomer Adrien Brody shocked Oscar handicappers by beating out Jack Nicholson, Michael Caine, Nicolas Cage, and Daniel Day-Lewis to take Best Actor for his role in *The Pianist* at the March 23, 2003, Academy Awards.

After an impromptu but passionate kiss with presenter Halle Berry, Brody confessed that he didn't write a speech because "every time I've done that in the past I didn't win." Brody then acknowledged that he was sad to be accepting an award at "such a strange time."

"My experiences of making this film made me very aware of the sadness and the dehumanization of people at times of war and the repercussions of war," he said. "Whoever you believe in, whether it's Allah or God, may he watch over you and let's pray for a peaceful and swift resolution [to the war in Iraq]. I have a friend in Queens who is a soldier in Kuwait and I hope you and your boys make it back real soon. I love you."

Brody's friend in Queens was American soldier Tommy Zarobinski, a childhood buddy. "We weren't watching the Academy Awards," said Zarobinski's father, Tom. "We have been glued to the war news coverage hoping not to hear mention of our son. Then there was a knock on the door and our neighbor said, 'Your son has just been mentioned on TV.' My first thought was, 'Oh my God, why would he be mentioned?' Then they told me that Adrien had mentioned him and I was thrilled. It's so nice that he should remember his old friend at this time. They used to be such good friends. One time I got mad at them for skipping out of school."

"Thank you, Adrien," added the soldier's mom, Ada, "you really made me feel good. Now we're just waiting for him to come home safe. I told him I don't want him to be a hero. He's already a hero to me."

"I'd like to Thank the Academy..."

When did Sean Penn attend the Academy Awards for the first time?

Despite three previous nominations, for *I Am Sam*, *Sweet and Lowdown*, and *Dead Man Walking*, Sean Penn had never gone to an Oscar ceremony until the February 29, 2004, fete. "I can't get up that red carpet without being embarrassed," Penn once said. "It's the same reason I don't like going to costume parties — because I'd feel silly." Up for Best Actor for his intense performance as the father of a murder victim in the Clint Eastwood–directed *Mystic River*, the reclusive actor told friends he would attend the gala to help support and publicize the film.

Penn ended up coming out ahead in the Best Actor race. Receiving a standing ovation from his peers as he made his way to the podium, he seemed genuinely moved. His speech was earnest and heartfelt — unlike when he accepted the 1996 Independent Spirit Award for his turn in *Dead Man Walking* with the joke "You tolerate me, you really tolerate me," a self-deprecating twist on Sally Field's famous Oscar speech.

"Thank you. If there's one thing that actors know, other than that there weren't any WMDs [weapons of mass destruction] — it's that there is no such thing as best in acting," he said at the dais. "And that's proven by these great actors that I was nominated with as well as the — as well as the Giamattis, Cages, Downey Jrs., Nicholsons, etc. that were not nominated. We know how great all of you were. My daughter Dylan and son Hopper find it presumptuous and embarrassing to write a speech, and so I'm gonna give it a go without. God, I really thank Clint Eastwood professionally and humanly for coming into my life. The great, great cast that I had to work with, my friends. Where do you go? Dennis Lehane, Brian Helgeland, Ma. Dad. Robin, for being an undying emotional inspiration on this roller coaster I'm learning to enjoy. Thank you all very much."

Who are the oldest performers to be nominated for a Best Actor Oscar?

At age seventy-eight *The Straight Story*'s Richard Farnsworth was the oldest person to be nominated for a Best Actor Academy Award. Billy Crystal singled out Farnsworth for praise at the 72nd Annual Academy Awards, saying that it was "great to see him and his nomination was a great story." Farnsworth started his film career as a stuntman in the 1930s, working on many notable films, including *Gone with the Wind*, before shifting his focus to acting in the 1970s. "I'm pretty limited in a lot of ways," he said, "but if I feel the character, it's damn easy to do."

George Arliss was sixty-three when he was nominated for, and won, the Best Actor kudo for the title role in *Disraeli* in 1930, and Art Carney was a relatively youthful fifty-seven when he was given the nod for *Harry and Tonto* in 1975.

Q Who is the only man to win a Best Actor Oscar for his film debut?

A Ben Kingsley, son of an Indian physician and English fashion model, was the first performer to win a Best Actor Oscar for a film debut, the title role in 1982's *Ghandi*. *Variety* raved that Kingsley's performance "has captured nuances in speech and movement which makes it seem as though he has stepped through black-and-white newsreel into the present Technicolor reincarnation."

After his win, Kingsley and his wife had to wait for half an hour for their limo to take them back to their hotel. While they were waiting several hecklers who had supported Paul Newman in his bid for the Oscar that year taunted the newly crowed Best Actor by yelling, "Fame is fleeting." Kingsley reportedly whispered to his wife, "A little fame is better than none," and, showing Ghandi-like restraint, ignored the insults.

Joe Morgenstern of the *Wall Street Journal* summed up the movie's Oscar success. "It made perfect sense," he wrote. "*Gandhi* was everything the voting members of the Motion Picture Academy would like to be — moral, tan and thin."

Kingsley was the first to earn a Best Actor Oscar on the first time out, but several women have taken top honours for their first film appearances: Shirley Booth for *Come Back Little Sheba*, Barbra Streisand for *Funny Girl*, and Marlee Matlin for *Children of a Lesser God*.

Q According to the Photoplay Awards, who was the Most Popular Male Star of the 1940s?

"I'd like to Thank the Academy..."

A Crooner Bing Crosby ruled the Photoplay Gold Medal Awards as Male of the Year through most of the 1940s, winning five in a row, from the inaugural year in 1944 through to 1948. He was eventually dethroned by a returning war hero, actor James Stewart. The Most Popular Female Star of the 1940s was Ingrid Bergman, who won Female of the Year three times, in 1946, 1947, and 1948.

Q Who are the only actors to be Oscar nominated for playing multiple characters in the same film?

A Only three actors have been nominated by the Academy for playing multiple roles in the same film. Lee Marvin won a Best Actor statue for his dual role as the gunfighter Tim Strawn and the boozing Kid Shelleen in the 1965 comedic western *Cat Ballou*.

Peter Sellers was the first actor to be nominated for a Best Actor Oscar for a film in which he portrayed three different characters. In Stanley Kubrick's Cold War satire *Dr. Strangelove or: How I Learned to Stop Worrying and Love the Bomb*, Sellers plays Group Captain Lionel Mandrake, President Merkin Muffley, and the title character, Dr. Strangelove. The multi-tasking comedian lost to Rex Harrison in 1964's *My Fair Lady*.

Nicolas Cage was recognized by the Academy for his yin and yang role as the twins Charlie and Donald Kaufman in Spike Jonze's *Adaptation*. Cage lost to Adrien Brody in the singular role of Polish Jewish musician Wladyslaw Szpilman in 2002's *The Pianist*.

Q How many times was Jack Nicholson nominated for a Golden Globe before he won?

A Jack Nicholson took home his first Best Actor Golden Globe on his fifth nomination at the January 25, 1975, ceremony. The wild-eyed actor won for his portrayal of Jake Gittes in the last film that Roman Polanski filmed in the United States, *Chinatown*, after losing for *Easy Rider* in 1970, *Five Easy Pieces* in 1971, *Carnal Knowledge* in 1972, and *The Last Detail* in 1974.

Chinatown also scored a gaggle of Oscar nods — Best Actor, Actress, Director, Picture, Art Direction, Cinematography, Costume Design, Film Editing, and Music — but produced only one winner, Robert Towne for Best Writing.

At the Golden Globes Nicholson was the only actor in the cast to be honoured with an award, although co-stars Faye Dunaway and John Huston were also nominated. Roman Polanski, who battled with his stars on the tumultuous shoot — once throwing Nicholson's portable TV out of his dressing room window and ripping some strands of Dunaway's hair from her head — won a Globe for guiding Nicholson's performance to the winner's dais.

"Every director implored me, 'Jack, can't you talk a little bit faster?' It was like a hot button for me and I would become hateful," Nicholson said when discussing his role in *Chinatown*. "So when Roman started to say it, I began and he said, 'Jack, this movie is 100-and-something pages long. To have a movie that is screenable, you'll have to talk a little faster.'"

Chinatown was voted the fourth greatest film of all time by *Entertainment Weekly*.

Which Best Actor Oscar winner "put on some makeup [and] stuffed Kleenex in my cheeks" to prepare for his most famous role?

Today it seems impossible to imagine anyone but Marlon Brando playing Don Vito Corleone in *The Godfather*, but he almost didn't get the part. Paramount studio head Stanley R. Jaffe did not want Francis Ford Coppola to cast Marlon Brando as the mafia boss. The studio bigwigs were still smarting from the budget overruns on *Mutiny on the Bounty*, for which Brando had been largely held responsible. Instead Laurence Olivier and Edward G. Robinson were suggested for the role. Coppola — who was nearly removed from the project for championing Brando — held fast, and Jaffe finally agreed to allow Brando to audition for the part.

To convince the studio heads — and himself — that he could do it, Brando went through a transformation to make Don Corleone look "like a bulldog."

"I went home and did some rehearsing to satisfy my curiosity about whether I could play an Italian," he said. "I put on some make-up, stuffed Kleenex in my cheeks, and worked out the characterization first in front of a mirror, then on a television monitor. After working on it, I decided I could create a characterization that would support the story. The people at Paramount saw the footage and liked it, and that's how I became the Godfather."

For actual filming, he got rid of the Kleenex and wore an appliance made by a dentist. The famous mouthpiece is now on display in the American Museum of the Moving Image in Queens, New York.

Brando won not only the Best Actor Golden Globe and Oscar for the role but also the respect of the movie's biggest fans. "I'd gotten to know quite a few Mafiosi," he said, "and all of them told me they loved the pictre because I had played the Godfather with dignity. Even today I can't pay a check in Little Italy."

Who got a big laugh at the January 2004 Golden Globes by saying in his acceptance speech that he'd recently canned his agents and suffered the loss of his personal trainer?

Bill Murray, who played an American actor having a mid-life crisis in Tokyo in *Lost in Translation*, wryly mocked his fellow actors who made sure to thank their agents in his Best Actor, Musical or Comedy acceptance speech.

"You can all relax. I fired my agents a couple of months ago. My trainer, my physical trainer, killed himself. I'd thank Universal and Focus Features, but there are so many people trying to take credit for [*Lost in Translation*], I wouldn't know where to begin.

"Too often we forget our brothers on the other side of the aisle — the dramatic actors," he said. "I'd just like to say: Where would our war, our miseries and our psychological traumas come from?"

It was the funniest speech of the night, but there was more than a grain of truth behind the laughs — Murray had severed ties with agents Jessica Tuchinsky and Rick Kurtzman of the Creative Artists Agency after making *Lost in Translation* and was an ex-client of the late

Raphael Picaud, the founder of Body Maxx, a celeb-catering gym in West Hollywood, California, who died in 2003.

Murray flew halfway around the world to collect his Best Actor award at Golden Globes ceremony in Hollywood at a cost of $180,000. The fifty-three-year-old actor started the trip in Italy — where he was filming the Wes Anderson film *The Life Aquatic* — flew to Teterboro Airport in New Jersey to pick up his wife, before moving on to Los Angeles for the glitzy gala. Following his win, the actor headed straight back to Rome to continue filming, dropping his wife off en route.

Murray was also nominated for an Academy Award for *Lost in Translation* but lost to *Mystic River*'s Sean Penn.

Q Which heroic Best Actor said he put everything into his most famous role, "all my feelings and everything I'd learned in 46 years of living"?

A Nominated for five Academy Awards in a career spanning nearly sixty years, Gregory Peck became synonymous with morally courageous heroes such as Atticus Finch, the right-minded southern lawyer in *To Kill a Mockingbird.*

Looking back on his 1962 Oscar-winning role as Finch, Peck said, "I put everything I had into it — all my feelings and everything I'd learned in 46 years of living, about family life and fathers and children, and my feelings about racial justice and inequality and opportunity."

His real-life image was so entangled with the role that he once joked, "They'll probably even put it on my tombstone."

Q Which actor gave his Best Actor in a Miniseries or Television Movie Golden Globe to Jack Lemmon?

A Ving Rhames was awarded the 1998 Best Actor Golden Globe for playing the title character in *Don King: Only in America*, but he gave his statue to screen legend Jack Lemmon, who was nominated in the same category for his performance in *Twelve Angry Men*. Rhames called Lemmon to the stage during the ceremony with the words, "I feel that being an artist is all about giving, and I'd like to give this to you, Mr. Lemmon." Rhames later explained that he felt that Lemmon's contributions to film exceeded his own. A surprised Lemmon responded, "This is one of the nicest, sweetest moments I've ever known in my life," and tried unsuccessfully to give the award back to Rhames. The Hollywood Foreign Press Association, which runs the Golden Globes, later announced that they would have a duplicate trophy made for Rhames.

The next year when Angelina Jolie won a Globe for her role in *Gia* she offered her award to Rhames. "I guess I should give this to you, shouldn't I?" she said.

"Nah," Rhames responded. "Maybe Jack Nicholson wants it."

Two years later Lemmon won a Golden Globe for Best Performance for his role as Henry Drummond in *Inherit the Wind*. "In the spirit of Ving Rhames," he joked in his acceptance speech, "I'm going to give this award to Jack Lemmon."

Who said, "First time an ulcer ever won the Oscar" about his role in *High Noon*?

In *High Noon* fifty-one-year-old Gary Cooper (who replaced the much younger Marlon Brando in the role) was playing opposite Grace Kelly, a starlet less than half his age. Nervous about being paired with the twenty-two-year-old Kelly, Cooper developed an ulcer.

His discomfort during the shoot led to an awkward scene where Cooper looked pained when the beautiful actress declared her love for him. The awkward scene didn't play well, and after a test audience burst into laughter during the sequence, a frantic editing job ensued. Kelly's close-ups were reduced and Gary Cooper's pained reaction shots were moved and placed in a more appropriate context — next to the bad guys who were threatening to kill him.

When Cooper won the Academy Award for Best Actor (his second) for the film he stated, "First time an ulcer ever won the Oscar."

Q Who received his Best Actor Oscar at the March 30, 1955, Oscars with the words, "It must be made of gold! It must be"?

A Marlon Brando was amazed at how heavy the Oscar statuette was when he won Best Actor for *On the Waterfront*. He "almost leaped to the stage to get the award for which he had been nominated three times previously," wrote *Variety*. "He fondled the statuette for a second before turning to the audience, 'It's much heavier than I imagined. I cannot ever remember anything in my life for which so many people are responsible. This is a wonderful moment and I'm certainly indebted.'

"Brando was unnerved as he walked offstage, clutching the Oscar, and muttering, 'It must be made of gold! It must be.'"

His role in *On the Waterfront* earned Marlon Brando his fourth Best Actor Oscar nomination and his first win.

Courtesy of AMPAS

Q Why did Charlie Chaplin refuse the New York Film Critics Circle Best Actor Award in 1940?

A Charlie Chaplin rebuffed the New York Film Critics Circle when they chose him as Best Actor for his dual performance as the dictator of Tomania and a Jewish barber in *The Great Dictator* because he was upset at the reviews they had given him when the film came out.

To add insult to Chaplin's injury, after the voting members of the critics group had been deadlocked for twenty-two Best Actor ballots one frustrated member of the group suggested they all side with Chaplin for the top acting honour simply because "he'd be a swell free attraction for us" at their Rainbow Room awards ceremony. When this bit of selfish promotion was revealed in the pages of the *New York Mirror* a hopping mad Chaplin fired off a letter to the group disparaging their "process of electioneering [because] such a procedure is, in my humble opinion, far afield from sound critical appraisal."

Charlie Chaplin's most famous character, The Tramp.

Which performer, born Marion Morrison, won a Best Actor Oscar for playing one-eyed U.S. marshall Rooster Cogburn?

A John Wayne called the role of the drunken lawman Rooster Cogburn in *True Grit* "the easiest of my career" when he picked up his first Best Actor Oscar at the 42nd Annual Academy Awards. "If I'd known this was all it would take, I'd have put that eye patch on forty years ago," he said in his acceptance speech.

Earlier in the night, before his win, Wayne told a reporter that the Oscar wasn't the most important thing for him. "You can't eat awards," he said. "Nor, more to the point, drink them." Later — perhaps after a few drinks — he seemed to change his tune: "The Oscar means a lot to me, even if it took the industry forty years to get around to it."

Wayne spent the rest of the awards night celebrating — by getting three sheets to the wind with one of the night's Oscar losers, Richard Burton.

Q How many Oscar nominations did Paul Newman receive for playing Fast Eddie Felson?

A Paul Newman was twice nominated for playing Fast Eddie Felson — the first time in *The Hustler* in 1961, which he lost to Maximilian Schell for *Judgment at Nuremberg,* and then again in *The Color of Money* in 1986. He won on the second try but didn't show up to collect his award in person.

"It's like chasing a beautiful woman for eighty years," he said, explaining his absence. "Finally she relents and you say, 'I am terribly sorry. I'm tired.'"

Q Which is the shortest performance to win a Best Actor Oscar?

A With less than sixteen minutes of screen time in 1991's *The Silence of the Lambs,* Anthony Hopkins's performance as Hannibal Lector was the shortest ever to win a Best Actor Oscar. After the win, backstage at the Oscars, Hopkins seemed to slip back into character when he told reporters, "If I hadn't won, you'd all be in trouble."

The Welsh actor claimed that his serial killer's steely reserve had been partially inspired by Katharine Hepburn. Hopkins first met

Hepburn twenty-three years earlier during the filming of *The Lion In Winter* in 1968. While they were on location making the historical epic, she swam twice a day in the freezing Irish Sea, explaining that it was so awful but she always felt great afterwards.

His nomination for playing Hannibal Lecter in *The Silence of the Lambs* was the first of four Best Actor Oscar nominations Anthony Hopkins (pictured here with *Variety* scribe Army Archerd) earned in the 1990s.

Who is the only male actor to be nominated for an acting award for a character that was not human?

In *Starman*, Jeff Bridges plays an alien who lands on earth and assumes the identity of a dead housepainter from Madison, Wisconsin, and is, according to one character in the film, "presently out tooling around the countryside in a hopped up orange and black 1977 Mustang." Bridges's E.T. lost the Best Actor Oscar to F. Murray Abraham for his role in *Amadeus*.

With Bridges's nomination, *Starman* became the only John Carpenter–directed film to earn an Academy Award nod.

Q Which Best Actor winner thanked boxer Jake La Motta "even though he's suing us"?

A On March 31, 1981, Robert De Niro won the top acting Oscar for his brutal portrayal of heavyweight boxer Jake "The Bronx Bull" La Motta in *Raging Bull*, a role De Niro packed on fifty pounds to play.

Courtesy The Hollywood Collection

"I'm a little nervous," he said. "I'm sorry. I forgot my lines so the director wrote them down." He went on to thank the usual suspects — his director, fellow actors — and Jake La Motta, "even though he's suing us." The La Motta family wasn't pleased with the way the boxer had been portrayed and sued. It was settled out of court.

Robert De Niro, a six-time Oscar nominee and two-time winner, says, "I don't like to watch my own movies — I fall asleep in my own movies."

"I want to thank my mother and father for having me," the actor continued, "and my grandmothers and grandfathers for having them..."

Q How many movies did John Wayne make before he won an Academy Award?

A John Wayne appeared in 138 films before receiving an Oscar for *True Grit* at the April 7, 1970, ceremony. "Oscar and I have something in common," said Wayne as he accepted his statue. "Oscar first came to the Hollywood scene in 1928. So did I. We're both a little weather beaten, but we're still here and plan to be around for a whole lot longer."

Q Who was the first performer to be nominated for a Best Actor Oscar posthumously?

"I'd like to Thank the Academy..."

On September 30, 1955, James Dean was killed in a crash while speeding his Porsche Spider to Salinas, California, to take part in a car race. Five months later, on February 18, 1956, Oscar nominations were announced, including the first-ever posthumous Best Actor nod for Dean's performance in *East of Eden*.

Gossip maven Hedda Hopper lobbied hard for Dean's family to receive an honorary award to acknowledge the dead actor but was rebuked by the Academy. President George Seaton told the columnist that nominees were excluded from accepting honorary awards. "We're sentimental, too," he said, "but that's the rule."

Although Dean was the emotional favourite to win, he lost to Ernest Borgnine in the lead role of *Marty*.

The following year he was once again posthumously nominated — making him the first actor to be twice nominated after death — for his portrayal of Jett Rink in *Giant*, and once again lost, this time to the follically challenged Yul Brynner in *The King and I*, whom *Redbook* called "the most exciting male on the screen since Rudolph Valentino." Brynner was so popular that boys were shaving their heads to emulate the star. In Des Moines, Iowa, fourteen boys were suspended from their high school for trying to achieve the "Yul Brynner look."

It was reported that when Brynner's name was announced as Best Actor, "his whole head flushed a deep red."

What do Orson Welles, Charlie Chaplin, and Sylvester Stallone have in common?

At the March 29, 1977, Oscar ceremony Sylvester Stallone followed in the footsteps of Welles and Chaplin by being only the third person to be nominated for Best Actor and Best Screenplay for the same film. Stallone's nominations were for *Rocky*, Chaplin earned the nods for 1940's *The Great Dictator*, while Welles was up for *Citizen Kane*. Of the three, Welles was the only one to take home an award. He split Best Original Screenplay for 1941's *Kane* with Herman J. Mankiewicz.

Q Who was the first person to direct himself to a Best Actor Oscar?

A At the March 24, 1949, Oscars Laurence Olivier's *Hamlet* won four awards — Best Art Direction, Best Costume Design, Best Actor, and Best Picture. The Best Actor win marked the first anyone had won for a film they had also directed.

Olivier was in London appearing onstage in *The School for Scandal* at the time of the win. When informed of the Oscar sweep he said, "It is incredibly generous of Hollywood to confer their highest honor upon the British film industry. I personally have not deserved this honor but my associates have and I am happy, proud and most grateful for their sakes and for my own."

When asked how he would celebrate he replied, "Oh, perhaps an extra drink after tonight's show."

The reaction in Hollywood wasn't quite as gracious. Upset that a British film had trumped all the American-produced entries, one Oscar guest grumbled, "Although the orchestra had opened the proceedings with 'The Star Spangled Banner,' in retrospect, maybe it was really 'God Save the King.'" *The Hollywood Reporter* moaned, "Hamlet's ghost stalked Hollywood last night and in the most ghoulish seventy-five minutes the picture business ever experienced waltzed off with a flock of golden Oscars. At midnight, merchants hereabouts reported a strong run on aspirin."

Q What is the only film in Oscar history to earn three nominations for Best Actor?

A The only film in Oscar history to receive three nominees for Best Actor is 1935's *Mutiny on the Bounty*. Clark Gable, Charles Laughton, and Franchot Tone were all nominated in the top acting category, although the award went to the only non-*Mutiny* nominee, Victor McLaglen for *The Informer*.

Mutiny on the Bounty is also one of only two films to have two separate versions nominated for Best Picture, the 1935 version and the Marlon Brando remake in 1962. The other film is *Moulin Rouge*. John

Huston's version lost to *The Greatest Show on Earth* in 1952, while Baz Luhrmann's 2001 remake was overshadowed by *A Beautiful Mind*.

Q Who was the first actor to be Oscar nominated twice for playing the same character?

A On March 15, 1945, when Bing Crosby accepted the Best Actor Oscar for playing Father Chuck O'Malley in *Going My Way*, he said, "I couldn't be more surprised if I won the Kentucky Derby." He must have been doubly surprised then to be nominated again the very next year for playing Father O'Malley in *The Bells of St. Mary's*. The second time around he lost to Ray Milland playing a binging drunk in *The Lost Weekend*.

Going My Way was actually written after its sequel *The Bells of St. Mary's*. In order to borrow Bing Crosby from Paramount for that film, RKO had to let Leo McCarey write and direct *Going My Way*, based on the same character. For some reason, however, *Going My Way* was released first.

Q Who physically threatened the producer of the 2002 BAFTAs after an acceptance speech was edited for the televised broadcast?

A Russell Crowe won the Best Actor BAFTA — the British equivalent of the Oscar — in 2002 for his role in *A Beautiful Mind*. As part pf his acceptance speech he read the poem *Sanctity* by the late Irish poet Patrick Kavanagh. Nominees had been instructed several times to keep their speeches short. Crowe didn't, and, since the show ran over by thirty minutes, editors at the request of BBC executives went ahead and eighty-sixed the poem.

Crowe was reportedly so incensed by the cut from the tape-delayed telecast that he roughed up one of the show's producers. The surly actor allegedly accosted director Malcolm Gerrie, shoving him up against a wall at an after-party at London's Grosvenor House Hotel. "Who on Earth had the audacity to take out the Best Actor's poem?" *Variety* quoted Crowe as yelling at Gerrie. "I'll make sure you never work in Hollywood!"

As it turns out Gerrie wasn't the hatchet man, and a few days after the incident Crowe apologized. "My language was excessive because I was livid [and] I behaved inappropriately. I was overreacting because I felt passionately about it at the time," London's *Sun* newspaper quoted Crowe as saying.

Gerrie graciously accepted Crowe's *mea culpa.* "I told him I didn't get any satisfaction out of the whole situation, and if he wanted to make it up to any of my family he could speak to my son," Gerrie told the *Sun.* "He then spoke to [my son] Oliver for about 15 minutes and told him all about the making of *Gladiator* and what it was like working with real tigers. Oliver was thrilled."

Crowe then suggested to Gerrie that they further make amends by getting together for a couple of drinks.

"He said we should go out for a few pints of Guinness when he was next there," said Gerrie. "I said, 'I know a great pub in Brentford where we could have a few quiet pints.' I couldn't believe it — it was a total contrast to how he had reacted the week before. It was like black and white. He sounded so humble and genuinely apologetic."

Later that year Academy Awards director Louis Horvitz announced that he would cut Crowe's Oscar acceptance speech short if he started reciting poetry. Asked if he had any concerns for his safety, the director said, "I'll be safe in my car!"

Who was the first person to win a Best Actor Oscar for a role he had played on both screen and stage?

Flamboyant U.K.–born George Arliss won a Best Actor statuette for his role as British Prime Minister Benjamin Disraeli in 1929's *Disraeli,* a role he knew well, having performed it on the British stage in 1911, then again in a 1921 silent film before making the talkie in 1929.

Arliss was a well-loved stage actor whose career really took off with the advent of talking pictures. Subsequent to the release of *Disraeli* he was billed as "The Finest Actor on the Screen," a nickname he apparently took to heart. Once, while testifying in court, he described himself as the world's best actor. When questioned about the veracity of the claim, he replied he had told the truth. "You see," he said, "I am under oath."

"I'd like to Thank the Academy..."

Q Who was the first person to win a Best Actor Oscar for a musical role?

A James Cagney — whose first performing job was as a female dancer in a chorus line — was the first song-and-dance man to take home an Oscar for Best Actor. He won the gold at the March 4, 1943, ceremony for his role as patriotic songwriter George M. Cohan in the film *Yankee Doodle Dandy*. "An actor is only as good or as bad as people think he is," said Cagney. "I am glad so many people think I was good." Cagney finished the speech using Cohan's famous line, "My mother thanks you, my father thanks you, my sisters thank you and I thank you."

Cagney was hand-picked for the part by the real-life Cohan after Fred Astaire turned it down.

Even though *Yankee Doodle Dandy* was based on Cohan's life, many facts were changed. After the film's premiere Cohan was heard to quip, "It was a good movie. Who was it about?"

Cagney went on to play George M. Cohan again a dozen years later in *The Seven Little Foys*.

The statue of "Give My Regards to Broadway" lyricist George M. Cohan in Times Square, New York City.

How many times was Al Pacino nominated for playing Michael Corleone?

In 1972 Al Pacino was nominated for Best Supporting Actor for playing Michael Corleone in *The Godfather*. He lost to Joel Grey for his role as the MC in *Cabaret*. Two years later he was once again nominated, this time for Best Actor, for playing Corleone in *The Godfather, Part II*. The second time around he lost to Art Carney's performance in *Harry and Tonto*. He did not receive a nomination for *The Godfather, Part III*.

Courtesy The Hollywood Collection

Al Pacino was apparently frequently referred to as "that midget Pacino" by producers of *The Godfather* who initially didn't want him for the part of Michael Corleone — a role twice recognized by the Academy. He earned Best Supporting Actor and Best Actor nominations but no Oscars.

"I'd like to Thank the Academy..."

Who was the first African-American actor to win a Best Actor Oscar?

Sidney Poitier became the first African-American performer to win a Best Actor Oscar at the April 13, 1964, ceremony for his performance in *Lillies of the Field*. In his unprepared acceptance speech, an emotional Poitier said, "It's been a long journey to this moment." As he was being ushered off stage by presenter Anne Bancroft she teased him by saying, "Enjoy it chum, it doesn't last long."

The win didn't transform Poitier's career overnight. His next film, *To Sir with Love*, was a troubled production, and he had to forego his salary just to get the film made at all. "The only real change in my career was in the attitude of the newsmen," said Poitier of his win. "They started to query me on civil rights and the Negro question incessantly. Ever since I won the Oscar, that's what they've been interested in — period."

In the 1995–96 awards season, who took home the following trophies: Best Actor, San Sebastian International Film Festival's Silver Seashell Award; Best Actor, New York Film Critics Circle Award; Best Actor, National Society of Film Critics Award; Best Actor, Chicago Film Critics Award; Best Actor, National Board of Review Award; Best Actor, Los Angeles Film Critics Association; Best Actor, Boston Society of Film Critics Award; Best Actor, DFWFC Association Awards; Outstanding Performance by a Male Actor in a Leading Role, Screen Actors Guild; Actor in a Leading Role - Drama, Golden Globes; Best Actor, Academy Awards; and Best Male Lead, Independent Spirit Awards?

Nicolas Cage's trophy case bulged with the awards he won for his performance as Ben Sanderson, a man determined to drink himself to death who unexpectedly falls in love with a hooker in *Leaving Las Vegas*. To prepare himself for the role Cage filmed himself drunk to scrutinize his speech pattern and studied what he considered to be "the great alcoholic four performances": Jack Lemmon in *The Days of Wine and Roses*, Albert Finney in *Under the Volcano*, Dudley Moore in *Arthur*, and Ray Milland in *The Lost Weekend*.

Years after winning his first Oscar for the role he was asked what the best thing was about winning the award. "When Jessica Lange wiped Patricia's [Arquette] lipstick off my mouth in the elevator after I'd won," he said.

Who said, "Mr. Beery and I recently adopted children. Under the circumstances it seems a little odd that we were both given awards for the best male performance of the year"?

There were two front-runners in the Best Actor Oscar race of 1931–32: Frederick March and Wallace Beery. But you can only have one winner — or can you? When the award was announced, presenter Norma Shearer called out March's name for his dual role in *Dr. Jekyll and Mr. Hyde*. Following his acceptance speech there was a commotion among the judges, who had been busy shuffling papers and recounting ballots. They asked Academy president Conrad Nagel to take the stage.

"Mr. Beery," Nagel said, "it is my pleasure to announce that you have tied for the best male performance of the year for your splendid portrayal in *The Champ*."

It was a shocking announcement — there had never been a tie before — and as Beery took the stage, March was heard to wisecrack, "Mr. Beery and I recently adopted children. Under the circumstances it seems a little odd that we were both given awards for the best male performance of the year."

Later it was discovered that the two actors hadn't exactly tied for first place — March had beaten Beery by one vote — but the Academy's rulebook declared that "the candidate or candidates who are within three votes of a tie shall be given an award." The following year that rule was abolished and a tie would have to be exactly that — a tie.

Which 1970 Best Actor nominee described the Academy Awards as "a two-hour meat parade, a public display with contrived suspense for economic reasons"?

"I'd Like to Thank the Academy…"

George C. Scott refused to attend the 1970 Academy Awards despite being nominated for Best Actor for *Patton*. In a public statement he dismissed the show as "offensive, barbarous and innately corrupt." Ironically, he won the award, which was accepted by producer Frank McCarthy. The next day when reporters asked if he had watched the broadcast, he shook his head no and said he had watched a hockey game and gone to bed early. He was the first actor in the history of the Oscars to refuse an award.

Two actors have been nominated for the Best Actor Oscar nine times. Who are they?

Laurence Olivier and Spencer Tracy were each nominated for Best Actor Oscars nine times. Laurence Olivier was nominated for *Wuthering Heights* (1939), *Rebecca* (1940), *Henry V* (1946), *Hamlet* (1948), *Richard III* (1956), *The Entertainer* (1960), *Othello* (1965), *Sleuth* (1972), and *The Boys From Brazil* (1978). He was also nominated for Best Supporting Actor for *Marathon Man* (1976). He took home the Best Actor statue for *Hamlet* (1948).

Spencer Tracy won Best Actor statues for *Captains Courageous* (1937) and *Boys Town* (1938). He was also nominated for *San Francisco* (1936), *Father of the Bride* (1950), *Bad Day at Black Rock* (1955), *The Old Man and the Sea* (1958), *Inherit the Wind* (1960), *Judgment at Nuremberg* (1961), and *Guess Who's Coming to Dinner* (1967).

How many times was Paul Newman nominated for an Academy Award before he finally won?

Paul Newman was a runner-up six times before he eventually won Best Actor for *The Color of Money*. Newman had previously been nominated for *Cat on a Hot Tin Roof* (1958), *Hud* (1963), *Cool Hand Luke* (1967), *Butch Cassidy and the Sundance Kid* (1969), *The Sting* (1973), *Absence of Malice* (1981), and *The Verdict* (1982). After such a losing streak Newman decided to skip the March 30, 1987, ceremony.

"I'm superstitious," he said. "I've been there six times and lost. Maybe if I stay away, I'll win."

Who is the youngest person to be nominated for a Best Actor Oscar?

Courtesy of AMPAS

Jackie Cooper's uncle, director Norman Taurog, gave the young actor the title role in *Skippy* based on a popular comic strip. The role earned Cooper a Best Actor Oscar nomination, making him the youngest actor to receive that honour, and he became a marquee star of the 1940s and 1950s.

"I'd like to Thank the Academy..."

A Jackie Cooper was just ten years old in 1931 when the Academy recognized his performance in *Skippy* with a Best Actor nomination. The ceremony dragged on past midnight, way past Jackie's bedtime, so when his category was announced he was fast asleep on the arm of Best Actress winner Marie Dressler. Just as well. The youngster didn't take home a statue that night, losing to Lionel Barrymore for his turn as a boozy lawyer who defends Clark Gable in *A Free Soul*.

In 1981 the former child star wrote a biography, *Please Don't Shoot My Dog*, taking the title from an incident on the set of *Skippy*. Jackie was having trouble with a crying scene, so the frustrated director, Norman Taurog (who was also Jackie's uncle), threatened to shoot his dog if he didn't well up. The tears flowed and the dog was spared.

Q Who suggested that each of the five Best Actor nominees should have to "do a soliloquy from *Hamlet* before an audience of voters"?

A When Humphrey Bogart was nominated as Best Actor for *The African Queen* in 1951 he quipped that a real race would see the five contestants doing a soliloquy from *Hamlet* before an audience of voters. Bogie beat out Montgomery Clift, Marlon Brando, Arthur Kennedy, and Frederick March to take home an Oscar that year, but later added that he wouldn't have floated the soliloquy idea "if Larry Olivier had been up."

1 "Hello, gorgeous." — Barbra Streisand to her Oscar in 1969

2 "I'd just like to say to all the other nominees in the audience, I don't think that I deserve it any more than the rest of you. I'd like to say that. I don't think that it would be true, though."

— Tom Green, accepting the 2002 Golden Raspberry for Worst Movie of the Year for *Freddy Got Fingered*

3 "Spencer Tracy is a fine actor, but he is most important because he understands why it is necessary to take orders from the front office."

— studio head Louis B. Mayer, accepting the 1937 Best Actor Oscar on behalf of Spencer Tracy

4 "I shall never waitress again, and you are my witnesses…"

— Mercedes Ruehl, accepting the Best Supporting Actress Golden Globe for *The Fisher King* in 1991

5 "To all those people who were happy to bankroll the film as long as I wasn't in it."

— Geoffrey Rush, accepting the 1996 Best Actor Oscar for *Shine*

6 "Now my kids won't think I'm just another bum — they'll know what I do for a living."

— Anthony Quinn, upon being told he had won the Best Supporting Actor Oscar for *Viva Zapata!* in 1952. He wasn't present at the ceremony.

SPEECH QUOTES

"The Academy asks that your speech be no longer than the movie itself."

— host Danny Kaye, 1952

7

"Having worked in a video store for five years, there's a whole full-circle, snake-swallowing-its-tail kind of thing about winning this award. All the guys who worked with me at Video Archives would be extremely proud of me right now."

— Quentin Tarantino, accepting the 2003 DVD Pioneer Award at the DVD Premier Awards, which honour the best direct-to-DVD movies and original programming

8

"If New York is the Big Apple, to me, Hollywood tonight is the Big Nipple."

— Bernardo Bertolucci, in his acceptance speech for Best Director for 1987's *The Last Emperor*

9

"A loaf of bread, two cans of tuna ... Oops, wrong sheet of paper!"

— Martin Sheen, accepting the New York Film Critics Circle's Best Actor award for *All of Me* in 1984

*"I don't deserve this award, but I have
arthritis and I don't deserve that either."*

— Jack Benny

10 "It couldn't have happened to an older guy."

— George Burns, in his 1975 acceptance speech for
Best Supporting Actor in *The Sunshine Boys*

11 "I'd like to thank the academy … oops, sorry. This is serious. It's
going to be so hard to talk out of my ass after this, but I'll
manage. You know what this means, don't you? I'm a shoo-in
for the Blockbuster Award."

— Jim Carrey, Golden Globe winner for Best Drama Actor
for *The Truman Show*, 1998

12 "Shame on you, Mr. Bush. Shame on you. And any time you got
the Pope and the Dixie Chicks against you, your time is up."

— Michael Moore, accepting the Best Feature Documentary
Oscar for *Bowling for Columbine* in 2003

13 "If I'd known this was all it would take, I'd have put that eye patch
on forty years ago."

— John Wayne, accepting the Best Actor Oscar for his portrayal
of the one-eyed lawman in *True Grit* in 1969

14 "I'll show you a pair of Golden Globes…"

— Bette Midler, accepting the Female Newcomer award in 1980

15 "I'm so loaded down with good luck charms I could hardly make it up the stairs."

— David Niven, in his Best Actor Oscar
acceptance speech for 1958's *Separate Tables*

16 "You like me — right now you like me!"

— Sally Field, in her 1984 Best Actress Oscar
acceptance speech for *Places in the Heart*

17 "You tolerate me. You really, really tolerate me."

— Sean Penn, winner of the Independent Spirit Award
for Best Actor for *Dead Man Walking* in 1995

18 "There has been so much niceness here tonight, that I am happy to say that I am entirely — and solely — responsible for the success of *The Philadelphia Story*."

— Donald Ogden Stewart, winner of the Best Screenplay
Oscar in 1940 for *The Philadelphia Story*

19 "I would like to thank my colleagues: Brahms, Bach, Beethoven, Richard Strauss…"

— Dimitri Tiomkin, winner of the Best Score of a
Dramatic or Comedy Picture Oscar in 1954 for *The High and the Mighty*

20 "I am in shock. I am so in love with my brother."

— Angelina Jolie, in her 1999 acceptance speech for the
Best Supporting Actress Oscar for *Girl, Interrupted*

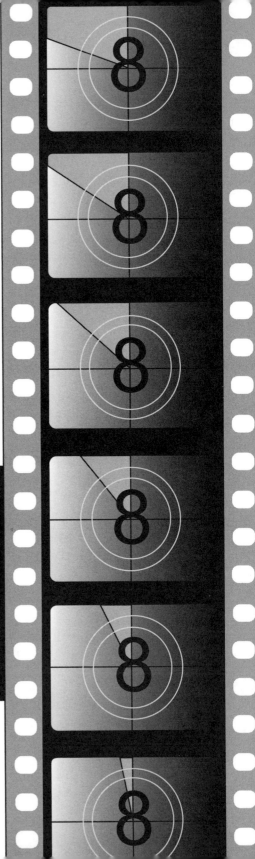

"*This is not an Academy Awards, ladies and gentlemen, it is a freak-out.*"

— Oscar show host Bob Hope, 1969

HOLLYWEIRD: THE GOOD, THE BAD, AND THE STRANGE

Hollyweird: The Good, the Bad, and the Strange

Which Oscar host announced that he was going to raffle off a car during the ceremony?

When late-night talk-show host David Letterman was given the job as host of the 67th Annual Academy Awards in 1995 he announced, "We're changing the format this year. The whole show will be forty minutes long and I'll be giving away cars."

He was at least halfway serious. Letterman planned to raffle off a car onstage in the middle of the show and originally wanted to fix the draw so that the elegant actress Jessica Tandy would win. When he was informed that Tandy had passed away six months previously, the edgy comedian decided Sally Field would be the recipient of the car. When the rigged giveaway didn't go well during rehearsal, it was scrapped.

Letterman's tongue-in-cheek promise that the show would only be forty minutes long didn't come to pass, either. Once the final award had been given out, the 67th Annual Academy Awards clocked in at three hours and thirty-two minutes.

Who backed out of the 2005 Golden Globes reportedly because of weight issues?

Spider-Man star Tobey Maguire dropped out of his appearance at the 2005 Golden Globe Awards minutes before the show, reportedly after he was advised to keep his recent weight gain private.

The *Spider-Man* star was scheduled to introduce a clip of Martin Scorsese's *The Aviator*, which went on to win the Best Drama prize. But just minutes before the ceremony he pulled out, allegedly at the insistence of his advisors, who wanted to keep him out of the spotlight until he lost the pounds he'd recently piled on. The Los Angeles awards' producers managed to recruit heartthrob Orlando Bloom to replace Maguire.

Who hired a plane to buzz the Oscar ceremony in 1997 to protest not being invited to the show?

Hustler publisher Larry Flynt caused a ruckus about not being invited to the 1997 Oscarcast despite multiple nods for the movie based on his life, *The People vs. Larry Flynt.* Columbia Pictures brass decided not to invite the pornographer for fear that he would do something embarrassing. Flynt railed against the company, accusing them of stealing his life story and then trying to censor him. At the last minute, Woody Harrelson (who played Flynt in the film) gave him his agent's ticket. Still heated, Flynt went ahead with his plan to embarrass the studio and hired a plane to buzz the Shrine Auditorium's red carpet with a banner reading, "Columbia Sucks — Larry Flynt."

A few years earlier another key player in one of the year's hottest movies hadn't been invited to the ceremony. In 1994 Winston Groom, the author of the *Forrest Gump* novel, wasn't offered a ticket and had to watch on TV as the movie adaptation of his book won six Academy Awards, including Best Picture, Best Director, and Best Actor. The sting of not being there to share the glory might have been dulled a bit if any of the winners had thanked the man who created the character of Forrest Gump, but shockingly, no one thought to mention his name.

Which movie duo was introduced at the 2003 MTV Movie Awards with the following: "This girl has just appeared as the cover girl of *FHM* magazine while this guy grossly masturbated before it"?

The presenters of the Best On-Screen Team award were *American Pie's* Alyson Hannigan and Jason Biggs. The racy introduction played off their onscreen personas from the teen hit.

What place does Stan Berman hold in Oscar history?

Berman, a cab driver from Brooklyn, N.Y., slipped by 125 police guards at the 34th Annual Academy Awards and handed Bob Hope a handmade Oscar onstage.

"Wearing evening clothes befitting the occasion, he mumbled into the mike that he was the world's greatest gate-crasher and that he had a statuette for emcee Bob Hope, for a pic he made in 1938," *Variety* reported. "The uninvited guest had the presenters and everyone else so surprised that nobody gave him the hook."

Hope responded with a quick one-liner. "Who needs Price Waterhouse," he wisecracked. "All we need is a doorman."

Berman later told reporters that he has to budget carefully to keep up with his expensive hobby. "I just spend thirty-five dollars a week on myself and save the rest for gate-crashing expenses."

Which Golden Globe winner made an alcohol-fuelled fool of himself at the 2004 Empire Film Awards in London?

Two-time Oscar nominee and 1979 Golden Globe winner for *Midnight Express* John Hurt was a drunken yob at London's Empire Film Awards in February 2004.

The previous night the sixty-four-year-old actor had been kicked out of a strip club for drunk and offensive behaviour and didn't appear to have mended his ways at the awards bash at the ritzy Dorchester Hotel.

Hurt presented a Lifetime Achievement Award to his *Alien* co-star Sigourney Weaver, but slurred as he struggled to read from the teleprompter as he introduced her. One guest told Britain's *Daily Mail*, "It was absolutely excruciating. You didn't know whether to feel sorry for him or just tell him to get on with it."

After his shameful performance the inebriated Hurt continued his bizarre behaviour, telling a *Daily Mirror* reporter that he likes to dress up in women's clothing. "Every man wants to be a woman," he said, "and ones who deny it are lying. I'd love to be a woman. You have beautiful clothes — all soft blouses and pretty skirts. I like dressing up."

He then went on to proposition the journalists, asking them, "Do you girls offer yourselves, do you, do you? You're a naughty one. What are we going to do with you? I bet you've got really big nipples. Show me."

At which awards show did Michael Moore first call George W. Bush a "fictitious president"?

REEL WINNERS

A In March 2003 Michael Moore's film *Bowling for Columbine* won the Independent Spirit Award for Best Documentary. "We have a fictitious president," he said in his acceptance speech, "who was put in office with fictitious results and he's now conducting a war for fictitious reasons. This is absolutely insane. The lesson for the children of Columbine this week is that violence is an accepted means to resolve a conflict and it's a sad, sick and immoral lesson." The next night Moore won the Best Documentary Oscar and ruffled a few feathers by reusing some of the inflammatory language from the Independent Spirit Award speech.

It was a night for political comment at the Independent Spirit Awards. After Elvis Costello received a standing ovation for kicking off the eighteenth annual ceremony with his anthem "Peace, Love & Understanding," host John Waters injected some humour to the proceedings. In his opening remarks he commented on "these scary times" and the war in Iraq but then added, "Saddam Hussein? George Bush? No one will stop me from getting my gift bag."

Others were more heartfelt. "I'd like to send out a prayer to the Iraqi people," said Best Supporting Actor winner Dennis Quaid, while Mexican actor Gael Garcia Bernal, winner of Best Foreign Film for *Y Tu Mama Tambien* added, "This time I get the opportunity to tell something for you the people from the United States to do, which is, 'The only way to stop this war, is you.'"

Q Which screenwriter won an Academy Award and a Razzie in the same week?

A On March 23, 1998, Brian Helgeland won an Academy Award for Writing (Based on Material from Another Medium) for *L.A. Confidential*. Later that same week, he allowed the founders of the Razzies to present him with the Worst Screenplay Golden Raspberry Award for Kevin Costner's *The Postman* in his Warner Brothers office. He was only the fourth person in Razzie history to voluntarily accept one of the awards.

When asked about winning both prizes Helgeland declared that he would display them side by side on his mantle — to remind him of the duality of Hollywood.

Hollyweird: The Good, the Bad, and the Strange

Q. Which acting legend overshadowed screenwriter Tom Schulman's Oscar win for *Dead Poets Society*?

A. Screenwriter Tom Schulman — writer of *Holy Man, 8 Heads in a Duffel Bag, Medicine Man, What About Bob?, Honey, I Shrunk the Kids*, and *Welcome to Mooseport* — picked up an Oscar for penning the script for *Dead Poets Society* on March 26, 1990.

"If I had any inclination to get a big head, the Oscars cured that," he said later. "The presenter who gave me the award was Jane Fonda. She had recently been in the news because she had started dating Ted Turner.

"She handed me the Oscar and I made my little speech and we went together into the press room where there was a small stage in front of bleachers filled with about 60 press members, who were supposed to ask the winner questions.

"Jane and I took the stage and she said, 'I'd like to introduce you to Tom Schulman, who's just won an Oscar for Best Original Screenplay. Do you have any questions?'

"There was a barrage of questions. 'Jane, what's it like with Ted? Are you getting married?' etc. and she said, 'Come on, this isn't my night, it's Tom's night. Please direct your questions to him.'

"So there's a little pause and somebody says, 'Tom, what's it like getting an Oscar from Jane? What's your thought — you think she'll marry Ted?'

"'That's it,' she said. 'Interview over!' and we walked out."

Q. At the 2004 Independent Spirit Awards who ran onstage and handcuffed host John Waters?

A. Jack Valenti, the long-time CEO of the Motion Picture Association of America — the fellow Robin Williams referred to as "the man you never heard of, but you have to listen to him anyway" — made a surprise appearance at the Independent Spirit Awards and jokingly handcuffed John Waters, who claimed to have lost a screening cassette. Valenti had spearheaded a campaign to ban screeners as a way to combat film piracy.

"When they called me, I said, 'Sure, whatever you want me to do.' I want to continue my rapport with the independents," said Valenti, who would retire from the MPAA later that year. "Handcuffing John Waters was their idea. It turned out to be a highlight. When I came out on the stage I saw Tom Cruise looking at me kind of funny, and then when I handcuffed Waters, [Tom's] jaw dropped. He was just totally surprised. But I'm not going to make acting my full-time job, I want you to know that."

Q Who was the only entrant at the 1990 Academy Awards ceremony who was not required to walk through a metal detector?

A The March 25, 1991, Oscar ceremony happened just five days after the ceasefire in the Persian Gulf and security was tight everywhere — particularly at high-profile events. The stars attending the awards that night were not exempt from security, and guests had to go through metal detectors and have their handbags searched. Everyone was checked, except for one: Hollywood legend Bob Hope, then eighty-seven years old, who was considered a safe enough bet to allow through unchecked.

Q What melee marred the January 22, 1954, Golden Globes ceremony?

A The 1954 Golden Globes ceremony turned into a punch-up when there was a shortage of seating for all the invited guests. For the first time ever the Hollywood Foreign Correspondents Association and the rival Foreign Press Association of Hollywood merged and presented one set of awards. Unfortunately, there weren't enough seats in the Club Del Mar for the members of both groups. As host Walter Pidgeon watched helplessly from the stage, *Variety* reported, "some left in a huff and a few in Cadillacs. Of those who stayed, the monocled Scandinavian twin correspondents, Gustaf and Bertil Unger, were the most noticeable. They exchanged blows with another set of twins. The Unger twins were distinguished by the fact that one wears a monocle in the right eye and the other wears a monocle in the left eye. When they departed at the end of the evening, one of them also was sporting a black eye."

The trade magazine also noted that "folk balladeer Burl Ives and thesp Gilbert Roland acted as peacemakers so the program could proceed on schedule."

Who did Dustin Hoffman call "a prick" while accepting a 2003 Empire Lifetime Achievement Award?

Four Weddings and a Funeral star Hugh Grant, who once said, "I think film acting's just a miserable experience. It's so long and so boring and so difficult to get right so that what you need above all is incredible willpower and strength of mind."

Dustin Hoffman caused a stir while accepting *Empire Magazine*'s 2003 Lifetime Achievement Award at the Dorchester Hotel in London. In a speech that rambled for nearly half an hour, Hoffman admitted that he'd never heard of the magazine, and when he heard that he'd got an Empire Lifetime Achievement Award he thought the British Empire was honouring him.

He made headlines, though, when halfway through his acceptance speech, fellow nominee Hugh Grant appeared to stifle a yawn. Hoffman turned to him and said, completely deadpan, "Yeah, he really is a prick." A dumbstruck Grant stared back, rubbing his eyes as if in disbelief. The next day Hoffman's spokesperson told the *New York Daily News* that he "was joking."

Q Which 1956 dialogueless film won a Best Screenplay Oscar?

A The thirty-four-minute dialogue-free *Le Ballon Rouge* (*The Red Balloon*) won the Best Original Screenplay Oscar on March 27, 1957. Albert Lamorisse's story of a young boy who keeps a red balloon as a pet beat out a distinguished list of nominees, including *The Bold and the Brave*, *Julie*, *La Strada*, and *The Lady Killers*.

Q Who said in 1970, "How in the hell would you like to have been in this business as long as I and then have one of your kids win an Oscar before you did?"

A Although Henry Fonda was a Hollywood legend, his track record at the Academy Awards was not good. By 1970 Fonda had been making movies for thirty-five years and had been nominated for only one acting Oscar — and that was in 1940 for *The Grapes of Wrath*. When his son, Peter, was nominated for Writing (Story and Screenplay Based on Material Not Previously Published or Produced) for *Easy Rider*, the elder Fonda vented his frustration to the press.

Peter didn't win the Oscar that year — *Butch Cassidy and the Sundance Kid* took home the gold — but another Fonda, Jane, beat her dad to the winner's podium, taking Best Actress in 1972 for *Klute*.

Q How did Oscar-winning screenwriter Frances Marion describe the Oscar statuette?

A Marion, writer of the screenplays for *The Big House* and *The Champ* and the first female to win an Academy Award for Best Original Screenplay, thought the Oscar statue was the perfect symbol of the film business, as it was a "powerful athletic body clutching a gleaming sword with half of his head — the part which held his brains — completely sliced off."

Q Which movie grossed more at the box office in 2004: Best Picture Oscar winner *Million Dollar Baby* or the Wayans Brothers comedy *White Chicks*?

A February 2005 Oscar host Chris Rock made the point that Oscar is out of touch with the movie-going public when, in a pre-recorded bit, he visited the Magic Johnson Theatre in South Central Los Angeles and asked ordinary people if they had seen any of the Oscar-nominated movies. Moviegoers mentioned *Alien vs. Predator*, *Saw*, *Chronicles of Riddick*, and *White Chicks* as their favourites, but hadn't seen any of the Best Picture nominees.

"I thought it was hilarious what Chris did," said *White Chicks* director Keenen Ivory Wayans. "I enjoyed having our movie represented on the Oscars, even in fun."

The Oscar-nominated films of 2005 — *Finding Neverland, Million Dollar Baby, Sideways, The Aviator*, and *Ray* — didn't burn up the box office. In fact, the gross of the previous year's Best Picture winner, *The Lord of the Rings: The Return of the King*, earned $364,115,612 through Oscar weekend in 2004, eclipsing the $344,807,085 total gross of all 2005 Best Picture nominees, while the critically maligned *White Chicks* — about two African-American FBI agents who pose as Caucasian socialites — took in almost $5 million more at the box office than the Oscar champ *Million Dollar Baby*.

Q George C. Scott was the first actor to refuse an Oscar, but who was the first non-performer to reject the award?

A Former New York newspaperman Dudley Nichols, the winner of Best Screenplay for *The Informer* in 1935, was the first person to decline an Oscar. He had resigned from the Academy in 1933 during a labour crisis and refused to accept his award because of the enmity between several industry guilds and AMPAS over union matters. As the president of the

Screen Writers Guild he felt that to accept the Oscar "would be to turn my back on nearly a thousand members of the Writers Guild."

Nichols would be nominated three more times — for *The Long Voyage Home* in 1940, *Air Force* in 1943, and *The Tin Star* in 1957 — and continue to write, direct, and produce films until the 1960s.

Which two award-winning films tied for the top prize at the 2004 Scripter Awards?

Mystic River and *Seabiscuit* were declared equal winners at the 2004 Scripter Awards. Established in 1988, the University of Southern California Scripter Award is bestowed annually by the Friends of the USC Libraries in recognition of the best film adaptation of a book or novella and is given to both the author and screenwriter.

The two films tied for the Best Movie Adaptation of a Book honour, and judges decided there must be one out-and-out winner. When a rematch failed to put one film ahead of the other, judges declared a tie. The award was presented to *Mystic River* screenwriter Brian Helgeland and author Dennis Lehane and *Seabiscuit* screenwriter Gary Ross and author Laura Hillenbrand.

Why was the controversial documentary *Fahrenheit 9/11* almost disqualified for consideration at the 2005 Academy Awards?

Michael Moore's anti–George Bush documentary *Fahrenheit 9/11* was almost banned from the Oscars in 2004 because a pirated version of the film aired on Cuban television. According to the Oscar rulebook, documentary films are ineligible for nominations if they are shown on TV or the Internet within nine months of release. The film's distributor had to convince the Academy that the airing was not authorized before the documentary could be considered for Oscar inclusion. "If somebody steals your movie and puts it on TV," said AMPAS spokesperson John Pavlik, "we're not going to penalize you for it."

Hollyweird: The Good, the Bad, and the Strange

Q Which former home of the Academy Awards had an underground tunnel to secret celebrities out of the building?

The famous sign at Mann's Chinese on Hollywood Boulevard.

A For three years — 1944, 1945, and 1946 — the Oscar ceremony was held at Sid Grauman's movie palace the Chinese Theatre — an unusual version of a classical Chinese temple, complete with quasi-Chinese motifs and inverted dragon tails — on Hollywood Boulevard. Celebrities could be seen entering the building via the red carpet but not exiting. Instead they escaped through an underground tunnel that led across the street to the Roosevelt Hotel — Sid Grauman also had an interest in the hotel. That way, celebrities could leave anonymously. Use of the tunnel was discontinued in the early 1970s, and in 2001 access to it from either end was sealed up when the subway was built under Hollywood Boulevard.

Q Why did the New York Film Critics Circle amend its "newspaper writers only" rule in 1962?

Membership in the NYFCC — which over the years has varied from eleven to thirty-one people and includes alumni like Pauline Kael, Judith Crist, Renata Adler, and Frank Rich — was once limited to critics published in daily New York newspapers, but the Big Apple's newspaper strike in 1962 crippled the industry and forced the group to extend its reach to include magazines or face extinction. By the end of the 1960s, critics writing for national magazines like *Newsweek*, *Playboy*, *The Saturday Review*, and *TV Guide* were members. In 1987, when *Time* critic Richard Schickel moved to Los Angeles, the association stretched itself geographically, to the point that the group now has members on both coasts.

Which two films hold the record for receiving the most Golden Globe nominations without winning a single award?

Who's Afraid of Virginia Woolf? (1966) and *The Godfather, Part III* (1990) scored the biggest Golden Globe shutouts with seven nominations each but no awards.

Which Disney film was given a special Golden Globe six years after its initial release?

In 1948, the Hollywood Foreign Press Association gave Walt Disney a Special Achievement Golden Globe for the Hindustani version of *Bambi*. Disney was cited for "furthering the influence of the screen."

Besides Best Actor and Best Supporting Actor, what are the two Oscar categories that no woman has ever won?

Two technical categories have never been won by a woman: Best Cinematography and Best Sound.

Hollyweird: The Good, the Bad, and the Strange

Q How many times during the twentieth century were the Academy Awards delayed or postponed?

A The Oscar ceremony has been delayed on only three occasions: for two weeks in 1938 because of floods; for two days in 1968 because of the assassination of Martin Luther King Jr.; and for twenty-four hours in 1981 because of the attempted assassination of President Ronald Reagan.

Q The New York Film Critics Circle has voted unanimously for an award winner only twice in its seventy-year history. Which awards were they?

A The only two winners to earn a unanimous victory from the members of the New York Film Critics Circle are *The Informer*, which won Best Picture in 1935, and Olivia de Havilland, who won the Best Actress award for *The Snake Pit* in 1948.

Q What is the most nominated film at the Independent Spirit Awards?

A Gus Van Sant's *Drugstore Cowboy* holds the record for most nominations at the Independent Spirit Awards, with a total of eight. The drug-fuelled road movie took home four awards — Best Cinematography for Robert D. Yeoman, Best Male Lead for Matt Dillon, Best Supporting Male for Max Perlich, and Best Screenplay for Gus Van Sant and Daniel Yost.

The all-time undefeated Independent Spirit champ is *Fargo*, which took in six awards from six nominations. Accepting the Best Picture award, producer Ethan Coen said, "Thanks. We deserve it."

Q Whose Best Supporting Oscar was stolen after it was sent out for cleaning?

A In 2002 Whoopi Goldberg's Best Supporting Actress Oscar for 1990's *Ghost* was stolen after it was sent out for cleaning. Goldberg had returned the statue to AMPAS, which sent it to the manufacturer for cleaning and replating.

The Academy packed up the Oscar and shipped it by United Parcel Service, but the box was empty when it arrived at R.S. Owens Co. of Chicago, the company that makes the statues.

A thief had opened the package, removed the Oscar, and then resealed the box. UPS officials reported that a security guard at the Ontario, California, airport found the Oscar in a trash bin.

UPS returned the Oscar to the Academy, which planned to send it back to Goldberg, who has discarded plans to have it cleaned in the future. "Polished or unpolished, the Oscar will never leave my house again," she said in a statement.

Q What was the first film to win all of the top five Golden Globe categories?

A *One Flew Over the Cuckoo's Nest* (1976) was the first film to win Globes in all five major categories: Best Drama Picture, Best Actor in a Drama for Jack Nicholson, Best Actress in a Drama for Louise Fletcher, Best Director for Milos Forman, and Best Screenplay for Laurence Hauben and Bo Goldman. Brad Dourif also won an award for Best Movie Debut, but that accolade is not included in the movie's tally.

Q How many films have achieved Oscar nominations in all four acting categories?

A Each of the following thirteen films had Oscar nominations in all four acting categories: *My Man Godfrey* (1936), *Mrs. Miniver* (1942), *For Whom the Bell Tolls* (1943), *Johnny Belinda* (1948), *Sunset Boulevard* (1950), *A Streetcar Named Desire* (1951), *From Here to Eternity* (1953), *Who's Afraid of Virginia Woolf?* (1966), *Guess Who's Coming to Dinner?* (1967), *Bonnie and Clyde* (1967), *Network* (1976), *Coming Home* (1978) and *Reds* (1981).

Q What is the only film in Academy Award history to be nominated in every eligible category?

Hollyweird: The Good, the Bad, and the Strange

A *Who's Afraid of Virginia Woolf* (1966) is the only film in Academy history to be nominated in every eligible category: Picture, Actor, Actress, Supporting Actor, Supporting Actress, Director, Writing (Adapted Screenplay), Art Direction (Black and White), Cinematography (Black and White), Sound, Costume Design (Black and White), Music (Original Score), and Film Editing.

Q Why was *Snow White and the Seven Dwarfs* awarded a special Oscar on February 23, 1939?

A *Snow White and the Seven Dwarfs* was not eligible for Best Picture — no animated films were allowed to compete — and it didn't fit in any other category, so the Academy gave Walt Disney a special award. The unique prize — a full-size Oscar flanked by seven miniature clones — was given in recognition of the film as "a significant screen innovation which has charmed millions and pioneered a great new field of entertainment field for the motion picture cartoon."

On hand to present the award to Disney was miniature megastar Shirley Temple.

"I'm so proud of it I could burst," said Disney.

"Oh, don't do that, Mr. Disney," ad libbed Temple to the delight of the audience.

Q Which voting body handed out an award for Best Film Promoting International Good Will?

A The Hollywood Foreign Press Association used to award a Golden Globe to the Best Film Promoting International Good Will. The first film to be so honoured was an eleven-minute short called *The House I Live In*, starring Frank Sinatra.

Sinatra, as himself, encounters a group of toughs who are bullying a young man because they don't like his religion. Sinatra talks to the boys and, through examples and reason, offers a lesson in tolerance.

The short also took home an honorary Oscar for Tolerance Short Subject.

Q Which Oscar winner also won the Best Use of Makeup to Uglify Rather than Beautify award at the 7th Annual Skinnies Awards?

A Once a year Dr. Vail Reese, a San Francisco–based dermatologist and film buff, awards the Skinnies to actors and their skin conditions. "It's something I started a few years ago," he explains, "as a tongue-in-cheek method of showing people the way skin conditions are used in movies, and to remind people that celebrities like Cameron Diaz — even though we tend to think of them as physically perfect — actually have skin like the rest of us. Truth is, that image of Cameron Diaz is not reality. It's an airbrushed fantasy. Cameron Diaz actually has very severe adult acne."

In 2004 Charlize Theron was honoured for Best Use of Makeup to Uglify Rather than Beautify for her role in *Monster*. Past winners include the "dark spot on Sean Penn's neck in *Mystic River*," which took home the Most Distracting Lesion award and "Demi Moore's stretch marks" which were honoured with a Best Hidden Comeback prize. For complete details on skin flicks — or rather, the skin in flicks — see Dr. Reese's website at Skinema.com.

Q Who accepted his Independent Spirit Award with the words, "This makes up for every chick who ever told me I had a small dick"?

A The often outrageous director Kevin Smith accepted his Best Screenplay Independent Spirit Award for *Chasing Amy* with the words, "This makes up for every chick who ever told me I had a small dick."

The Generation X romantic comedy *Chasing Amy* was the third installment in writer/director Smith's New Jersey trilogy, which began with the Sundance and Cannes Film Festival award–winning *Clerks* and the so-so *Mallrats*. Produced independently by Smith's View Askew Productions for $250,000, *Chasing Amy* introduces Holden (Ben Affleck) and Banky (Jason Lee), creators of the cult hit comic book *Bluntman and Chronic*. Things become complicated when Holden meets cute comic book creator Alyssa (Joey Lauren Adams) and must deal with her complex sexual history as well as Banky's enraged response to the affair.

Hollyweird: The Good, the Bad, and the Strange

Q Which association has taken flak over the years because of the cash bar at its awards ceremony?

A Since 1975 the Los Angeles Film Critics Association — made up of Los Angeles–based professional film critics working in print and electronic media — have hosted a yearly awards ceremony that, unlike any other, features a cash bar. In 1998, after Bill Murray accepted the Best Supporting Actor award for his role in *Rushmore*, he reached into his wallet and left a hundred-dollar bill on the podium, telling the group they could put it toward having an open bar the next year.

When Russell Crowe took home Best Actor in the 1999 race for *The Insider*, he couldn't help but chide the group. Having just arrived from Australia, he said, "It's bloody lovely to come all the way over here to a function with a cash bar."

Q Which blonde and buxom sex kitten stood in for an absent Pierre Boulle when he won the Oscar for Best Screenplay for 1957's *The Bridge on the River Kwai*, accepting the award with the words, "This is the closest I'll ever get to one of these"?

A It was no secret in Hollywood that the screenplay for the wartime drama *The Bridge on the River Kwai* was written by Michael Wilson and Carl Foreman, two blacklisted writers with suspected Communist ties. Columbia Pictures, however, afraid of upsetting the House Un-American Activities Committee, kept their names off the movie, instead crediting Pierre Boulle, the author of the original French novel.

Boulle publicly acknowledged that he didn't write the screenplay — he didn't speak English — and refused to show up at the Oscar ceremony. The studio sent Kim Novak — who isn't in the movie — to accept the award in his absence.

"This is the closest I'll ever come to one of these," said the sultry star of *The Amorous Adventures of Moll Flanders*.

In 1984 the Academy retrospectively awarded the Oscar to Wilson and Foreman. Wilson did not live to see this; Foreman died the day after it was announced. Later, when the film was restored, their names were added to the credits.

Q Who used a pseudonym to pen the 1984 Best Writing (Adapted Screenplay) Oscar nominee *Greystoke, The Legend of Tarzan, King of the Apes*?

A Robert Towne, the legendary scriptwriter responsible for the *Chinatown*, *Shampoo*, and *Marathon Man* screenplays, to name just a few classics, used the name of his sheepdog, P.H. Vazak, as his credit on *Greystoke* because he was displeased with the finished film. He lost the award that year to Peter Shaffer for *Amadeus*.

Q What prompted Rita Moreno to throw her shoe at Jack Nicholson at the 1997 National Board of Review Awards ceremony?

A Bad boy Jack Nicholson started his National Board of Review Best Actor acceptance speech for *As Good as It Gets* by complaining that he was bored of the staid proceedings. He then tried to spice things up by launching into a raunchy story about oral sex. Presenter Rita Moreno's efforts to shut him up only spurred him on to remind everyone that Moreno had once played a hooker who was forced to service him several times in the movie *Carnal Knowledge*.

He continued in that vein, which, according to the *New York Daily News*, "provoked Moreno to go into spitfire mode and hurl a thick red binder of introductory remarks at the actor's skull. Nicholson was shaking off that missile when he was struck by Moreno's shoe."

Q Which legendary party-boy said he might show up drunk to pick up his Oscar — if only the Academy would ever nominate him?

A John Barrymore was the only one of the three Barrymore siblings — John, Ethel, and Lionel — never to be nominated for an Academy

Award. He was considered to be the most talented of the three, but his wild reputation might have worked against him with the Academy. "This town is filled with hypocritical old biddies who are afraid that if I win, I'll show up drunk to accept it," he said. "And I just might."

Barrymore was an unrepentant sot — often arrested and locked up for vagrancy, specifically for being drunk and going through his rich neighbour's trash cans to find scraps for his pet buzzard — who drank himself into an early grave. Near the end of his life, when a doctor suggested that he abandon "wine, women and song," he asked if he had to quit everything at once. "No, you can taper off," the doctor said. "Then I shall quit singing," said Barrymore.

Q Why did Oscarcast producer Allan Carr say he didn't think he'd care for Best Picture winner *The Deer Hunter*?

A "It's two things I didn't care about: Vietnam and poor people," said manager/producer Carr of *The Deer Hunter*, director Michael Cimino's three-hour look at a group of Pennsylvania steelworkers sent off to war.

Q Who was recruited to fill in at the last minute when guest host Charlton Heston was late for the 45th Annual Academy Awards?

A On March 27, 1973, four people were scheduled to host the Academy Awards — Carol Burnett, Michael Caine, Rock Hudson, and Charlton Heston — trouble was, with just minutes to air Heston was nowhere to be found.

Producer Howard Koch spotted Clint Eastwood in the front row and asked him to sub for the tardy actor.

He agreed and began the show by explaining to the audience that he was a last-minute replacement because one of the hosts was late. "So, who did they get?" he asked rhetorically. "A guy who hasn't said three lines in 12 movies."

Heston, who had gotten a flat tire on the way to the show, arrived a few minutes later and took over from the taciturn Eastwood.

Q: Who disrupted the January 12, 1991, New York Film Critics Circle Awards ceremony?

A: The January 12, 1991, New York Film Critics Circle Awards ceremony at the Pegasus Room in Rockefeller Center was infiltrated by nine members of a gay activist group. According to *The Village Voice*, the uninvited guests "ingeniously dressed in tuxes and passed out angry leaflets." The group's ire was directed at the nominations for *The Silence of the Lambs,* a film they claimed fed "the myth that drag queens, since they wear dresses, must be sick."

The pamphleteers made a hasty exit and no arrests were made. Later, *Lambs* director Jonathan Demme expressed admiration for the gate-crashers. "I thought that was exceptionally gracefully achieved," he said.

The Silence of the Lambs went on to win four awards that night — Best Picture, Best Director, Best Actor for Anthony Hopkins, and Best Actress for Jody Foster — the first time in the group's fifty-six-year history that one movie swept the major awards.

Q: Which was the longest Oscar ceremony in history?

A: The 74th Annual Academy Awards, honouring the films of 2001, was a record-breaker, running a mind-numbing four hours and eighteen minutes. Johnny Carson's joke from years before that the Oscars were "two hours of sparkling entertainment spread over four hours" seemed very appropriate that night.

Prior to that marathon show, the 1999 telecast ran four hours and eight minutes, one of only three to run past four hours. In her closing monologue that night, host Whoopi Goldberg joked that while they did the show, "another century went by." The 1998 telecast ran four hours and two minutes.

Q: In 2000 how many Oscars were stolen en route from the manufacturer in Chicago to Los Angeles?

The oversized Oscars used to dress the set at the 77th Annual Academy Awards ceremony waiting to be loaded into storage until the following year. In 2000 52 Oscars statuettes were stolen, only to be found later in a dumpster.

Photo by Richard Crouse

On March 10, 2000, six cases, weighing 470 pounds and containing fifty-five Oscars, mysteriously vanished while they were being shipped from Chicago to the organizers of the show in Los Angeles. Nine days later, fifty-two of the stolen statuettes were discovered next to a dumpster in the Koreatown section of Los Angeles.

Willie Fullgear told CBS TV that he found the Oscars still wrapped in plastic and in individual white boxes.

"I found a lot of white stuff out there which were a lot of Styrofoam boxes and I picked one up and busted it open — Oscar!" Mr. Fullgear said.

The trophy disappearance was the second snafu to strike in 2000. Earlier that month, sacks containing four thousand nomination ballots were misrouted after delivery to the Beverly Hills branch of the United

States Postal Service. The Academy was forced to print and mail new ones and extend the deadline for returning the ballots from March 21 to March 23.

Academy president Bob Rehme said, "Well, it's certainly been an interesting year, or at least an interesting last few weeks in which the focus in Hollywood shifted from who in the world's going to win the least predictable year in memory to what in the world are we going to present them with?"

During the Oscarcast that year host Billy Crystal made numerous jokes about the theft of the Oscar statues and loss of the ballots, including the suggestion that presenter Erykah Badu had concealed one of the statues in her oversized hat. "Who's in charge of security?" he joked. "Probably the same guys who protected Sonny Corleone at the tollbooth."

When the camera focussed on Fullgear, Crystal said, "Willie got $50,000 for finding the fifty-two Oscars. Not a lot of money, when you realize that Miramax and Dreamworks are spending millions just to get one."

Which of the Baldwin brothers was nominated for an Academy Award and a Golden Raspberry in the same year?

In the 2004 awards season Alec Baldwin, the oldest and least embarrassing of the Baldwin acting clan, was nominated for, but lost, a Best Supporting Oscar for his work in *The Cooler* and a Worst Supporting Actor Razzie dishonour for *The Cat in the Hat*, which one critic called "82 of the most wretched minutes ever imprinted on celluloid."

Who accepted the 2000 Golden Raspberry Awards for the film *Wild, Wild West*?

According to "Ye Olde Head Razzberry" John J.B. Wilson, Bob Conrad, the former star of the television series *Wild, Wild West*, offered to collect any dishonours the film picked up at the Razzies.

In a press release Wilson described the phone call from the star. "'This is Bob. Bob Conrad. I'd love to accept the Razzies if *Wild, Wild West* wins any.' Well, ya coulda knocked us over with a feather! Of course, we said 'YES!'"

The feud between Conrad and the film, which was based on his sci-fi western series, which ran from 1965 to 1969, stems from an offer made by director Barry Sonnenfeld. Apparently Conrad was approached by the director to make a cameo appearance in the film as President Ulysses Simpson Grant but turned down the role, citing poor writing and lack of respect for the original series it was based on.

Conrad then became very public about his disdain for the film, and critical reaction proved him right — Roger Ebert likened the movie to "watching money burn on the screen."

On the night of the awards *Wild, Wild West* cleaned up, taking home five Razzies — Worst Picture of 1999, Worst Director of 1999 for "Berry" Sonnenfeld, Worst Screenplay of 1999, Worst "Original" Song of 1999, and Worst Screen Couple of 1999 for Kevin Kline and Will Smith.

Conrad took the stage three times to accept awards on behalf of the film. "And we couldn't have found a Better Bitter Banterer if we'd cast it ourselves," said Wilson. "Funny, self-deprecating and superbly snide, Conrad's three speeches are all howlers."

Accepting for Worst Picture, Conrad said sarcastically, "I can't tell you how happy this makes me."

Which fictional character was nominated for a Golden Globe and an Academy Award in 2003?

Donald Kaufman, the fictitious twin brother of real-life screenwriter Charlie Kaufman, was given a screenwriting credit on the film *Adaptation* and was also nominated for Golden Globe and Oscar screenwriting awards. This is the first time in Oscar history that a nomination has been bestowed upon a fictional character.

Adaptation didn't win either the Globe or the Oscar, but the Academy made it known that, in the event of a win, the two brothers would have to share one statue. The make-believe brothers did, however, share screenwriting prizes at the BAFTAS, the Boston Society of Film Critics Awards, the Golden Satellite Awards, and the New York Film Critics Circle Awards.

Q What 1981 award is generally acknowledged as the lowest point in the history of the Golden Globes?

A The documentary *The Golden Globes: Hollywood's Dirty Little Secret* points to Pia Zadora's Newcomer of the Year award in 1981 as the darkest stain on the reputation of the Golden Globes. She won for her performance in the bomb *Butterfly*, prevailing over Kathleen Turner for *Body Heat* and Elizabeth McGovern for *Ragtime*.

Now, mistakes happen, but this award was tainted when it was revealed that Zadora's husband, billionaire Meshulam Riklis, had flown the voting members of the HFPA to Las Vegas and entertained them at his hotel-casino in an attempt to "buy" the award.

There had always been rumblings that the association's members were at times more influenced by the perks they receive than the quality of the work they are appraising. In 1975 several members even admitted that they "always remember which studios are extra nice to us," but the Zadora gaffe was pushing the limits of credulity.

Zadoragate seriously damaged the reputation and credibility of the Golden Globes; in fact, the awards ceremony wasn't even broadcast on television for fourteen years, from the post-Pia show in 1982 to 1996. Since then the group has worked to clean up its act, hiring a leading accounting firm to supervise the voting and refusing excessive favours from the studios and artists.

In hindsight it almost seems like much ado about nothing. These days Pia Zadora is better remembered as the person who bought and demolished Mary Pickford's legendary Pickfair mansion than as a performer, but in 1981 she had some heat to her career. *Playboy* labelled her "Zadorable," and *Variety* raved about "her little girl looks and Lolita sensuality." Her albums did well on the charts and she was even nominated for a Grammy (for Female Rock Performance) for the tune "Rock It Out." The Golden Globes fiasco tarnished the shine not only of the awards but also of Zadora's career. She became an industry joke and went into semi-retirement in the late eighties.

Q Which reality television star literally made a splash at the pre-Oscar bash for *The Lord of the Rings: The Return of the King*?

A Hotel heiress and *Simple Life* star Paris Hilton had her spirits dampened when she gatecrashed the *Lord of the Rings: The Return of the King* pre-Academy Awards dinner in 2004 and blundered into a wading pool.

Hilton screamed, "Oh my God," as she splashed into a Japanese pool carpeted in rose blossoms at New Line Cinema boss Bob Shaye's ultra-modern estate in Beverly Hills. After climbing out of the pond, Hilton whined, "God, I didn't see the pool. Why does he have a pool there? At least I didn't go in the big pool." She was then overheard telling her sister Nicky on her rhinestone-encrusted cellphone, "Guess what? I just fell into a little pond! It's soooo embarrassing."

The socialite — who achieved notoriety when a videotape of her having sex with former boyfriend Rick Solomon surfaced on the Internet — didn't soak her swanky ball gown but did get her Louis Vuitton shoes wet. As she bent over to dry her silver stilettos, she was heard to say, "Oh, my new Vuitton shoes! Well, at least they're clean now."

"Now I can say I know literally two things about Paris Hilton," said partygoer Andy Serkis. "She's some sort of reality television star in America, and she splashed in the water over there."

"If you were to think of it in the terms of Freudian psychiatry," said Peter Jackson, "you would look at the size and the shape of Paris' puddle and try and decipher their larger meaning. You would show the puddle to people and ask them to tell you what it means — just like an ink-blot test."

Another anonymous guest was reported to have joked, "I guess she just likes to be wet."

The party's host was baffled by Hilton's presence. "She wasn't even invited," he said.

Q Which classic musical — and winner of the 1940 Best Music Oscar — was allegedly the inspiration for Pink Floyd's *The Dark Side of the Moon*?

A The almost perfect synchronization of *The Dark Side of the Moon* album and the movie *The Wizard of Oz* is just a really weird coincidence. The deal is that if you start the album just as the MGM lion roars for the third time the music seems to fit the story. If you do it right, during "Time" Dorothy starts to jog at the line "no one told you when to run." When Dorothy leaves the fortune teller to go back to her farm, the album is playing "home, home again." "The Great Gig in the Sky" matches up to the tornado sequence. "Money" begins just as the film switches from black and white to colour. Glinda, the sweet Good Witch of the North, appears in her bubble just as the band sings "Don't give me that do goody good bullshit." The Good Witch confronts the Wicked Witch as Gilmour sings "And who knows which is which." The song "Brain Damage" starts at almost the same time as the scarecrow launches into "If I Only Had a Brain," and as Dorothy listens to the Tin Man's chest we hear the heartbeat at the end of the album.

As cool as it may be, the band denies any connection between the two. "Some guy with too much time on his hands had come up with this idea of combining *Wizard of Oz* with *Dark Side of the Moon*," says guitarist David Gilmour. Album engineer Alan Parsons has a less terse answer. "We didn't talk at all about the *Wizard of Oz* during the recording of the album," he said. "There simply wasn't mechanics to do it. We had no means of playing videotapes in the room at all. I don't think VHS had come along by '72, had it?"

Q How many performers from the 1989 Oscarcast "stars of tomorrow" musical number actually went on to win Academy Awards?

A On the same show that featured the now legendarily horrible "Snow White" opening number, producer Alan Carr also assembled a group of twenty up-and-comers to sing a tribute to Oscar called "I Wanna Be an Oscar Winner." The fifteen-minute production number featured Corey Feldman doing a Michael Jackson impersonation; Chad Lowe, whose brother Rob had humiliated himself earlier in the night "singing" a duet with Snow White, crooned the line, "I'm a thespian in the classic sense"; while Tyrone Power Jr. performed sword fight with Christian Slater. Other youngsters forced to sing inane lyrics about becoming a "super-trouper, super-duper Oscar winner" included Savion Glover, Carrie Hamilton, Blair Underwood, Tracey Edwards, Melora Hardin, Matt Lattanzi, Holly Robinson, Joey Fisher, Keith Coogan, Corey Parker, Patrick O'Neal, Tricia Leigh Fisher, Tracy Nelson, Ricki Lake, and D.D. Pawley, none of whom have been invited back to pick up an award.

Why did author and comedian Scott Kerman sue AMPAS in 1998?

Scott Kerman, author of *No Ticket? No Problem! How to Sneak into Sporting Events and Concerts*, was busted the day before the 1997 Oscars for trespassing at the Shrine Auditorium. A so-called expert on how to steal into events of all kinds, Kerman made it known prior to the 1997 Academy Awards that he submitted several of his home movies to the Academy for Oscar consideration, and although he received no response, he decided to crash the ceremony anyway. When he was caught and arrested, he sued the Academy and a number of its representatives, charging that the organization had embarrassed him.

Two and a half years and tens of thousands of dollars of legal fees later, the courts ruled that the Academy's actions were thoroughly within its rights. On each of Kerman's charges the court found for the defendants.

"Kerman is now personally liable for everybody's court costs," said David Quinto of the Academy's legal firm, Quinn Emanuel Urquhart Oliver & Hedges. "That's $20,000 for the Academy alone."

In his book Kerman claimed to have "snuck into over 300 concerts and sporting events" as well as the 1996 Academy Awards. In testimony, however, he stated that the book was mostly creative writing and that he'd never snuck into any events apart from movies as a child, Quinto reported.

"He had an opportunity to say he wouldn't go anywhere near the event, and he didn't. It's our responsibility to create a safe, secure environment for those who are invited," said Academy spokesman Rick Robertson. "If you're not invited, stay home. It's televised."

Which *Star Wars* character was honoured with a Lifetime Achievement Award at the 1997 MTV Movie Awards?

Chewbacca (Peter Mayhew) was honoured with a Lifetime Achievement Award for his roles in *A New Hope*, *The Empire Strikes Back*, and *Return of the Jedi*. Actor Mayhew, who portrayed the two-hundred-year-old Wookie in the original trilogy, was a hospital attendant in England with only one film to his credit when he took on the role that made him famous.

"The film started a revolution in the film industry. I'm proud of it," says Mayhew. "You look at any movie or history book, it is one of the top 10 movies of the century ... I am Chewie, and people respect me for it ... I will go on and on because nothing can touch it."

What does the Palm Dog Award pay tribute to?

"Dogs are more than indispensable to the big screen," says Toby Rose, a British journalist who created the spoof Palm Dog Award, presented at the Cannes Film Festival each year. "Animals do have key roles but are never in a position to be recognized."

The award identifies the best canine performance of the year as judged by five British and French journalists. Winners receive a black leather Palm Dog collar with gold lettering. Past honourees include the flatulent bulldogs Edgar and Hoover from the Jonathan Nossiter documentary *Mondovino* and the dog that dramatically expires in the Coen brothers film *The Ladykillers*.

Rose cites Lassie and Rin Tin Tin as contenders for the greatest canine performance ever but favours the dog in *As Good As It Gets*. "Helen Hunt and Jack Nicholson were up for Oscars," he says. "The dog never had a chance."

Hollyweird: The Good, the Bad, and the Strange

Q Scientifically speaking, who lives longer, Oscar winners or losers?

A Canadian scientists showed that those who win the golden statue live almost four years longer than those who do not.

While watching the Academy Awards one year University of Toronto epidemiologist Donald Redelmeier noticed how homogeneously healthy the Oscar nominees seemed to be. "The people up on stage didn't look anything like the type of patients I see in the hospital," he said. "It was the way they walked and gestured and talked. They just seemed so much more alive, for lack of a better word."

That observation sparked his interest. Accepted theories indicated that money, social status, and survival were inherently linked, so the doctor asked himself, "Do extra triumphs add years to the lives of already successful people?"

With the help of Sheldon M. Singh, BSc, from the Institute for Clinical Evaluative Sciences, a list of every actor and actress that had been nominated for a leading or supporting role by the Academy was assembled. For each film the nominated actors were in, they picked another non-nominated actor of a similar age to create a total list of 1,649 performers.

The duo then researched the birth and death dates of each actor and actress in the sample (and used a statistical curve to include those who were still alive) and were able to determine that movie stars who have won multiple awards have a survival advantage of 3.9 years. Award winners, on average, lived 79.7 years, while nominees tended to live 76.1 years. Performers who were never recognized by the Academy averaged 75.8 years. Scientifically speaking, the 3.9-year gap is huge. "If you were to cure all cancers in all people in North America for all time," Redelmeier says, "you would add maybe 3.5 years to life expectancy."

In a separate study the researchers discovered that Oscar-winning directors live about two years longer than those who were just nominated, the result of a 24 percent decrease in the risk of death over their lifetimes. Those who won more than once saw their average risk of death decrease 48 percent compared to those with only a single statuette. It was also determined that directors lived 4.5 years longer than actors, while actors who dabbled in directing saw their mortality decrease 34 percent.

The study couldn't definitively determine why an Oscar victory had such a significant effect on lifespan. One study argued that being successful is less stressful and provides a profound boost to health, while another suggested that differences in lifestyle and material wealth could explain the longevity of award winners.

Who was voted the Worst Rock-Star Actor of All Time by the readers of *Blender Magazine* in 2004?

Fresh from her Golden Raspberry win as Worst Actress of the 20th Century, Madonna took top dishonours in *Blender Magazine*'s 25 Worst Rock-Star Actors of all Time poll.

Blender said of the singer, "She is invariably cast as an irresistible femme fatale — yet cannot do sexy. Instead, she adopts the glassy-eyed expression of someone on a cocktail of prescription drugs and delivers her lines as if she were reading aloud from the letters of a stalker."

The Material Girl topped the iconic list of rock legends. At #2 is Bob Dylan for a long list of widely panned performances, culminating with 2003's snorefest *Masked and Anonymous*, about which it was noted that the singer "walks around as if the camera were causing him physical pain"; Mariah Carey's groan-inducing performance in *Glitter* earned her a #3 berth; rocker Jon Bon Jovi rings in at #4; Elvis Presley is at #5; Britney Spears came in at #6 for her work in *Crossroads*, which one reviewer called "so mind-numbingly awful that you hope Britney won't do it one more time, as far as movies are concerned"; in the #7 slot is white rapper Vanilla Ice, whose film debut, 1991's *Cool as Ice*, was a poorly received rap-oriented remake of *Rebel Without a Cause*; at #8 is Neil Diamond, who became the first winner of a Worst Actor Razzie Award for his one and only theatrical film, *The Jazz Singer*; Kiss bassist Gene Simmons ranked ninth based on a string of poor performances, including *KISS Meets the Phantom of the Park*, about which one writer said, "This film is so wonderfully cheesy that the band should've changed their name to KITSCH"; and rounding out the top ten is Master P, basketball player–turned-rapper-turned-actor for a string of performances that suggest he should stick to playing basketball.

Hollyweird: The Good, the Bad, and the Strange

Q In 2005, which Internet muckraker ran a news item with the headline "Host Chris Rock Shock — Only Gays Watch Oscar"?

A Matt Drudge, the webmaster of the Drudge Report, tried to fan the flames of controversy by running a story that claimed 2005 Academy Awards host Chris Rock was tarnishing the reputation of the Academy. In the weeks before he took the stage as MC Rock poked fun at the Oscars.

"Come on, it's a fashion show," the comic said in *Entertainment Weekly*. "What straight black man sits there and watches the Oscars? Show me one. And they don't recognize comedy, and you don't see a lot of black people nominated, so why should I watch it?"

Oscarcast producer Gil Cates defended Rock as Oscar host and put to rest rumors that Academy members wanted Rock to resign, as Drudge had hinted at on his site.

"The Academy is excited about Chris Rock hosting this year's Oscar telecast and looking forward to a very funny evening with him," Cates said in a statement. "Chris's comments over the past few weeks are meant to be humorous digs at a show that some people, obviously including Chris himself, think may be a bit too stuffy."

"The Academy has heard no grumbling from its members and has no intention of even suggesting that Chris step aside," Cates added.

The Gay and Lesbian Alliance Against Defamation also came to Rock's defense, suggesting the Drudge item was trying to make something of nothing.

"Chris Rock isn't making fun of gays — he's poking fun at the Oscars," said GLAAD executive director Joan Garry. "It's shtick."

The *Hollywood Reporter* also weighed in. "It isn't homophobia that's getting [Rock] into trouble but a lack of deference to the event. This is the same problem that got another guy who hangs out in New York, David Letterman, into trouble during his infamous stint at the Oscar helm. He was an outsider who failed to gauge the tolerance a Hollywood crowd would have for a guy poking harmless but pointed fun at their revered institution — and the crowd turned on him."

"The fact that Rock is the best thing that could happen to the way-too-full-of-its-bloated-sense-of-self-importance Academy Awards is undeniable," the *Reporter* wrote.

"He's a pro. He knows how to behave himself. ... I promise that he won't be ruining your precious Oscars. But please don't ask him to be a Boy Scout, either. You can't hire a pit bull and expect a poodle to show up."

Rock has a turbulent history with Drudge. In March 2003, the comedian lambasted the Internet writer for an online report alleging studio bosses at DreamWorks asked Rock to avoid making any comments against President Bush and the war in Iraq before his comedy *Head of State* hit theatres.

At the time, Rock said: "I don't know Matt Drudge, I never met Matt Drudge, but if I see Matt Drudge, I'm going to take my red-blooded American foot and put it up his un-American ass for trying to disrupt the opening of my movie."

How did 2005 Oscarcast host Chris Rock offend presenter Sean Penn?

Chris Rock upset Sean Penn during the 2005 Oscarcast by making a joke about his friend Jude Law. In his opening monologue Rock said that filmmakers should wait for better talent instead of rushing bad movies into theatres.

"Clint Eastwood's a star, OK? Tobey Maguire's just a boy in tights," Rock riffed.

"You want Tom Cruise and all you can get is Jude Law? Wait. You want Russell Crowe and all you can get is Colin Farrell? Wait. *Alexander* is not *Gladiator*.

"You want Denzel [Washington] and all you can get is me? Wait," he joked. "Denzel's a fine actor. He woulda never made *Pootie Tang*."

"Who is Jude Law?" the comedian continued. "Why is he in every movie I have seen the last four years? He's in everything. Even the movies he's not acting in. If you look at the credits, he makes cupcakes, or something."

Later in the show, when Sean Penn took the stage to present the Best Actress Oscar, he asked for the audience's forgiveness for "eschewing" his sense of humour and said that Law was "one of our finest actors." At the time Law and Penn were in production on the film *All the King's Men*, based on the Robert Penn Warren novel about the life of populist

Southerner Willie Stark, a political figure loosely based on Governor Huey Long of Louisiana.

The hot-headed actor then introduced the category by saying, "What Jude and all other talented actors know is that for every great, talented actor, there are five actresses who are nothing short of magic."

Onstage Rock tried to diffuse the situation by telling Penn, "My accountants would like to speak with you" — referring to two burly actors he had on stage with him earlier as part of a gag — while backstage the comic and the actor cleared the air.

"He said 'cause he's working with Jude on a movie right now he felt the need to [stand up for him]. I don't know," Rock said. "It's kinda funny."

"Jude Law probably made a skillion dollars this year," Rock added. "I'd never hit a person that's down."

Which 2004 televised awards show gave a prize to *Bruce Almighty* for Most Divine Miracle in a Movie?

The irreverent MTV Movie Awards: Mexico gave away some very unusual prizes at their second annual ceremony in 2004. Up for Milagro más Divino en una Película, or Most Divine Miracle in a Movie, were Willem Dafoe in *The Last Temptation of Christ* for the water into wine sequence; Jim Caviezel as Jesus in *The Passion of the of Christ* for the scene in which Christ heals Peter's injured ear; and the part in *Bruce Almighty* where Bruce (Jim Carrey) causes Grace's (Jennifer Aniston) chest to grow several cup sizes. Mexican audiences voted, and *Bruce Almighty*'s miracle took the prize.

Other awards were given to Funniest American in Japan (Gringo/a más Gracioso en Japón) — nominees included Tom Cruise in *The Last Samurai* — and Best Colin Farrell in a Movie (Mejor Colin Farrell en una Película) which was given to his performance in *S.W.A.T.*

At the 2005 Oscars who did Adam Sandler say looked "incredibly sexy tonight"?

Courtesy of AMPAS

Academy Awards host Chris Rock and *The Longest Yard* star Adam
Sandler goof around at the 77th Annual ceremony.

In one of the raunchier moments at the 2005 Oscars Adam Sandler
presented the Adapted Screenplay award while fellow *Saturday Night
Live* alumnus and Oscar host Chris Rock stood in for an absent
Catherine Zeta-Jones.

As Sandler took the stage to present the trophy, it was announced that
Catherine Zeta-Jones would be joining him, but the actress was a no-show.

So, in a pre-planned gag, Rock came in from the wings and offered
to read Zeta-Jones's teleprompter lines.

"Catherine," said Sandler, reading from the teleprompter, "may I
just say your dress looks incredibly sexy tonight."

"Why thank you, Adam," Rock replied. "It's Versace."

"Well, with you in it, it should be Ver-sexy," said Sandler.

Continuing to read from the stilted script, Rock teased that Sandler needed a spanking for being so naughty. Sandler responded, "Sign me up, Mrs. Douglas."

Q What was the original name of the Independent Spirit Awards?

A The Findie ("Friends of Independents") Awards were founded in 1984. The statue was a Plexiglas pyramid containing suspended shoestrings representing the paltry budgets of independent films. The Findies were renamed the Independent Spirit Awards in 1986. They usually take place the day before the Oscars.

The Spirit statuette is an abstract of a bird with a strip of film in its talon. Spirit ceremony host Buck Henry noted that the award represents "circumventing the establishment, then choking it to death."

Q How did Robert Opel steal the spotlight from David Niven during the 1974 Oscarcast?

A Robert Opel was an unemployed actor who moonlighted as a professional streaker. For a few dollars he would spice up swinging parties in Beverly Hills by running naked through the homes of the rich and famous. Ann-Margaret's agents had hired him once, although for that run he wasn't exactly nude — he wore a gold lamé cape — and he was later hired by flamboyant producer Allan Carr to streak at a party for dancer Rudolph Nureyev.

On April 2, 1974, he did his highest profile gig. While David Niven was preparing to introduce Elizabeth Taylor, who would then present the Best Actor trophy, Opel ran across the stage, flashing a peace sign and nothing else. "Isn't it fascinating that probably the only laugh that man will ever get is by stripping off his clothes and showing his shortcomings," Niven ad libbed.

Opel got away with baring himself at the Oscars but pushed his luck too far when he streaked in front of the Los Angeles city council and was arrested for public lewdness. He was put on a four-year probation, after which he left L.A. and opened a sex paraphernalia shop called Fey Way in San Francisco. On July 9, 1979, he was gunned down by armed robbers who raided his store, taking his life for five dollars, a used camera, and a backpack.

Q Which Canadian-born comedian swept the 2001 Stinkers Bad Movie Awards?

A The Stinkers Bad Movie Awards have been handed out every year since 1978 by film freaks Mike Lancaster and Ray Wright. There is no ceremony or acceptance speeches, just a website — thestinkers.com — that reflects the founder's low tolerance for crappy movies.

"I just hate that the studios are always lying to us," says Lancaster. "*Gigli* was not the 'romantic comedy of the year,' but they told us it was in that ad campaign. *Pluto Nash* was not, and never will be the 'comedy event of the decade,' but that's how they described it. The studios keep giving us crap, so they deserve all the crap we shoot back at them."

In 2001 Canadian comedian Tom Green and his directorial debut *Freddy Got Fingered* took top honours at the Stinkers, earning Worst Film, Worst Sense of Direction, Worst Performance by an Actor in a Lead Role, Most Painfully Unfunny Comedy, and Worst On-Screen Couple (Tom Green and any person, animal, or foreign object).

Winners are sent a certificate, but so far the only response has been from Tom Green's people. "We got an angry e-mail from Tom Green's manager," Lancaster says. "He didn't think it was very funny — but then, the movie wasn't very funny either."

Q Why did comic Robin Williams run onto the stage at the 2005 Oscars with tape covering his mouth?

A Wildcard actor Robin Williams took the stage at the 2005 Oscarcast to present the award for Best Animated Feature with a large piece of tape covering his mouth to protest the network's censorship of one of his gags.

ABC reportedly refused to allow Williams to sing a song poking fun at a conservative group that had criticized children's cartoon *SpongeBob SquarePants*.

Earlier in the year SpongeBob was among several cartoon characters featured in a video produced by the We Are Family Foundation featuring cartoon characters singing the disco-era song "We Are Family." The video's producers say it was designed to encourage tolerance and diversity, but religious conservatives say it advocates a pro-homosexual agenda.

James Dobson, one of the most vocal critics of the religious conservative group Focus on the Family, complained that the motive for using SpongeBob was "to desensitize very young children to homosexual and bisexual behavior."

Williams wasn't allowed to sing his song, but he did crack wise on the subject. "They tell me now that SpongeBob is gay," he said. "SquarePants is not gay. Tight pants maybe. SpongeBob HotPants? You go, girl!"

Courtesy of AMPAS

Robin Williams on the red carpet at the 77th Annual Academy Awards. During the show he was annoyed when a song he wanted to sing was cut by the show's producers. "For a while you get mad," he said, "then you get over it. They're afraid of saying Olive Oyl is anorexic. It tells you about the state of humor. It's strange to think: how afraid are you? We thought that they got the irony of it. I guess not."

Who invented the term "the Oscar jinx"?

Although some sources list Hollywood columnist Hedda Hopper as the inventor of the "Oscar jinx," it was actually created by gossip rival Louella Parsons. Parsons coined the term to describe the career of the "Viennese Teardrop," Luise Rainer. Rainer, the one-time wife of playwright Clifford Odets and star of *The Great Ziegfeld* and *The Good Earth*, was the first person to win back-to-back Oscars. "For my second and third pictures I won Academy Awards," said Rainer. "Nothing worse could have happened to me."

There are several theories as to why the pixie-faced Rainer's career took a nosedive after winning her second Oscar. Despite being a contract star at MGM, the German-born actress never fit into the studio system. She rejected not only the glitzy image that the studio manufactured for her, preferring a sloppy style of dress to gowns and tailored clothes, but also the advances of studio chief Louis B. Mayer. Rumour has it that when Rainer tried to renegotiate her contract after winning the second Oscar she refused to sit on Mayer's lap. Apparently he was so incensed at her rejection that he personally saw to it that she was never offered another decent role.

A less salacious story cites Academy political intrigue for her post-award blues. Up until the mid-1930s studio heads held sway over the Academy and ultimately had a say in who would take home an award. That changed in 1937, when Academy president Frank Capra tried to democratize the awards and opened the voting to fourteen thousand background players, writers, and movie insiders. For the first time studio heads couldn't directly control the outcome of the awards.

The newfound Academy members voted with their hearts and chose Rainer over the more accomplished actresses Greta Garbo, Irene Dunn, Janet Gaynor, and Barbara Stanwyck. Since MGM had never planned for Rainer to win, they didn't treat her as a winner, and her career withered and died.

Rainer was by no means the first award winner to fall victim to Oscar's fickle finger of fate. Predating Rainer were Mary Pickford and Warner Baxter, who won the Best Actress and Best Actor awards respectively in the 1928–29 contest. Pickford retired a mere three years later for lack of suitable roles, and Baxter watched his career swirl down the toilet after taking home the gold. He suffered a nervous breakdown less than ten years after his win.

In the days since then the jinx has slowed more than a few careers. Dancer-turned-actor George Chakiris won a Best Supporting Actor award for *West Side Story*, only to be doomed to make a series of career-nuking films including *Kings of the Sun*, *Flight from Ashiya*, and *The Bug Cube*.

On March 25, 1985, it appeared that Cambodian physician-turned-actor Haing S. Ngor was at the beginning of a successful career. "This is unbelievable, but so is my entire life," he said when he was awarded the Best Supporting Oscar for his portrayal of photographer Dith Pran in *The Killing Fields*. His story inspired hundreds of inches of column space — he survived torture and imprisonment at the hands of the Khmer Rouge — and was the first non-professional actor to win an Oscar in fifty years. Unfortunately that night was the high-water mark of his career and he spent the next decade taking any work he could find, often playing roles that were unflattering depictions of Asians. Ngor was murdered in Los Angeles in 1996.

Many others have had their careers stalled by an Oscar win — Marisa Tomei, Cuba Gooding Jr., Roberto Benigni, and Mira Sorvino, whose attempt to play Daisy in the television adaptation of *The Great Gatsby* has been called "perhaps the worst post-Oscar performance ever captured on film" by *Film Threat* magazine.

When asked what he would do if he could go back in time and change his Oscar acceptance speech, who said, "I would have pulled out a huge flag with a hammer and sickle on it and started waving it madly, or perhaps I should have leapt into the orchestra pit and slain every one of them in the name of the Lord. Nah, I probably should have just kissed Diane Lane when she handed me the Oscar and got the hell out of there"?

Michael Moore drew both applause and boos when he accepted his Oscar for Best Documentary for *Bowling for Columbine* by lambasting President George Bush.

"I have invited my fellow documentary nominees on the stage with us," he said. "They're here in solidarity with me because we like nonfiction. We like nonfiction and we live in fictitious times. We live in the time where we have fictitious election results that elect a fictitious president. We live in a time where we have a man sending us to war for fictitious reasons. Whether it's the fiction of duct tape or fiction of orange alerts, we are against this war, Mr. Bush. Shame on you, Mr. Bush. Shame on you. And any time you got the Pope and the Dixie Chicks against you, your time is up."

When host Steve Martin took the stage after Moore's speech, he joked, "It was so sweet backstage, you should see it. The teamsters are helping Michael Moore into the trunk of his limo."

Michael Moore later recalled the first words he heard after leaving the stage after collecting his Best Documentary Oscar: "They've got two interns standing there," he said. "The first one is holding a thing of champagne and she goes, 'Champagne?' and the other person says, 'Breath mint?' As an Oscar winner, these are the first two words that you hear. Except I heard a third word. A stagehand came up to me and in my ear, he says, 'Bullshit!' 'Champagne, breath mint, Bullshit!'"

"Last time I was on your show," Moore told *Tonight Show* host Jay Leno a few months later, "this man comes up to me backstage and says, 'I'm the spotlight operator here on alternative weeks and I'm the man who uttered that word in your ear at the Oscars and I just want to say I'm really sorry.' He said, 'It was the first week of the war and you said we were being led to war for fictitious reasons. I couldn't believe that was true.' I said, 'Listen, you didn't do anything wrong. You did something right. You believed your president. You should be able to believe your president. So you don't need to apologize.' So it was a very nice moment."

There were reports in the media that many were incensed by Moore's speech, but the director insists he was sent letters of support by many Hollywood bigwigs.

"Some complained about it on TV — James Woods and others, just horrible, disgusting people," said Moore. "I was glad they didn't like it. I got incredible notes, phone calls, e-mails and letters from Jonathan Demme, Jeff Bridges, Martin Scorsese, Meryl Streep — I could go down a whole list, but I don't know if I should out them. Then, when everyone was saying that any person who criticized America at a time of war would be shunned and boycotted and ignored and vilified, the sales of my books and movies went through the roof."

Q Which sexy 1996 film took home a Golden Raspberry Award as Worst Film of the Decade?

A According to the Golden Raspberries, the worst film of the 1990s was *Striptease*, the Demi Moore movie about a divorced mother who takes a job as a stripper to raise money for a court appeal after losing custody of her daughter to her unscrupulous ex-husband.

Striptease topped many of "worst of" lists in 1996, and in addition to winning six Razzie dishonours, critics also had a field day with it. "The movie is as lifeless as Demi's breasts," wrote one, while another said, "For a movie with more bare breasts than any two tattered issues of *Playboy* and *Hustler*, *Striptease* is the flattest offering of the year."

Other nominees included 1998 five-time Razzie champ *An Alan Smithee Film: Burn, Hollywood, Burn!*; *The Postman*, a five-time winner; *Showgirls*, a seven-time winner in 1995; and *Hudson Hawk*, which won three Razzies in 1991.

Q What was the first film to garner acting Oscar nominations in all four categories?

A 1936's *My Man Godfrey* was not only the first film to earn Academy Award nominations in all four acting categories — William Powell for Best Actor, Carole Lombard for Best Actress, Mischa Auer for Best Supporting Actor, and Alice Brady for Best Supporting Actor — but also the only movie to be nominated for all of the acting categories, as well as Writing and Directing, without being nominated for Best Picture.

Q In 2002 who became the first onscreen talent to show up and collect a Razzie Award in person?

REEL WINNERS

Shock comedian Tom Green was the first performer to attend a Razzie ceremony to collect an award. In 2002 his film *Freddy Got Fingered* was nominated for five Razzies, including Worst Picture. "When we set out to make this film we wanted to win a Razzie, so this is a dream come true for me," Green said at the time. The comedian followed the lead of director Paul Verhoeven, who received in person his award as the filmmaker behind *Showgirls*. The Raspberry Awards have been dishonouring bad films since 1980.

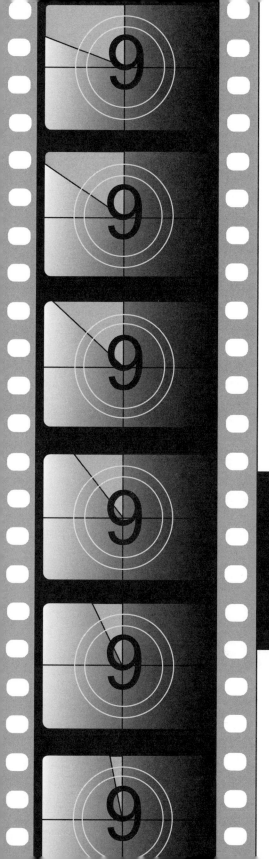

*"Shoot a few scenes out of focus.
I want to win the foreign
film award."*

— Billy Wilder

"I'M KING OF THE WORLD!"

Best Director Trivia

Q Who are the only women nominated for top honours by the Directors Guild of America?

A The only women nominated for top honours by the Directors Guild of America are Lina Wertmuller (real name: Arcangela Felice Assunta Wertmuller von Elgg Spanol von Braucich) for *Seven Beauties* in 1976, Randa Haines for *Children of a Lesser God* in 1986, Barbra Streisand for *The Prince of Tides* in 1991, Jane Campion for *The Piano* in 1993, and Sofia Coppola for *Lost in Translation* in 2003.

Q Why didn't William Wyler pick up his Best Director Oscar for *Mrs. Miniver* in person?

Courtesy of AMPAS

Director William Wyler (seen here with Stephen Boyd on the set of *Ben-Hur*) earned twelve Best Director Oscar nominations but often complained about making movies. "It's a miserable life in Hollywood," he said. "You're up at five or six o'clock in the morning to be ready to start shooting at nine. The working hours aren't arranged to suit the artists and the directors; they're for the convenience of the technicians. If you go to a party at night, you'll never find anyone there who's shooting a picture; they're all home in bed."

A Wyler's wife, Margaret, had to accept his Best Director Oscar in 1942 because he was stationed overseas with the air force. He had enlisted shortly after the completion of *Mrs. Miniver* and was stationed with the Ninety-First Bomber Group near Oxford, England.

The day after the ceremony Wyler received a call from the editor of *Stars and Stripes*, who requested a recent photograph of the director. Wyler didn't have one and wondered out loud why *Stars and Stripes* wanted a photograph of him.

"You won the Academy Award," he explained. "Didn't you hear?"

"No!" Wyler said. "When?"

"Last night in Hollywood," the editor replied, "at the Academy Awards."

Wyler was taken aback. He had been nominated for Best Director every year since 1937 and had dutifully attended the ceremony each year. "I went in with a suitcase to bring home the Oscars and got nothing," he explained. "Now I get one, and I'm not there."

Q Which two directors have won back-to-back Oscars?

A John Ford won back-to-back directing Oscars for *The Grapes of Wrath* and *How Green Was My Valley* in 1940 and 1941 respectively. "I like making pictures but I don't like talking about them," said Ford, explaining why he wasn't on hand to collect his award in 1940.

Joseph Mankiewicz made two consecutive trips to the winner's circle for *A Letter to Three Wives* and *All about Eve* in 1949 and 1950. Actress Ida Lupino presented the director with the first of his two back-to-back prizes. "Thank you, brother Lupino," said the director. "She's listed in the membership list of the Directors Guild as Irving Lupino."

Q Who are Oscar's most honoured film directors?

A William Wyler has twelve nominations for Best Director — the most for any director — with three wins: *Mrs. Miniver* (1942), *The Best Years of Our Lives* (1946), and *Ben-Hur* (1959).

John Ford has won more Academy Awards for directing, taking home four Oscars out of six nominations. Ford was always well known for his Westerns, but amazingly his four directing Oscars came for films that were unlike the films we usually associate with him: *The Informer* (1935), *The Grapes of Wrath* (1940), *How Green Was My Valley* (1941), and *The Quiet Man* (1952).

Who was named Film Icon of the Decade in 2005 at the Empire Awards?

Director Quentin Tarantino was named Film Icon of the Decade at the Empire Awards ceremony in London in March 2005. Tarantino, who helmed *Reservoir Dogs*, *Pulp Fiction*, *Jackie Brown*, and *Kill Bill*, was given the honour after twelve thousand readers of *Empire Magazine* voted in an online poll.

While accepting his award, the maverick announced plans to retire from movie directing in fifteen years to become a movie theatre manager.

"The fact that England has embraced me as one of its own is really cool," Tarantino said. "I hope to give you at least 15 more years of movies, but I'm not going to be this old guy that keeps cranking them out. My plan is to have a theatre by that time in some small town and I will be the manager — this crazy old movie guy. I've made enough money that nobody even needs to show up at the theatre. It's just having something to do."

Who tap-danced as he received his honorary Oscar in 1997?

Legendary director Stanley Donen — best known for his lush musicals — sang and tap-danced part of his acceptance speech for his honorary Oscar. The award paid tribute to Donen's "body of work marked by grace, elegance, wit and visual innovation."

Starting off as a choreographer on Broadway, Donen got into the film business with dancer Gene Kelly, and together they revolutionized the Hollywood musical with such films as *On the Town*, *Love Is Better than Ever*, and *Singin' in the Rain*.

When Martin Scorsese handed Donen the award, the director said, "Marty, it's backwards. I should be giving this to you, believe me."

He went on to thank the board of governors and said, "Tonight words seem inadequate. In musicals that's when we do a song, so…" He then sang a few bars of "Cheek to Cheek," tap-dancing and holding his Oscar to his cheek when he sang the chorus to rafter-shaking applause.

Switching back to his speech he continued, "I'm going to let you in on the secret of being a good director. For the script you get Larry Gelbart or Peter Stone or Huyck and Katz or Frederic Raphael, like that. If it's a musical, for the songs you get George and Ira Gershwin, or Leonard Bernstein and Comden and Green, or Alan Lerner and Fritz Loewe, like that.

"And then you cast Cary Grant or Audrey Hepburn, Fred Astaire, Gene Kelly, Sophia Loren, Richard Burton, Rex Harrison, Gregory Peck, Elizabeth Taylor, Burt Reynolds, Gene Hackman or Frank Sinatra, like that.

"And then the filming starts, you show up, and you stay the hell out of the way. But you've gotta show up, you've gotta show up. Otherwise you can't take the credit and get one of these fellas. Thanks you very much."

Donen's speech was the highlight of the evening. Gene Siskel called it a classic Oscar moment, while *Entertainment Weekly* said it "pointed out the resounding gracelessness of most of his fellow honorees."

Later Donen said, "I didn't want to do something boring and list people. I figured I'd sing and dance, since I've done a little bit of that before."

Who are the only women to be nominated for Best Director Academy Awards?

Lina Wertmuller was nominated in 1976 for the film *Seven Beauties*, Jane Campion got a nod in 1993 for her movie *The Piano*, and Sofia Coppola made the list for 2004's *Lost in Translation*.

Several films directed by women have been up for Best Picture but have failed to earn a Best Director kudo as well — both Randa Haines and Penny Marshall were snubbed for their nominated films, *Children of a Lesser God* and *Awakenings* respectively.

Q What was the first film from a first-time filmmaker to win the Palme d'Or at the Cannes Film Festival?

A Steven Soderbergh's *sex, lies and videotape* — about a young, impotent man whose only physical pleasure comes from watching taped interviews of women talking about their sexual habits — was the surprise hit of 1989 and helped resurrect the independent film movement.

The background story of *sex, lies and videotape* is now part of movie folklore. Writer/director Steven Soderbergh, aged twenty-nine, wrote the screenplay in eight days during a trip to Los Angeles and made the film for a paltry $1.2 million. In 1989 it won the Palme d'Or at the Cannes Film Festival — a first for a debut film — as well as the best actor prize for star James Spader.

Q Which two directors have been nominated more than once in the same year?

A The Actors Branch of the Academy stipulates that an actor may receive only one nomination per year. Not so with the Directors Branch, which allows multiple nominations in a given year. Surprisingly a multiple nomination has only happened twice in the history of the awards. In 1938 Hungarian-born actor-turned-director Michael Curtiz was nominated for two films — *Angels With Dirty Faces* and *You Can't Take It With You*. The two nominations cancelled one another out and he went home empty-handed.

Sixty-two years later Steven Soderbergh grabbed a pair of nominations for his work on *Erin Brockovich* and *Traffic*. "I see it as a terrific party," he declared before the ceremony, "with a great door prize."

Although it appeared inevitable that his two nominations would work against him, he was able to overcome the odds, taking home the Oscar for his work on *Traffic*. A surprised Soderbergh later told the press, "I was having a great time. I got to see a lot of friends go up there. This is going to take a long time to process."

"I'm King of the World!"

Q Who was the first British filmmaker to win a Best Director Oscar?

A David Lean, voted the 34th Greatest Director of all time by *Entertainment Weekly*, became the first Brit to win a Best Director Oscar when he took home a statue for 1957's *The Bridge on the River Kwai*.

Lean, whose strict religious upbringing prohibited watching movies, began his career in motion pictures as a tea boy on set, before working his way up to editor and eventually, in 1943, co-director (with Noel Coward) of the propaganda film *In Which We Serve*. Over the next couple of decades, Lean's films — including *Blithe Spirit, Brief Encounter, Great Expectations, Oliver Twist, Lawrence of Arabia, Doctor Zhivago,* and *A Passage to India* — won twenty-eight Academy Awards.

Lean was working on a movie adaptation of Joseph Conrad's *Nostromo* when he passed away at age eighty-three in 1991.

The Bridge on the River Kwai was originally set to be directed by Howard Hawks, but Hawks withdrew after the box-office failure of his film *Land of the Pharaohs*. The movie was his first commercial crash, and the box-office buzzkill prompted him to take a break from directing and travel through Europe for four years. *Bridge on the River Kwai* tempted him — he thought critics would like the movie — but he didn't make another film until *Rio Bravo* in 1959.

Q Which 2005 Best Director Oscar winner attended the ceremony accompanied by his ninety-six-year-old mother?

A When Clint Eastwood accepted the 2005 Best Director Oscar for *Million Dollar Baby* he began by thanking his wife — TV news anchor Dina Ruiz — and Francesca Ruth Eastwood, his ninety-six-year-old mother, who was sitting in the audience.

He looked down at her in the audience and said that she had been by his side when he won the Best Director prize for *Unforgiven* over a decade ago. "She was only 84 then. But she's here with me again tonight. And she just — so, at 96, I'm thanking her for her genes," he said.

At age seventy-four, Eastwood — the oldest Best Director winner ever — was at the age when most directors and actors are collecting honorary awards for their life's work, not raking in the gold in the competitive categories. "[I'm] lucky to be still working," he said in his speech. "And I watched Sidney Lumet, who is 80, and I figure, I'm just a kid. I'll just — I've got a lot of stuff to do yet. So thank you all very much. Appreciate it."

Courtesy The Hollywood Collection

At age seventy-four Clint Eastwood is the oldest Best Director Oscar winner. In his acceptance speech he joked, "I'm just lucky to be here. Lucky to be still working. And I watched Sidney Lumet, who is eighty, and I figure, I'm just a kid. I've got a lot of stuff to do yet."

What is the only movie to share the Best Director Oscar between its two directors?

Rosalind Russell presented the only shared Best Director Oscar in history at the April 9, 1962, ceremony to Jerome Robbins and Robert Wise for the star-crossed romance *West Side Story*.

The film version of *West Side Story* was an epic undertaking for United Artists, so it was decided that two directors were needed. The pair were brought to the project to exploit their individual strengths. Wise was a strong dramatic director with almost twenty years' experience. He began his career as a sound and music editor and was nominated for an Oscar for editing *Citizen Kane*. Robbins was a Tony Award–winning choreographer who had brought the gravity-defying choreography to the original Broadway run of the show. The original arrangement was for Robbins to direct all the musical and dance sequences while Wise directed everything else.

Unfortunately Robbins's inclination to shoot and re-shoot scenes, using miles of films as he strove for perfection, led to monetary and schedule problems. That, coupled with his confrontational personality, led to problems on the set. In his autobiography, Oscar-winning composer, arranger, and musical director Saul Chaplin discussed Robbins's confrontational personality: "Jerry was by far the most exciting choreographer I had ever watched. He seemed to have an endless stream of exciting ideas.... At the same time, he was such an insane perfectionist that it was impossible for any of the dancers to achieve the standards he demanded immediately. To make matters worse, he had a very low tolerance point. When he was displeased, he heaped such verbal abuse on the dancers that the place took on the atmosphere of a concentration camp. They didn't dance out of joy, they danced out of fear.... I wondered how he ever got anyone to work for him until I asked one of the dancers. The reply was 'How else would I ever get a chance to dance like that?' I didn't invent the notion, but it's further proof that being a successful dancer requires a certain degree of masochism."

Robbins struggled through 60 percent of the picture before being let go by Mirisch Pictures. Wise completed the filming solo.

The animosity between the two former collaborators was so great that at the Oscar podium neither man mentioned or thanked the other.

What Oscar distinction do Delbert Mann, Jerome Robbins, Robert Redford, James L. Brooks, Kevin Costner, and Sam Mendes share?

The first director to win an Oscar for his debut film was Delbert Mann for 1955's *Marty*. He was followed by Jerome Robbins for 1961's *West Side Story*, Robert Redford for 1980's *Ordinary People*, James L. Brooks for 1983's *Terms of Endearment*, Kevin Costner for 1990's *Dances with Wolves*, and Sam Mendes for 1999's *American Beauty*.

Q: Who is the most nominated director by the Directors Guild of America?

A: Steven Spielberg holds the record for most nominations, at nine, and has won top honours three times. Alfred Hitchcock, Billy Wilder, and Fred Zinnemann tie for second place with eight noms. Hitchcock never won the guild's top annual prize, but he did win a quarterly award.

Q: Who is the youngest person to be nominated for a Best Director Academy Award?

A: In 1991 *Boyz in the Hood*'s John Singleton became not only the youngest person to be nominated for Best Director, at just twenty-four years of age, but also the first African-American to be so honoured. The previous record-holder was Orson Welles, who was nominated for *Citizen Kane* when he was twenty-five.

"I think what it did for me was that I really took filmmaking very seriously," Singleton says of his nomination. "That culminated in *Rosewood*, with me being real fucking serious. It was an honor and then a crutch also, because at a young age, I was like, I guess I'm a serious filmmaker. I never set out to be a serious filmmaker. I just set out to make movies.

"And so if you look at *Higher Learning*, which I was 25 years old making it, I'm like chock full of everything that would concern young people: lesbianism, and racism, and everything I could put in that movie. It was a great movie. A fun movie to do. But you could never get that movie made now. Never. The guy shoots everybody, know what I mean? Then *Rosewood* hit with that, and it was too powerful for some people. So then I was like, you know what? I'm just going to go and have some fun, and approach filmmaking from an emotional standpoint. Whatever I feel like doing, whether or not it's a fun movie or a serious movie. I'm just gonna go and do it. That's what I'm doing now."

Q: Three writer/director/producers have shared the honour of winning three Oscars in a single night. Who are they?

Billy Wilder had to make room for three more Oscars on his mantle after the April 17, 1961, ceremony. He won for co-writing, directing, and producing *The Apartment*.

On April 8, 1975, Francis Ford Coppola made three trips to the stage to collect Oscars for co-writing, directing, and producing *The Godfather, Part II*. "I almost won this a few years ago for the first half of the same picture, but that's not why we did part two," said Coppola, accepting the Best Picture award.

"I feel like I've been beaten up," said James L. Brooks as he accepted the Oscar for Best Director, just one of three he would earn at the April 9, 1984, Oscars for writing, directing, and producing *Terms of Endearment*.

Who was the first Japanese director to be nominated for a Best Director Oscar?

At the April 18, 1966, Oscar ceremony *Woman in the Dunes* helmer Hiroshi Teshigahara became the first Japanese filmmaker nominated for Best Director. He lost to *The Sound of Music*'s Robert Wise.

Who was the first American woman to be nominated for a Best Director Oscar?

Actor Bill Murray toasted Sofia Coppola's accomplishment of becoming the first American woman to be nominated for a Best Director Oscar by joking he and other crew members wanted to quit while shooting *Lost in Translation* on location in Japan. Murray — himself nominated for Best Actor for the movie — teased that several team members lacked confidence in Coppola's leadership and came close to pulling out of the project. "Four days into shooting," he said, "certain members of our Tokyo crew politely asked if they could quit the film. They did not feel that the director knew what she was doing. We were politely refused. We continued to follow her and her devoted cameraman up and down the back stairs and service elevators of a five star Tokyo hotel in the middle

Courtesy of AMPAS

Sofia Coppola is one of the few A-listers in Hollywood to have won an Academy Award (Best Screenplay for *Lost in Translation*) and a Razzie Award (Worst New Star and Worst Supporting Actress for *The Godfather, Part III*).

of the night, stealing shots and a little piece of the heart of Tokyo. There are still some of us who think the director should have been replaced — [which] would have [only] cost us one week. We could have picked it right up again. Tonight, she becomes the first American girl ever to be nominated for Best Director and her film for Best Picture."

Coppola lost the Oscar to Peter Jackson and *The Lord of the Rings: The Return of the King*, but she made Oscar history simply by being nominated. Besides being the first American woman to be nominated for Best Director, she and her then-husband Spike Jonze (who was nominated for *Being John Malkovich* in 2000) were also the first married couple to both earn Best Directing nods.

She didn't win the directing trophy, but she did grab a Best Screenwriting Oscar for *Lost in Translation*, which made hers only the second family — the Hustons were the first — to have Oscar winners in three generations. The winning streak began with her father, Francis Ford Coppola, who is a five-time winner, continued with grandfather Carmine Coppola, who was nominated twice and won once for Best Score for *The Godfather, Part II*, and helped along by her cousin, *Leaving Las Vegas* Best Actor Nicolas Cage.

Q How many times did director Jonathan Demme use the word "uh" during his Oscar acceptance speech for *Silence of the Lambs*?

A "In the context of my movie-making life, this is unanticipated," said a flustered Demme as he accepted his award at the March 30, 1992, ceremony. He stumbled through the rest of his five-minute speech, using the word "uh" almost forty times.

Why couldn't Roman Polanski pick up his 2002 Academy Award for Best Director in person?

"Roman Polanski won the best director Oscar for his film *The Pianist* although he couldn't come to the Unites States to pick up the statue," Conan O'Brien joked in March 2003. "Apparently Polanski said, 'Picking up something that small is what got me into trouble in the first place.'"

O'Brien was referring to Polanski's 1977 conviction for the statutory rape of a thirteen-year-old girl during a dinner party at Jack Nicholson's mansion. The director fled from America to Europe to avoid going to jail.

Polanski received the Best Director Oscar five months after the ceremony when Harrison Ford, his friend and the star of his film *Frantic*, delivered the statue to him at his home in France. In a written acceptance speech Polanski said, "I am deeply moved to be rewarded for the work which relates to the events so close to my own life, the events that led me to comprehend that art can transform pain. I believe this still holds true today. My most heartfelt thanks to the members of the Academy for this wonderful award."

Only one lead actor and one supporting actor were ever nominated by the Academy for a role in a Stanley Kubrick film. Who are these actors and what films were they in?

Peter Ustinov won the Best Supporting Actor Oscar for his role in 1960's *Spartacus*. Judging by his speech, Ustinov was quite unprepared for the win. "Having been educated in English schools," he said, "we were taught for at least fifteen years of our lives how to lose gracefully, and I've been preparing myself for that all afternoon…. Now I don't know quite what to say."

Another Peter, Peter Sellers, earned a nomination for Best Actor for his work in 1964's *Dr. Strangelove, or: How I Learned to Stop Worrying and Love the Bomb*.

For the record, Kubrick, who passed away in 1999, earned Best Director nominations for *2001: A Space Odyssey*, *A Clockwork Orange*, *Barry Lyndon*, and *Dr. Strangelove*. *A Clockwork Orange*, *Barry Lyndon*, and *Dr. Strangelove* were also nominated for Best Picture. He won only one Oscar, for Special Visual Effects in 1968 for *2001: A Space Odyssey*.

Q Director Louis Malle worked with a famous explorer on *The Silent World* (*Le Monde du silence*), the Best Documentary Feature Oscar winner for 1956. Who was he?

A Celebrity oceanographer Jacques-Yves Cousteau co-directed *The Silent World* (*Le Monde du silence)* with acclaimed French filmmaker Louis Malle. Cousteau, inventor of the modern Aqua-Lung, also won Oscars in 1959 for the live-action short *The Golden Fish (Histoire d'un poisson rouge)* and in 1964 for the documentary *World Without Sun (Le Monde sans soleil)*.

Louis Malle was nominated for an Academy Award three times: Writing (Best Story and Screenplay based on factual material or material not previously published) in 1972 for *Le Souffle au Coeur* (*Murmur of the Heart*), Directing in 1981 for *Atlantic City*, and Writing (Best Screenplay Written Directly For the Screen) in 1987 for *Au Revoir, Les Enfants (Goodbye, Children)*.

Q Who are the only twins to share an Oscar win?

A Twins Julius J. and Philip G. Epstein shared the shared the Best Screenplay Oscar (with Howard Koch) for *Casablanca*. The brothers were popular and prolific screenwriters in the Golden Age of Hollywood, collaborating on more than two dozen scripts, including *The Man Who Came to Dinner*, *The Strawberry Blonde*, *Yankee Doodle Dandy*, *Arsenic and Old Lace*, and *Romance on the High Seas*.

When they were working on their most famous assignment, the script of *Casablanca*, they didn't think they were writing a classic, just another big-name release.

"Just a routine assignment," said Julius. "Frankly, I can't understand its staying power. If it were made today, line for line, each performance as good, it'd be laughed off the screen. It's such a phony picture. Not a word of truth in it. It's camp, kitsch. It's just ... slick shit!"

Julius Epstein wrote close to fifty screenplays in a fifty-year writing career and was nominated for four Academy Awards spanning forty-four years — in 1938 for *The Four Daughters*, in 1942 for *Casablanca*, in 1972 for *Pete 'n' Tillie*, and in 1983 for his particularly witty adaptation of Peter DeVries's wry novel *Reuben, Reuben*.

Philip passed away in 1952.

Which *Best Years of Our Lives* Oscar-winning producer once told a reporter, "I'm willing to admit that I may not always be right ... but I'm never wrong"?

In the early days of the film business Samuel Goldwyn was Hollywood's leading "independent" producer. Goldwyn earned Best Picture Oscar nominations for *Arrowsmith*, *Dodsworth*, *Dead End*, *Wuthering Heights*, and *The Little Foxes*. He won an Oscar for *The Best Years of Our Lives* in 1946, received the Irving G. Thalberg Memorial Award that same year, and took home the Jean Hersholt Humanitarian Award in 1957.

In Hollywood circles he was as well known for his unusual sayings, sometimes known as "Goldwynisms," as he was for his films. The oft-quoted sayings were famous for their unintentional wit, which was partially a result of his poor understanding of the English language. Some of his more famous manglings included: "We've all passed a lot of water since then," "I'll believe in color television when I see it in black and white," "A verbal contract isn't worth the paper it's written on," and "Let's have some new clichés."

Even Bob Hope used to joke about Goldwyn and his way with words. When Bing Crosby was nominated for Best Actor for *Going My Way*, Hope wisecracked, "Crosby winning an Oscar is like hearing Sam Goldwyn lecturing at Oxford."

Q: Which dignified 1970 honorary Oscar recipient also dropped LSD every weekend for two years, starting in 1957?

A: Cary Grant, the beloved star of over seventy films, including *Charade*, *North By Northwest*, and *Arsenic and Old Lace*, started taking LSD while under the care of Dr. Mortimer Hartman (whom the actor referred to as "my wise Mahatma") at the Psychiatric Institute of Beverly Hills.

Grant claimed that taking the drug for medicinal purposes completely changed him. "I was an utter fake, a self-opinionated bore, a know-it-all who knew very little." His acid revelations ranged from the pithy realization that "the only way to remain happy is know nothing or everything. Unfortunately, it is impossible to know nothing for very long," to the off-the-wall "I imagined myself as a giant penis launching off from Earth like a giant spaceship."

Years later soon-to-be-ex-wife Dyan Cannon accused him of being an "apostle of LSD" who told her that the new her "could be created through LSD."

Grant rarely discussed his acid trips in public, although he did tell one reporter that his intention in taking LSD was "to make myself happy. A man would have to be a fool to take something that didn't make him happy."

"When picture makers vote their own preferences, they are not for the sensational, the tawdry, the cheap, the sexy."

— *Los Angeles Herald*, 1932

"AND THE WINNER IS..."

Best Picture Trivia

Q: Which two films tied for Best Picture at the March 16, 1949, Golden Globes?

A: *The Treasure of the Sierra Madre* and *Johnny Belinda* tied for top honours at the March 16, 1949, Golden Globes. Both films were also nominated for Best Picture Oscars but lost out to Laurence Olivier's *Hamlet*.

One of the most famous movie lines comes from *The Treasure of the Sierra Madre*, but it is often misquoted. Alfonso Bedoya, as the bandit leader, never actually says, "Badges? We don't need no stinking badges!" He says, "We don't need no badges. I don't have to show you any stinking badges."

Q: Which film won the inaugural Independent Spirit Award for Best Feature?

A: In 1986 *After Hours*, a Kafkaesque black comedy that plays on the paranoia and dread of everyday life in the Big Apple from director Martin Scorsese, was the first-ever Best Feature at the Independent Spirit Awards.

Q: About which film did an *Entertainment Weekly* writer joke, "It got 14 [Oscar] nominations — one per lifeboat"?

A: At the March 23, 1998, Oscar ceremony *Titanic* — the biggest box-office hit in film history, grossing more than $1 billion worldwide — received fourteen nominations, tying with *All about Eve* for the most nominations for a single motion picture.

It was nominated for Best Picture, Best Director for James Cameron, Best Actress for Kate Winslet, Best Supporting Actress for Gloria Stuart, Best Music (Original Song) for "My Heart Will Go On," Best Music (Original Dramatic Score) for James Horner, Best Sound, Best Makeup, Best Film Editing, Best Visual Effects, Best Sound Effects Editing, Best Art Direction, Best Cinematography, and Best Costume Design. The movie took home eleven of the fourteen awards — it failed to win the acting and makeup awards — tying *Ben-Hur* for the most honoured movie of all time.

"And the Winner Is..."

Titanic may have tied with *Ben-Hur* for Oscar wins, but it did break several other records — mostly at the box office. On its way to becoming the highest grossing film in North American box-office history ($600,788,188), it was number one at the U.S. box office for a record fifteen consecutive weeks, from December 19, 1997, to April 2, 1998. It also had the longest cinematic release in movie history — it stayed on U.S. movie charts from December 19, 1997, until September 25, 1998, a record 281 days.

Q Which three Best Picture Oscar winners have the longest running times?

A According to one mathematician the nominated movie with the longest running time wins the Best Picture Oscar 44 percent of the time. The facts and figures seem to add up when you look at a list of the Best Picture winners and note that three Best Picture winners run more than three and a half hours — *Gone with the Wind*, *Lawrence of Arabia*, and *Ben-Hur*.

BEST PICTURE:
MOVIES ABOUT SHOW BUSINESS THAT HAVE BEEN NOMINATED FOR BEST PICTURE

1.	*The Great Ziegfeld*	10.	*Lenny*
2.	*Stage Door*	11.	*Nashville*
3.	*A Star Is Born*	12.	*The Turning Point*
4.	*All about Eve*	13.	*All That Jazz*
5.	*Sunset Boulevard*	14.	*Coal Miner's Daughter*
6.	*The Country Girl*	15.	*Tootsie*
7.	*Funny Girl*	16.	*Amadeus*
8.	*Hello, Dolly!*	17.	*Shine*
9.	*Cabaret*	18.	*Shakespeare in Love*
		19.	*Moulin Rouge*

Q Ten films have won Best Picture without receiving acting nominations for any of their casts. What were they?

A *Wings, All Quiet on the Western Front, Grand Hotel, An American in Paris, The Greatest Show on Earth, Around the World in 80 Days, Gigi, The Last Emperor, Braveheart,* and *The Lord of the Rings: The Return of the King* were all nominated for Best Picture without recognition for any of the actors.

Q Which organization had more of their Best Picture picks included on the AFI list of the 100 Best Movies Ever Made — the Academy Awards or the New York Film Critics Circle?

A The American Film Institute's 100 Best Films Ever Made list was compiled in 1996 by a vote of fifteen hundred movie industry professionals. The list, topped by *Citizen Kane,* features thirty-three Academy Awards (formed in 1928) Best Pictures versus only twenty picks from the New York Film Critics Circle Awards (formed in 1935).

Q What was the first film to be released on video before winning a Best Picture Oscar?

A In 1992 the video market was still relatively new, and it was the general practice to hold off on video releases of Oscar-calibre movies until after awards season. But since a horror film had never won Best Picture, MGM decided to release 1991's *The Silence of the Lambs* before the nominations were announced. The volume of nominations it received — seven in total, including the marquee categories of Best Picture, Director, Actor, and Actress — might have been directly linked to Academy voters having had the chance to rent the movie and watch it in the comfort of their homes. Rentals of *The Silence of the Lambs* jumped by 70 percent after the Oscars. Total spending on rental of that title during the eight weeks surrounding the Oscar ceremony was approximately $33 million. The film was so popular that rental locations couldn't get enough copies of the film to meet the demand.

"And the Winner Is..."

According to the Guinness Book of World Records, which Best Picture Oscar winner was the fastest movie to gross $1 billion?

2004 Best Picture Oscar winner *The Lord of the Rings: The Return of the King*, the final instalment of director Peter Jackson's trilogy, shattered box-office records, taking in $1 billion (£536.7 million) at the international box office in just nine weeks and four days from its release on December 17, 2003.

The New Zealand–shot fantasy film is only the second film in history to break the billion-dollar barrier, the first being *Titanic*, which took eleven weeks to make the same amount of money.

What was the first documentary in almost fifty years to win the Palme d'Or at the Cannes Film Festival?

Quentin Tarantino headed the jury at the Cannes Film Festival that presented Michael Moore with the festival's highest honour, the Palme d'Or, for his anti–George W. Bush documentary *Fahrenheit 9/11*. Moore's film is only the second documentary — and the first American documentary — to win the top prize in Cannes. The first was Jacques-Yves Cousteau and Louis Malle's *Le Monde du silence* in 1956.

Tarantino had to publicly defend the decision to those who thought the controversial film — which received what some observers called "the longest standing ovation in the history of the festival" — was chosen for political reasons.

"When I was on stage with Michael Moore," said Tarantino, "I knew all this politics crap would be brought up. I just whispered in his ear and said, 'I just want you to know it was not because of the politics that you won this award. You won it because we thought it was the best film that we saw.'"

According to the Guinness Book of World Records, which Best Picture Oscar winner is the world's most valuable script?

On December 15, 1996, Steven Spielberg shelled out a record-breaking $244,500 for Clark Gable's personal film script from *Gone with the Wind* at Christie's, Los Angeles, California. The script was sold by Gable's estate along with his 1934 Oscar for *It Happened One Night* as part of a day-long auction of Hollywood memorabilia that raised more than $1.8 million.

CLASSIC MOVIES THAT WERE NOT NOMINATED FOR BEST PICTURE:
MOVIES THAT OSCAR FORGOT

1. ***Modern Times*:** The final appearance of Charles Chaplin's Little Tramp character, and the comedian's first full sound film, failed to garner any notice from the Academy.

2. ***Meet Me in St. Louis*:** The movie that brought Vincente Minnelli and Judy Garland together, professionally and personally, earned four Oscar nominations — Best Cinematography (Color), Writing (Screenplay), Music (Song), and Music (Score) — but was overlooked for Best Picture.

3. ***To Have and Have Not*:** Howard Hawks was one of the most prolific and successful directors of the Golden Age of Hollywood — Leonard Maltin called him "the greatest American director who is not a household name" — but his work was seldom recognized by his peers at the Academy. He was only nominated once, in 1942 for *Sergeant York* — he lost to John Ford — and this film was ignored completely.

4. ***Singin' in the Rain*:** Musicals have regularly gone unnoticed by the Academy — in the first seventy-five years of the awards only eight song-and-dance movies took Best Picture — but to ignore this film seems almost inconceivable. It did earn — and lose — two nominations for Best Supporting Actress and Best Music (Score), but decades later it was acknowledged by the American Film Institute, which voted *Singin' in the Rain* the #10 movie of all time. It was the highest rated musical on the list. The AFI also selected three tunes from the score — "Singin' in the Rain," "Good Morning," and "Make 'em Laugh" — for its Top 100 Movie Songs list.

5. ***A Star Is Born*** (1954 remake): James Mason and Judy Garland were both nominated for their work in *A Star Is Born*, and while

both won Golden Globes there were no Oscars in sight. Regarded by some as the greatest musical ever made, this movie might have cast too jaundiced an eye on Hollywood and the price of fame for the comfort of Academy voters.

6. ***Rear Window:*** Nominated for four awards — Best Director, Sound, Writing, and Cinematography (Color) — the Academy stopped short of giving this Hitchcock classic a Best Picture nod. In fact, Hitchcock had a miserable time with the Academy, receiving six nominations — including one for *Rear Window* — but no wins. To make nice they gave him the Irving Thalberg Award — an honorary award for producing, not directing — in 1968, but that hardly makes up for the egregious absence of a competitive trophy.

7. ***The Searchers:*** A cover story in *New York Magazine* called *The Searchers* the most influential movie in American history, and while hindsight reveals it to have some, let's say, antiquated views on racial issues, the film's beautiful camera work and one of John Wayne's best performances should have earned it some respect from the Academy.

8. ***The Sweet Smell of Success:*** When this movie was released in 1957, it was seen as a thinly veiled attack on Walter Winchell, who for decades had been the most famous gossip columnist in America, so perhaps it was out of some misguided sense of respect for the powerful columnist that the Academy completely ignored the film, not even appreciating the superb performances of Tony Curtis and Burt Lancaster, who both could have easily earned Best Actor nods.

9. ***A Touch of Evil:*** It won the Best Film at the 1958 Brussels World Fair but stateside it disappeared after being buried as the bottom half of a double bill. It was director Orson Welles's fifth Hollywood film — and after its failure, it was his last American studio film. Criticized in its day as a pretentious yet sleazy pulp fiction B movie, the film's reputation was rehabilitated by video and DVD releases and is now regarded as a classic.

10. ***The Manchurian Candidate*** (1962 original): Hailed by many critics as a masterpiece and "one of the best and brightest of modern American films," it might come as a surprise that it was not nominated for Best Picture or Best Director. Angela Lansbury picked up a Best Supporting Actress nomination and the Academy threw a bone to the editor, Ferris Webster, both of whom went home empty-handed.

11. *Rosemary's Baby*: Roman Polanski's first American film is a spine-tingling story of devil worship in New York City that rivals Hitchcock in suspense. The film's macabre tone and sense of danger should have produced a Best Picture nod, but the Academy has a hard time with genre pictures. Only two thriller/horror films, *Rebecca* and *The Silence of the Lambs*, have taken the top prize in the history of the awards.

12. *Brazil*: Terry Gilliam's surreal movie won the Los Angeles Film Critics' Best Picture but was virtually ignored by the Academy, which gave it only two nominations, for Best Art Direction and Best Screenplay, both of which it lost.

13. *Do the Right Thing*: Despite being one of the most original — if not controversial — filmmakers in America, Spike Lee has never been nominated for Best Director, nor have any of his films been up for Best Picture. Lee expected at least a nomination for this film. When he accepted the Los Angeles Film Critics Association Awards for Best Picture and Best Director he said those wins would "help us definitely with the Oscar nominations [since] 85 percent of the academy voting members live here in the L.A. area." Unfortunately the Academy didn't do the right thing and the film was shut out.

14. *Hoop Dreams*: Critic Roger Ebert called *Hoop Dreams* "one of the great moviegoing experiences of my lifetime," and yet it garnered only an Editing nomination. "It was the St. Valentine's Day Massacre," said *Hoop Dreams* director Steve James of the snub. "We just joined a pretty prestigious club. There seems to be a history of not nominating the year's best documentaries. At least we were named in the editing category — which is a vote of our peers." The omission of *Hoop Dreams* from the Best Documentary roster prompted a long-overdue re-examination of the doc nomination process. As a result, the rules were changed so that documentary filmmakers, and not a group of retired volunteers, vote in this category.

Only one film version of a Shakespeare play has ever won the Best Picture Oscar. What was it?

At the March 24, 1949, Oscar ceremony Sir Laurence Olivier's version of *Hamlet* became the first (and so far only) Shakespearean film to win Best Picture. The film also holds the distinction of being the only film in which the winner of the Best Actor Oscar directed himself to win the award. *Hamlet* also won Oscars for black and white Art Direction and Costume Design. Other Shakespearean films to win Oscars include 1935's *A Midsummer Night's Dream* for Best Cinematography and Best Film Editing, *Julius Caesar* in 1953 for Best Art Direction (Black and White), and 1989's *Henry V* for Costume Design.

What Oscar distinction does the 1969 film *Z* hold?

Z, the Costa-Gavras political drama, is the first film to be nominated for Best Picture and Best Foreign Film in the same year.

Based on a novel by Vassilis Vassilios, *Z* was Greek director Costa-Gavras's first foray into political drama. The film tells the more or less true story of the 1963 murder of the Greek pacifist, physician, and politician Gregory Lambrakis and the efforts to bring his killers to justice. True to the film's pseudo-documentary style, the opening credits even contain a reversal of the normal movie disclaimer: "The screenwriters proclaim that any similarity to actual events or persons is *intentional.*" *Z*'s mesmerizing mix of conspiracy, action, violence, and valour helped the film take an Oscar for Best Foreign Film of 1969 and come in fourteenth in terms of box-office success for the year.

After the success of *Z*, Costa-Gavras was offered a chance to direct *The Godfather*. He declined after the studio refused to make changes in the script that he believed were necessary to prevent the film from glorifying the Mafia.

Which BAFTA Award nomination for Best Animated Film was covertly funded by the CIA?

The CIA acquired the film rights to George Orwell's classic satire on Stalinism, *Animal Farm*, after the writer's death and secretly funded the production as anti-Communist propaganda. Directed by John Halas and Joy Batchelor, *Animal Farm* was the first animated feature produced in England, beginning its production in 1951 with a release date of

December 1954. The movie is quite faithful to the book, right up to the end: the CIA softened the theme of the novel by adding an epilogue where the other animals successfully revolt against the pigs.

Q What was the first movie to earn Best Picture nods from the Oscars, the Golden Globes, the New York Film Critics Circle, and the National Board of Review?

A In 1954, Elia Kazan's *On the Waterfront* earned nominations from all the major prize-giving organizations. It was the first time — and remains the only time — that all of these independent groups had agreed on one film. Bosley Crowther wrote of the New York Film Critics that "their hasty and happy agreement was almost unprecedented. So far as this member can recall, the ladies and gentlemen of the scribe tribe have never been in sweeter harmony." *On the Waterfront* went on to win all major awards that year, convincingly claiming the title of top movie of the year.

The acclaimed movie, inspired by the Pulitzer Prize–winning *Crime on the Waterfront* series by Malcolm Johnson, wouldn't have been made at all if Darryl Zanuck at 20th Century Fox had his way. He turned down the script because the gritty drama didn't fit well with his strategy of creating only lush productions for the studio's Cinemascope format. Columbia picked up the film, which earned eight Oscars and was voted the seventeenth greatest film of all time by *Entertainment Weekly*.

Q What was the first film from China to win Taiwan's Golden Horse Award?

A *Hoh Xil: Mountain Patrol*, also known as *Kekexili*, beat out two Hong Kong blockbusters — *Infernal Affairs III* and *2046* — at the forty-first edition of the Golden Horse Awards, the Oscar for Chinese-language cinema.

As the result of a long-standing political feud between Taiwan and China — they were split by a civil war in 1949 — few films from mainland China have entered the competition, and before this, none had taken the top prize.

Lu Chuan, who directed the story about volunteers protecting Tibetan antelope from ruthless poachers in remote western China, made no mention of the bad blood in his acceptance speech. "I hope you can continue to trust me," he said, "because I will certainly make different movies."

In a more light-hearted moment, Hong Kong heartthrob Daniel Wu accepted his Best Supporting Actor award for *New Police Story* by saying that when he started in movies, he was "a fool with no ideas. Now I am a fool with an award."

Q Which films are eligible to win the Golden Reel Award?

A The Golden Reel Award is presented by the Academy of Canadian Cinema & Television to the Canadian film that earns the highest domestic box-office revenue of the year. The trophy is awarded during the annual Genie Awards ceremony.

Past recipients of the Golden Reel Award are *Meatballs* (1980), *The Changeling* (1981), *Heavy Metal* (1982), *Porky's* (1983), *Strange Brew* (1984), *La guerre des tuques* (1985), *The Care Bears Movie* (1986), *Le déclin de l'empire américain* (1987), *The Gate* (1988), *La grenouille et la baleine* (1989), *Jésus de Montréal* (1990), *Ding et Dong, le film* (1991), *Black Robe* (1992), *La Florida* (1993), *Louis 19, le roi des ondes* (1994), *Johnny Mnemonic* (1995), *Crash* (1996), *Air Bud* (1997), *Les Boys* (1998), *Les Boys 2* (1999), *The Art of War* (2000), *Nuit de Noces* (2001), *Les Boys III* (2002), *Séraphin: Un homme et son péché* (2003), *Resident Evil* (2004).

Q Which classic film lost out on a Best Picture Oscar because of a smear campaign by the Hearst press syndicate?

A In what has become known as the mother of all bad Academy calls, *Citizen Kane*, nominated for nine awards, was shut out, save for Best Writing (Original Screenplay) in the 1942 Oscar race. How could a film that Andrew Sarris called "*the* great American film" strike out so badly with an organization that is supposed to honour "excellence in the motion picture arts and sciences"? By offending one of the most powerful media moguls in the world, that's how.

Tipped off by gossip hound Louella Parsons, who thought that *Citizen Kane* was a slanderous account of his life, newspaper magnate and sometime politician William Randolph Hearst blew a gasket.

Hearst felt the film was an affront to him personally, and it's not hard to imagine why. Although, in truth, the character of Charles Foster Kane is a composite of any number of powerful, colourful, and influential American individualists and financial barons in the early twentieth century, the similarities to Hearst are undeniable. Kane was the owner of the *New York Inquirer*, while Hearst owned the *San Francisco Examiner* and the *New York Journal*. Both shared political aspirations and ran for the position of governor of New York and lived in opulent mansions — or rather castles — filled with priceless art collections, but it was the film's sneering attitude toward Kane's wife, which Hearst believed to be based on his mistress Marion Davies, that fanned the burning embers of the newspaperman's hatred of the film and its creator, Orson Welles.

Davies was represented in the film by Susan Alexander as a pathetic, talentless drunk. Welles also had the temerity to include one precious intimate detail from their personal life. According to a Gore Vidal essay in the *New York Review of Books* "Rosebud" was Hearst's name for Davies's clitoris. (Screenwriter Herman J. Mankiewicz insisted that he took the name from a bicycle he owned as a child.) Welles later admitted that this portrayal was cruel to Davies and that the actress was nothing like the fictional Mrs. Kane, but the damage was done.

Hearst banned any advertising of the film — and all other RKO movies — in his newspapers and offered to buy the negative from studio head George Schaefer in order to burn it. RKO wisely refused Hearst's offer, buoyed by the rave reviews the film was garnering from influential industry figures who had seen the film prior to its release.

Because of Hearst's heavy-handed tactics — refusing to accept advertising from any theatre that showed *Citizen Kane* — the studio had a hard time finding screens to exhibit the film. It was granted a limited theatrical release, and when major theatre chains refused to carry the movie, in at least one instance a makeshift theatre was created expressly for the purpose of showing the film.

Hearst was relentless in his campaign of intimidation to squash the film. He threatened to bring to light long-buried Hollywood scandals his newspapers had repressed at the request of the studios. His papers were ruthless, using Welles's private life against him, making blunt references to communism and questioning Welles's willingness to fight for his country.

By the time the Academy Awards came around in 1942, Hearst's smear campaign and the twenty-six-year-old Welles's arrogance had taken their toll. Whenever Welles or his film was mentioned at the ceremony, they were booed. Nominated for nine awards, *Citizen Kane* lost in every category except one — Welles shared the award for Best Screenplay with Herman Mankiewicz.

After the Academy's denunciation of *Citizen Kane*, RKO consigned the film to its vaults.

Hearst's ban on the film lasted for years after his death. *Citizen Kane* was not reviewed in any Hearst newspaper until the mid-1970s, when the *Los Angeles Herald-Examiner* gave it a belated rave review.

What qualifies a film to be considered for Best Picture by AMPAS?

Each year AMPAS considers hundreds of films — in 2001, 248 films were eligible for Best Picture — with a very precise set of eligibility rules. To qualify for a Best Picture Oscar, a movie must have a running time longer than forty minutes and be projected on 35-mm or 70-mm film or an approved digital format in a commercial theatre in Los Angeles between January 1 and December 31 for a minimum of seven consecutive days.

Which Best Picture Oscar, Golden Globe, and National Board of Review–winning movie did legendary critic Pauline Kael suggest should have been called *Plays with Camera*?

The famously influential *New Yorker* movie critic Pauline Kael was never afraid to speak her mind, even if it went against conventional wisdom. Her savage skewering of *The Sound of Music* got her fired from *McCall's* in 1966, but during her twenty-four-year tenure at the *New Yorker* she could rescue a film from obscurity with just a few kind words. In print she nurtured careers, championing the early work of Steven Spielberg, Brian De Palma, Martin Scorsese, and Robert Altman.

Kael retired in 1991, citing the discouraging quality of current moviemaking, but let it fly in one of her last columns. The subject was *Dances with Wolves*, the crowd-pleasing award magnet directed by Kevin Costner. Kael called the movie an "epic made by a bland megalomaniac — the Indians should have named him Plays with Camera." Her attack continued, using phrases like "childishly naïve" and commenting that "Costner has feathers in his hair and feathers in his head."

Despite Kael's lambasting, *Dances with Wolves* proved very popular with audiences and became a regular on the awards circuit. In February 1991 it walked away with Oscars for Best Picture, Best Adapted Screenplay for Michael Blake, Best Cinematography for Dean Semler, Best Director for Kevin Costner, Best Editing for Neil Travis, Best Score for John Barry, and Best Sound for Jeffrey Perkins, Bill W. Benton, Greg Watkins, and Russell Williams. The Directors Guild of America saw fit to give Costner its Best Director prize, as did the National Board of Review, which also named it Best Picture. The Golden Globes were somewhat more reserved, doling out only Best Screenplay and, you guessed it, Best Picture (Drama) trophies. Almost a decade after its release the accolades continued to roll in when the AFI ranked it #75 on its list of 100 Great American Movies.

Q Which Independent Spirit Award–winning Best Picture did the *New York Times* erroneously report had been retitled *I'm a Drunk, and You're a Prostitute* for the Chinese market?

A In 1998 the *Wall Street Journal* ran a piece on some of the outrageous translations of movie titles from English into foreign languages. It was noted that *Boogie Nights* was called *His Powerful Device Makes Him Famous* for the Mandarin market, while *The Full Monty* became *Six Naked Pigs*, and *As Good As It Gets* was called *Mr. Cat Poop*. As funny or unusual as those titles sound, they are legit. The trouble started when a cyber jokester attached a list of bogus titles to the *Wall Street Journal* online article. Suddenly really crazy titles started popping up in copycat articles in newspapers and on television.

The *New York Times* fell for the hoax and printed a story that quoted the Chinese title of the indie hit *Leaving Las Vegas* as *I'm a Drunk, and You're a Prostitute*, and *The Crying Game* — an Independent Spirit winner for Best Foreign Film — as *Oh No! My Girlfriend Has a Penis*. Even Peter Jennings of the venerable ABC news got sucked in, when on January 5, 1999, he closed his broadcast with a kicker — a funny little story to end off the news. "And finally, the new title for *Babe* reminds us that in China the communists are still in charge," he said. "*Babe* is now *The Happy Dumpling-to-be Who Talks and Solves Agricultural Problems*."

Soon afterward the mix-up was exposed by Howard Kurtz of the *Washington Post*.

Which movie won Best Picture at the inaugural MTV Movie Awards in 1991?

Terminator 2: Judgment Day scooped the top prize at the first-ever MTV Movie Awards on June 10, 1992. Other nominees included *Backdraft*, *Boyz N the Hood*, *JFK*, and *Robin Hood: Prince of Thieves*.

The sci-fi flick also won Best Action Sequence for the L.A. freeway chase, Best Breakthrough Performance for star Edward Furlong, Best Female Performance and Most Desirable Female for Linda Hamilton, and Best Male Performance for Arnold Schwarzenegger. The future "governa-tor" was paid $15 million for the role, which was composed of a total of seven hundred words of dialogue. That breaks down to $21,429 per word — "Hasta la vista, baby," for instance, earned him $85,716.

What was the first foreign film to be named Best Picture by the Los Angeles Film Critics Association?

Wo hu cang long, better known in North America as *Crouching Tiger, Hidden Dragon*, was the first non-American film to win the top prize from the Los Angeles Film Critics Association.

The film also holds the record for the most Oscar nominations for a foreign film. It was nominated for ten Oscars, including Best Picture, Best Director, Best Music (Original Song), Best Writing (Adapted Screenplay), Best Film Editing, and Best Costume Design, taking home four: Best Cinematography, Best Art Direction, Best Foreign Language Film, and Best Music (Original Score).

"I saw *Crouching Tiger, Hidden Dragon*, and I was surprised because I didn't see any tigers or dragons, and then I realized why," said comedian Steve Martin at the Oscar ceremony later that year, "they're crouching and hidden."

"To me," he continued, "*Crouching Tiger, Hidden Dragon* sounds like something Siegfried and Roy do on vacation."

Which is the only film to win both the Grand Jury Prize and the Audience Award in the drama competition at the Sundance Film Festival?

Three Seasons, the debut feature of Vietnamese American filmmaker Tony Bui, was the hot ticket at the 1999 Sundance Film Festival, becoming the only film to win both the Grand Jury Prize and the Audience Award in the drama competition at the Utah fest. The film — an American-made movie about the renewal of life in post-war Saigon — also won a cinematography award for Lisa Rinzler.

At which film festival did Kevin Smith win the Filmmaker's Trophy and a distribution deal for his film *Clerks*?

In 1994, *Clerks* — a day in the life of two convenience and video store clerks and the eccentric drug dealers who hang out outside the stores — debuted at the Sundance Film Festival, becoming the breakout hit of the event. *Clerks* was Kevin Smith's first film, and introduces several characters, notably Jay and Silent Bob, who reappear in his later films. The black and white film was made on a budget of $26,800 — financed largely by credit cards and money borrowed from Smith's family and friends — and became a surprising success after it was taken on by Miramax Films.

Which 1957 Golden Globe and Oscar Best Picture employed 90 animal handlers to deal with 3,800 sheep, 2,448 buffalo, 950 donkeys, 800 horses, 512 monkeys, 17 bulls, 15 elephants, 6 skunks, and 4 ostriches?

Around the World in 80 Days employed the talents of what was at that time the most animals in any film. Shot on location in the Persian Gulf, Saudia Arabia, Japan, Pakistan, Iraq, Bangkok, and Afghanistan, as well as aboard the Denver & Rio Grande Railroad in Durango, Colorado, this 175-minute epic provided the origin of the word "cameo" to mean a brief appearance of a star in a minor role. Among the credited performers were Buster Keaton, Frank Sinatra, Cesar Romero, Marlene Dietrich, John Gielgud, Red Buttons, Joe E. Brown, Glynis Johns, Peter Lorre, Ronald Colman, Beatrice Lillie, and dozens of others.

When producer Mike Todd picked up the Best Picture Oscar for the film he was quoted as saying, "Imagine this — and being married to Liz [Taylor] too!"

Which New York Film Critics Circle's 1950 pick for Best Foreign Film was labelled "blasphemous" by New York's Cardinal Spellman?

Roberto Rossellini's *L'Amore* (also known as *Ways of Love*) is divided into two parts: a monologue called *The Human Voice* and the controversial *The Miracle*.

The Miracle — about a homeless woman who believes she is carrying the child of Saint Joseph — earned the ire of the good Cardinal, prompting him to declare it "blasphemous" and to use his juice to get New York City to ban the film and threaten to revoke the licence of any movie house that played it.

When the film critics announced that they planned to reward *L'Amore* with a scroll at a ceremony at Radio City Music Hall, religious leaders threatened to storm the hall with picketers. The critics opted for a smaller ceremony at the Rainbow Room, where they quietly presented *L'Amore*'s American distributor with a scroll. The distributor called the honour "a tribute to the integrity of people who really care about films."

Q Which 1959 Best Picture winner was considered to be the most expensive picture made to that date?

A At $15 million, William Wyler's 1959 epic *Ben-Hur* was the most expensive movie to date to win Best Picture. Shot in Rome over the course of ten months, the production required the construction of over three hundred sets and employed eight thousand extras. The film was one of the first to involve marketing tie-ins, including hundreds of toys, as well as, if you can believe it, Ben-His and Ben-Hers towels.

Q Which actor appeared in only five films, all of which were nominated for, or won, the Best Picture Oscar?

A Italian-American actor John Cazale made only five films during his career before succumbing to bone cancer in March 1978.

In New York he won two Obie Awards for his work in the off-Broadway stage productions of *The Indian Wants the Bronx* and *The Line* before his long-time friend Al Pacino invited him to audition for *The Godfather*. Starting with the role of Fredo Corleone, who falls from grace with his smarter younger brother Michael, Cazale became typecast, usually playing likeable but doomed oddballs.

Each of the five films he appeared in garnered Best Picture nominations — *The Godfather*, *The Conversation*, *Dog Day Afternoon*, *The Deer Hunter*, and *The Godfather, Part II* — and although he was never nominated for an Oscar, his turn as Sal the bank robber in Sidney Lumet's *Dog Day Afternoon* earned him Golden Globe consideration.

Cazale was so weakened by his illness during the shooting of *The Deer Hunter* that director Michael Cimino shot all his scenes first in case his condition worsened. When the studio discovered he was suffering from terminal cancer they insisted he be removed from the film, but his co-star and fiancée Meryl Streep threatened to quit if he was fired.

Cazale died shortly after filming was completed.

Q What 1961 film was the first musical to win top honours from the New York Film Critics Circle?

A *West Side Story*, the tuneful update of *Romeo and Juliet*, was the first musical Best Picture in the New York Film Critics' twenty-seven-year history. The musical about two youngsters from rival NYC gangs who fall in love also took Best Picture at the Oscars, beating out *Fanny*, *The Guns of Navarone*, *The Hustler*, and *Judgment at Nuremberg*.

Q What film took home top honours at the first New York Film Critics Circle Awards in 1936?

A The New York Film Critics Circle founded their own awards in 1935 as an antidote to the more commercially minded Academy Awards. Their first choice for Best Picture was an unlikely one: *The Informer*, a glum melodrama about a drunken brute who gives up his best friend for a few dollars during the Irish revolt of 1922, was a box-office flop on its original release.

Later, when the film was recognized by the Academy — it took Best Actor, Best Director, Best Adapted Screenplay, and Best Musical Score — the NYFCC took full credit for championing the movie. "It was conceded in the industry that the picture had little chance of winning," wrote the *New York Times*, "but with the disturbance caused by the Broadway lads the picture could not be ignored."

Following the Oscar kudos RKO re-released *The Informer*, hoping that a handful of Academy Awards would stir some public interest. They were right, and the film earned back its $243,000 budget in just eighteen days, making it the first film to benefit financially from winning awards.

Q: What was the first colour film to win an Academy Award for Best Picture?

A: In 1939, *Gone with the Wind* became the first colour — Technicolor, actually — film to win Best Picture. To achieve the vivid Technicolor hues the movie was shot on three strips of negatives that were combined to make one colour film.

When the movie made its world premiere at Atlanta's Fox Theatre in December of 1939, the mayor declared it *Gone with the Wind* Day and gave all civic employees and school children the day off. Over three hundred thousand people turned up to catch a glimpse of the glamorous cast and the movie's producer, David O. Selznick.

Q: The black and white film *The Apartment* won Best Picture in 1960. What was the next black and white movie to take the top Oscar?

Courtesy of AMPAS

Jack Lemmon and Shirley MacLaine in *The Apartment*, the first Best Picture winner to refer to a previous winner. Lemmon tries to watch *Grand Hotel* on television but gets frustrated because of all the commercial interruptions.

A: Thirty-three years after *The Apartment* won the gold, Steven Spielberg's black and white *Schindler's List* won Best Picture in 1993. "Oh, wow. This is the best drink of water after the longest drought of my life," said Spielberg, referring to years of being passed over by the Academy.

"And the Winner Is..."

The last black and white film to win an Oscar from Hollywood's heyday, *The Apartment* was directed by Billy Wilder and stars Jack Lemmon, Shirley MacClaine in her film debut, and Fred McMurray and was later made into a Broadway musical, *Promises, Promises*. The movie is cited by filmmaker Cameron Crowe as his favourite film of all time. Crowe is such a fan of the film and its director that he actually tried to convince Billy Wilder to make his acting debut as Tom Cruise's mentor, Dicky Fox, in *Jerry Maguire.*

Who was the first woman to walk away from the Oscar ceremony with a Best Picture Oscar?

On April 2, 1974, *The Sting* producer Julia Phillips became the first woman to win a Best Picture Oscar. "You can imagine what a trip this is for a Jewish girl from Great Neck," she said. "I get to win an Academy Award and meet Elizabeth Taylor at the same time."

Phillips, who died at age fifty-seven in 2002, also produced both Martin Scorsese's *Taxi Driver* and Steven Spielberg's *Close Encounters of the Third Kind*, but it was her outrageous memoir of the movie industry, *You'll Never Eat Lunch in This Town Again*, that brought her to public attention and ended her career in films.

What was the first American film to win the Palme D'Or at the Cannes Film Festival?

In 1955 Ernest Borgnine won a Best Actor Oscar for his role as a Bronx butcher who gives up on love — until he meets an equally lonely schoolteacher. *Marty* garnered a total of four Oscars, including Best Picture, and was the first American film to take home the Palme d'Or, the top honours of the Cannes Film Festival.

Marty, which the *New York Times* called "warm and winning," was also the only movie in film history for which the producers spent more on an Oscar campaign — $400,000 — than they did on making the movie, whose total budget was $343,000. When producer Harold Hecht picked up the Best Picture award, he said, "We are very fortunate to live in a country where any man, no matter how humble his origin, can become president — and in an industry where any picture, no matter how low the budget, can win an Oscar."

What is the longest film to win an Oscar?

Clocking in at a mind-bending six-plus hours, the 1968 Best Foreign Film winner *War and Peace* (U.S.S.R.) is the longest film to win an Oscar. Presented with three intermissions, the five-hundred-minute film features more than a quarter-million extras and in today's dollars would have cost close to $1 billion to make.

The longest films to win Best Picture were 1939's *Gone with the Wind* at three hours and fifty-eight minutes, and 1962's *Lawrence of Arabia* at three hours forty-two minutes.

What do the following films have in common: *All about Eve, Titanic, From Here to Eternity, Mary Poppins, Who's Afraid of Virginia Woolf?, Forrest Gump, Shakespeare in Love, The Lord of the Rings: The Return of the King,* and *Chicago*?

All these films earned thirteen or more Academy Award nominations. *All about Eve* and *Titanic* both earned fourteen nods, while the others each raked in thirteen noms.

What movie has the shortest title of any film to win the Oscar for Best Picture?

Vincent Minnelli's 1958 Best Picture winner *Gigi* is the film with the shortest title to win the top prize at the Oscars. Shot on location in Paris, *Gigi* was a hit worldwide — everywhere but in France.

Often called the last great movie musical, it was nominated for nine Oscars and won all of them, a record at the time. Based on a novella by the French novelist Colette, the movie tells the story of a young girl in Belle Epoque Paris who is raised and educated to go into the family business of being a courtesan.

Q Which movie won the 1985 Los Angeles Film Critics Association Award for Best Picture, even though it hadn't yet been released?

A *Los Angeles Times* critic Jack Mathews was a champion of Terry Gilliam's film *Brazil* and arranged a secret screening of the film for his colleagues at the Los Angeles Film Critics Association. The screening occurred just before the group was to vote on their annual awards, and in a move that stunned the industry, they awarded the film Best Picture, Best Director, and Best Screenplay.

The awards were controversial because the picture had not even been scheduled for release. Universal chairman Sid Sheinberg and Terry Gilliam disagreed over the film; Sheinberg insisted on radically re-editing the movie to give it a happy ending, which Gilliam strongly resisted.

The movie was shelved by Universal, but after it won the Los Angeles Film Critics Association Awards Universal finally released Gilliam's version in 1985. "You gave us the stamp," said *Brazil*'s producer as he accepted the Best Picture award at the official ceremony several weeks after the nominations had been announced. "For us it made the difference between being dead or alive."

Q What is the only Alfred Hitchcock film to win a Best Picture Oscar?

A Academy members responded to *Rebecca*'s interesting mix of suspense and romance. It was the first film Hitchcock made in Hollywood and the only one that won a Best Picture Oscar. Hitchcock made the film under the watchful — some would say controlling eye — of producer David O. Selznick. Years after the win, Hitch said, "When I came to America to direct *Rebecca*, David Selznick sent me a memo ... I've just finished reading it. I think I may turn it into a motion picture... I plan to call it *The Longest Story Ever Told*."

Alfred Hitchcock security gate on a store on Hollywood Boulevard. When producer David O. Selznick insisted that Hitchcock show smoke forming the letter R coming out of a chimney in *Rebecca* (1940), the director refused. Instead the Master of Suspense showed flames licking at a pillow embroidered with the letter R.

What was the first X-rated film to win a Best Picture Oscar?

John Schlesinger's *Midnight Cowboy* broke a lot of ground. The film was rated X before that rating became the domain of the porno industry, so there is a truckload of trivia about it. At the April 7, 1970, ceremony it was the first, and so far only, X-rated film to win the Best Picture Oscar; Jimmy Carter requested it be shown in the White House screening room, making it the only X-rated film to be shown to a U.S. president while in office; and it was the first X-rated film to be shown on television, although the film's rating had been changed to R by the time it had its television premiere.

The Academy of Motion Picture Arts and Sciences selected the wartime drama *Wings* as the winner of its inaugural Best Picture Award in 1927–28. What other distinction does this film hold in Oscar history?

A *Wings*, directed by William A. Wellman and starring Clara Bow, Charles Buddy Rogers, Richard Arlen, Jobyna Ralston, Gary Cooper (in his first substantial role), Arlette Marchal, and El Brendel — about two young men from different backgrounds who love the same woman and become fighter pilots in the First World War — was the first film, and the only silent movie, to win the Best Picture Oscar. Technically the film wasn't completely silent. A soundtrack of sound effects and music — but no speech — was available to theatres with the equipment to handle it.

If you put aside the saccharine love story, *Wings* is worth a look for some of the best flying sequences ever captured on celluloid. Twenty-eight-year-old director William Wellman, himself a wartime aviator, shot the spectacular fight scenes with the full co-operation of the U.S. War Department.

Wings was also the first film to win Best Picture without taking Best Director or any acting awards.

Also nominated in the 1st Annual Academy Awards were *The Last Command, The Racket, The Way of All Flesh*, and *7th Heaven*.

Q Which Billy Wilder Best Picture winner was allegedly the target of a $5-million bribe from the liquor industry?

A Director Billy Wilder claimed the liquor industry offered Paramount $5 million to not release *The Lost Weekend*, his gritty look at the miserable life of a chronic alcoholic on a four-day drinking binge. Wilder also intimated that he would have accepted the cash had it been offered to him.

The Lost Weekend won Best Picture at the March 7, 1946, Oscar ceremony, beating out *Anchors Aweigh, The Bells of St. Mary's, Mildred Pierce*, and *Spellbound*.

Q Who appeared dressed as Spider-Man at the 2004 MTV Movie Awards to present the Best Movie award?

A At the 2004 MTV Movie Awards it was announced that Kirsten Dunst would co-present the Best Movie award with Tobey Maguire, her co-star in the movie *Spider-Man 2*. When she came on stage she was accompanied by someone in a Spider-Man suit. "You're not Spider-Man," the blonde actress said, "you've got tatas!"

It was then revealed that the co-presenter was not Maguire but comic Ellen DeGeneres in Spidey drag. The comedienne explained that Maguire had strep throat and had asked her "to come and save the day," and went on to say how comfortable the suit was.

When Maguire joined them a moment later he remarked that he "noticed his Spidey suit was missing."

"You have one too?" replied DeGeneres in mock surprise.

Q What movie has the longest title of any film to win the Oscar for Best Picture?

A Peter Jackson's 2004 winner *The Lord of the Rings: The Return of the King* — with thirty-five letters — has the longest title of any film to take Best Picture at the Oscars. Stanley Kubrick's *Dr. Strangelove, or: How I Learned to Stop Worrying and Love the Bomb*, up for Best Picture in 1964, has the longest title of any film to be *nominated*, with fifty-four letters.

The longest film title in history is the 1967 Patrick Magee film *The Persecution and Assassination of Jean-Paul Marat as Performed by the Inmates of the Asylum of Charenton Under the Direction of the Marquis de Sade*, most commonly referred to as *Marat/Sade*. It wasn't nominated for any Oscars but did win the Silver Ribbon for Best Direction awarded by the Italian National Syndicate of Film Journalists and a Special Mention at the Locarno International Film Festival.

Q Which was the first (and so far only) film to win a Best Picture Oscar without a single other nomination?

At the 1931–32 Oscars the star-studded *Grand Hotel* took home the top honour — Best Picture — despite not having garnered any other nominations.

MGM claimed they had "more stars than there are in Heaven," and to prove it they cast many of the biggest names from their galaxy of actors — John and Lionel Barrymore, Greta Garbo, Joan Crawford, Wallace Beery, Lewis Stone, and Jean Hersholt — in this extravagant movie. Comedy and drama are mixed in this classic film directed by Edmund Goulding about occupants of a beautiful between-wars Berlin hotel, who are all struggling with issues of finances, health, or social standing.

It was as a depressed ballerina in the *Grand Hotel* that top-billed star Greta Garbo uttered the famous line that would forevermore come to define her career and reclusive nature: "I want to be alone."

Courtesy of AMPAS

A studio headshot of Greta Garbo. When Garbo retired at age thirty-six it was reported that when asked why she was leaving public she said, "I want to be alone." Not so. "I never said, 'I want to be alone.' I only said, 'I want to be left alone,'" she noted. "There is a world of difference."

Garbo suddenly retired from film at age thirty-six, completely disappearing from public life — refusing all appearances and comment. Garbo left Hollywood for New York City and stayed out of sight, dying in 1990 after nearly fifty years of solitary retirement.

Q What do *Doctor Zhivago*, *One Flew Over the Cuckoo's Nest*, and *A Star Is Born* have in common?

A They were all nominated and won in the five top Golden Globe categories, including Best Picture.

Q What was the first western to win an Oscar for Best Picture?

A *Cimarron*, starring Richard Dix and Irene Dunn, a film that Pauline Kael of the *New Yorker* called "one of Edna Ferber's heartfelt, numbskull treks through the hardships and glories of the American heritage," became the first western to win Best Picture honours at the 1930–31 ceremony. The story of early Oklahoma settlers who take part in the famous 1889 land grab cost $1.5 million, making it Hollywood's most expensive picture at the time.

Q What was the first movie to win the Oscar "grand slam" — Best Picture, Best Actor, Best Actress, Best Director, and Best Screenplay?

A On February 27, 1935, *It Happened One Night* became the first film to sweep all the top categories at the Academy Awards — Best Director and Picture for Frank Capra, Best Actor for Clark Gable, Best Actress for Claudette Colbert, and Writing (Adaptation) for Robert Riskin. Not bad for a movie that almost closed after its first week at Radio City Music Hall in New York. It was held over only after word of mouth got around.

From the sounds of it, leading man Gable wouldn't have been too upset if the movie had closed early. He had been loaned to Columbia Pictures to make the film and wasn't enthusiastic about it. The actor had never played a comedic role before and felt he was being punished, grimly saying on the first day of shooting, "Let's get this over with."

Q What was the first foreign film to be nominated for a Best Picture Oscar?

"And the Winner Is..."

The 1937 Jean Renoir classic *La Grande illusion* (*The Grand Illusion*) was the first non-American film to take an Oscar nomination for Best Picture. Renoir's commentary on war, class struggle, racism, and the commonality of mankind lost at the February 23, 1939, ceremony to Frank Capra's romantic comedy *You Can't Take It with You*.

The movie may have come last in the Oscar derby, but it scooped up several other top awards, including Best Foreign Film from both the National Board of Review and the New York Film Critics Circle and Best Overall Artistic Contribution at the Venice Film Festival.

Writing about French film decades later, Roger Ebert said, "Apart from its other achievements, Jean Renoir's *Grand Illusion* influenced two famous later movie sequences. The digging of the escape tunnel in *The Great Escape* and the singing of the *Marseilles* to enrage the Germans in *Casablanca* can first be observed in Renoir's 1937 masterpiece."

Albo, Mike, Clark Collis, Andrew Harrison, Steve Kandell, Ben Mitchell, James Slaughter, and Jonah Weiner. "And the Oscar Doesn't Go To… The Worst Rock-Star Actors of All Time." *Blender*, January / February 2005.

Aulier, Dan. *Hitchcock's Notebooks: An Authorized and Illustrated Look Inside the Creative Mind of Alfred Hitchcock*. New York: Harper*Entertainment*, 1999.

Barbour, Alan G. *Humphrey Bogart: The Illustrated History of the Movies*. London: W.H. Allen Ltd., 1974.

Biskind, Peter. "Making Crime Pay: The Making of The Godfather." *Premiere: The Movie Magazine*, August 1997.

Biskind, Peter. "Midnight Revolution." *Vanity Fair*, March 2005.

Bona, Damien. *Inside Oscar 2: 6 New Years of Academy Awards History: 1995-2000*. New York: Ballantine Books, 2002.

Campbell, Bruce. *If Chins Could Kill: Confessions of a B Movie Actor*. Los Angeles: LA Weekly Books, 2001.

Catos, J.M. Gregory. *From Moses to Monkey Men: Charlton Heston*. *Filmfax*, Dec. / Jan. 1991.

Corman, Roger. *How I Made a Hundred Movies in Hollywood and Never Lost a Dime*. New York: Random House, 1990.

"Disastrous, Disgraceful or Just Plain Dumb: The 50 Most Disturbing Moments in Movie History." *Premiere*, November, 2004.

Selected Bibliography

Edmonds, Ben. *No Exit. Mojo: The Music Magazine*, June, 2002.

Fierman, Daniel. "Kings, Queens and Wild Things." *Entertainment Weekly*, Issue 793. November 19, 2004.

Fredrik, Nathalie. *The New Hollywood and the Academy Awards*. Beverly Hills: Hollywood Awards Publications, 1974.

Gardetta, Dave. "*Mr. Indelible*." *Los Angeles Magazine*, February, 2005.

Harmetz, Aljean. *The Making of The Wizard of Oz: Movie Magic and Studio Power in the Prime of MGM — and the Miracle of Production #1060*. New York: Delta, 1977.

Higham, Charles. *Brando: The Unauthorized Biography*. New York and Scarborough, ON: The New American Library of Canada, 1987.

Higham, Charles. *Charles Laughton: An Intimate Biography*. New York: Doubleday & Company, 1976.

Jordan, Rene. *Clark Gable: The Illustrated History of the Movies*. London: W.H. Allen Ltd., 1974.

Jordan, Rene. *Marlon Brando: The Illustrated History of the Movies*. London: W.H. Allen Ltd., 1973.

Juneau, James. *Judy Garland: The Illustrated History of the Movies*. New York: Jove Publications, 1974.

Kinn, Gail and Jim Piazza. *And the Oscar Goes to… The Academy Awards*. New York: Black Dog & Leventhal Publishers, 2002.

Levy, Emanuel. *All About Oscar: The History and Politics of the Academy Awards*. New York: Continuum, 2003.

Mann's Chinese Theatre. C.P., 1992

McGilligan, Patrick. *Alfred Hitchcock: A Life in Darkness and Light*. New York: Regan Books, 2003.

Moser, Margaret, Michael Bertin and Bill Crawford. *Movie Stars Do the Dumbest Things*. Los Angeles: Renaissance Books, 1999.

Moss, Robert F. *Karloff and Company: The Horror Film*. London: Pyramid Publications. 1973.

Nashawaty, Chris. "Fight Club" *Entertainment Weekly*, Issue 803. January 28, 2005.

O'Neil, Tom. *Movie Awards: The Ultimate, Unofficial Guide to the Oscars, Golden Globes, Critics, Guild & Indie Honors*. New York: Perigee Books, 2003.

Peretz, Evgenia. "The Sky's the Limit" *Vanity Fair*, December, 2004.

Pond, Steve. *The Big Show: High Times and Dirty Dealings Backstage at the Academy Awards*. New York: Faber and Faber Inc, 2005.

Salisbury, Mark. "Cannes is Burning." *Premiere*, September 2004.

Sandford, Christopher. *McQueen: The Biography*. New York: HarperCollins*Entertainment*, 2001.

Schruers, Fred. "Women in Hollywood: Angelina Jolie". *Premiere*, October, 2004.

Skal, David J. and Elias Savada *Dark Carnival: The Secret World of Tod Browning, Hollywood's Master of Disguise*. New York: Anchor Books, 1995.

Staggs, Sam. *Close-Up on Sunset Boulevard: Billy Wilder, Norma Desmond and the Dark Hollywood Dream*. New York: St. Martin's Griffin, 2002.

Taraborrelli, J. Randy. *Once Upon A Time: Behind the Tale of Princess Grace and Prince Rainier*. New York: Rose Books, 2003.

"The Total Film Readers' Awards 2004" *Total Film: The Ultimate Movie Magazine*, Issue 96. December, 2004.

Topalocih, Maria. *And the Genie Goes to... Celebrating 50 Years of the Canadian Film Awards*. Toronto: Stoddart Publishing Company, 2000.

Brown, Peter H. and Jim Pinkston. *Oscar Dearest*. New York: Harper & Row, 1987.

Selected Bibliography

Wiley, Mason and Damien Bona. *Inside Oscar: The Unofficial History of the Academy Awards*. New York: Ballantine Books,1986.

Wulf, Steve. "Oscar 2005: Morgan Freeman" *Entertainment Weekly*, Issue 804/805. February 4, 2005.

Yanni, Nicholas. *W.C. Fields: The Illustrated History of the Movies*. London: Pyramid Publications, 1974.